Blackstone's Police Manual

Road Policing

Blackstone's Police Manual

Volume 3

Road Policing

2012

Simon Cooper

MA, LLB

and

Michael Orme

BA

Consultant Editor: Paul Connor

OXFORD
UNIVERSITY PRESS

OXFORD
UNIVERSITY PRESS

Great Clarendon Street, Oxford OX2 6DP

Oxford University Press is a department of the University of Oxford.
It furthers the University's objective of excellence in research, scholarship,
and education by publishing worldwide in

Oxford New York

Auckland Cape Town Dar es Salaam Hong Kong Karachi
Kuala Lumpur Madrid Melbourne Mexico City Nairobi
New Delhi Shanghai Taipei Toronto

With offices in

Argentina Austria Brazil Chile Czech Republic France Greece
Guatemala Hungary Italy Japan Poland Portugal Singapore
South Korea Switzerland Thailand Turkey Ukraine Vietnam

Oxford is a registered trade mark of Oxford University Press
in the UK and in certain other countries

Published in the United States
by Oxford University Press Inc., New York

© Oxford University Press, 2011

First published 1998
Fourteenth edition published 2011

British Library Cataloguing in Publication Data
Data available

Library of Congress Cataloging in Publication Data
Data available

Typeset by Glyph International, Bangalore, India
Printed in Great Britain
on acid-free paper by
CPI William Clowes, Beccles

ISBN 978-0-19-969606-2

10 9 8 7 6 5 4 3 2 1

Foreword for 2012 Blackstone's Police Manuals

The *Blackstone's Police Manuals 2012* have been written in consultation with police forces across England and Wales and are endorsed by the National Policing Improvement Agency (NPIA). It is the official study guide and an essential learning resource for police officers. The Manuals cover the entire Objective Structured Performance Related Examination (OSPRE®) syllabus and should therefore be your first port of call when revising.

The role of a police officer has become more technical and more demanding over the last decades. To be properly qualified as a frontline officer, particularly a frontline supervisor and manager, there is a huge quantity of law, legal precedent and its interpretation that is required. Unlike a barrister, solicitor or judge, who have the books to hand or a website one click away with their mouse, a police officer frequently has to make crucial legal decisions with partial knowledge of all the facts, the pressure of time and events and the presence of a none-too-cooperative citizen. It is a testimony to the training that officers receive that they get the decisions right most of the time.

The training, however, is crucially dependent on the quality of the training materials. These Manuals are the product of a partnership between the NPIA and Blackstone's. The NPIA has a key role in promoting learning, and the development of leadership in policing. It is building on more than two decades of national expertise in supporting learning for police officers, and now has responsibility for improving every aspect of learning in policing from recruit training to the most senior ranks. Alongside Blackstone's we are committed to ensuring that the public is served by qualified, well-trained and well-led officers and police staff. These Manuals are a key part of that mission.

Nick Gargan
Chief Executive of the National Policing
Improvement Agency

Preface

Road policing covers many areas of community life and, given the high usage of transport networks, brings the police into contact with a significant percentage of the population. Using the roads in England and Wales is a highly regulated activity, heavily reliant upon documentation, registration and notification. Those tasked with road policing are given a whole array of practical powers, from inspecting documentation and checking registration details to stopping and redirecting traffic and removing vehicles. As the ACPO Road Policing Strategy makes clear, all these features present the police with a valuable opportunity, not only to pursue the immediate priorities associated with traffic policing (such as safety and traffic management), but also to disrupt the activities of serious and organised criminals and terrorists. Although much of the activity is high profile, the information that can be obtained from road policing is capable of providing invaluable criminal intelligence within the National Intelligence Model. Add to this the considerable numbers of people killed or injured on the roads each year, together with the impact of dangerous, aggressive or simply anti-social driving on the quality of life in the community, and road policing acquires a very important role.

Operational police officers, their supervisors and managers need to know a vast and growing volume of law and procedure. One effect of the highly regulated nature of road policing is that the underpinning legislation can be painfully detailed and precise in parts. However, the aim of this Manual is to condense what is an overwhelming mass of local, national and European law and strip it back to its bare essentials, considering the key elements in a practical and pragmatic context—without losing the specific meaning and applicability along the way.

If we have achieved that, it is thanks to the contributions of the many police officers and staff, lawyers and practitioners who have helped in the development of this Manual, now in its fourteenth edition; if we haven't, it is not for the want of trying.

The Blackstone's Police Manuals are the only official study guides for OSPRE® Part I Police Promotion Examinations—if the law is not in the Manuals, it will not be in the exams.

All the Manuals include explanatory keynotes and case law examples, providing clear and incisive analysis of important areas. As well as covering basic law and procedure they take full account of the PACE Codes of Practice and human rights implications. They can also be used as a training resource for student police officers, special constables and PCSOs or as an invaluable reference tool for police staff of all ranks and positions.

Oxford University Press are always happy to receive any useful written feedback from any reader on the content and style of the Manual, especially from those involved in or with the criminal justice system. Please email this address with any comments or queries: police.uk@oup.com.

The law is stated as at 1 June 2011.

Acknowledgements

The authors would like to thank the many people who assisted in the production of this year's Manual. Particular thanks go to the staff at the National Policing Improvement Agency.

Also, thanks to the production, editorial and marketing team at OUP, especially Peter, Emma, Lucy and Katie.

Simon Cooper and Michael Orme

Contents

Table of Cases

Table of Statutes

Table of Statutory Instruments

Table of Codes of Practice

Table of European Legislation

Table of International Treaties and Conventions

How to use this Manual

Volume numbers for the Manuals

The 2012 Blackstone's Police Manuals each have a volume number as follows:

Volume 1: *Crime*
Volume 2: *Evidence and Procedure*
Volume 3: *Road Policing*
Volume 4: *General Police Duties*

The first digit of each paragraph number in the text of the Manuals denotes the Manual number. For example, paragraph 2.3 is chapter 3 of the *Evidence and Procedure* Manual and 4.3 is chapter 3 of the *General Police Duties* Manual.

All index entries and references in the Tables of Legislation and the Table of Cases, etc. refer to paragraph numbers instead of page numbers, making information easier to find.

Material outside the scope of the OSPRE® syllabus—blacklining

These manuals contain some information which is outside the scope of the OSPRE® Part I exams. A full black line down the margin indicates that the text beside it is excluded from Inspectors' examinations.

Any feedback regarding content or other editorial matters in the Manuals can be emailed to police.uk@oup.com.

Length of sentence for an offence

Where a length of sentence for an offence is stated in this Manual, please note that the number of months or years stated is the maximum number and will not be exceeded.

OSPRE® Rules and Syllabus Information

The rules and syllabus for the OSPRE® system are defined within the OSPRE® Rules & Syllabus document published by the National Policing Improvement Agency (NPIA) Examinations and Assessment on behalf of the Police Promotions Examination Board (PPEB). The Rules & Syllabus document is published annually each September, and applies to all OSPRE® assessments scheduled for the calendar year following its publication. For example, the September 2010 Rules & Syllabus document would apply to all OSPRE® Part I and Part II assessments held during 2011.

The document provides details of the law and procedure to be tested within the OSPRE® Part I examinations, information on the Part II assessment centre, and also outlines the rules underpinning the OSPRE® system.

All candidates who are taking an OSPRE® Part I examination or Part II assessment are strongly encouraged to familiarise themselves with the Rules & Syllabus document during their preparation. The OSPRE® Part I rules also apply to candidates who take Part I and then go on to apply for their force's work-based assessment promotion trials.

The document can be downloaded from the Recruitment, Assessment & Selection Section of the NPIA website, which can be found at www.npia.police.uk. Electronic versions are also supplied to all force OSPRE® contacts.

If you have any problems obtaining the Rules & Syllabus document from the above source, please email the OSPRE® Candidate Administration Team at: exams.ospre@npia.pnn.police.uk.

Usually, no further updates to the Rules & Syllabus document will be issued during its year-long lifespan. However, in exceptional circumstances, NPIA (on behalf of the PPEB) reserves the right to issue an amended syllabus prior to the next scheduled annual publication date.

For example, a major change to a key area of legislation or procedure (e.g. the Codes of Practice) during the lifespan of the current Rules & Syllabus document would render a significant part of the current syllabus content obsolete. In such circumstances, it may be necessary for an update to the syllabus to be issued, which would provide guidance to candidates on any additional material which would be examinable within their Part I.

In such circumstances, an update to the Rules & Syllabus document would be made available through the NPIA website, and would be distributed to all force OSPRE® contacts. The NPIA will ensure that any syllabus update is distributed well in advance of the examination date, to ensure that candidates have sufficient time to familiarise themselves with any additional examinable material. Where possible, any additional study materials would be provided to candidates free of charge.

Please note that syllabus updates will only be made in *exceptional* circumstances, an update will not be made for every change to legislation included within the syllabus. For further guidance on this issue, candidates are advised regularly to check the NPIA website, or consult their force OSPRE® contact, during their preparation period.

3.1 Classifications and Concepts

3.1.1 Introduction

The majority of the most common road traffic definitions can be found in ss. 185 and 192 of the Road Traffic Act 1988. However, there are some other definitions which are specifically set out in the relevant piece of legislation, the most obvious examples being those relating to the construction and use of road vehicles (**see chapter 3.9**) and driving licences (**see chapter 3.10**).

The definitions that follow in this chapter are critical to police officers when dealing with road traffic offences.

The definition of a particular vehicle will generally be determined by its size, weight and construction; on occasions it will also be determined by the way in which the vehicle is used.

In approaching any situation involving road traffic legislation it is critical to establish the exact definition *as it applies to that particular piece of legislation*.

This chapter sets out the more commonly encountered definitions which are referred to, where appropriate, throughout the rest of this book. Where different definitions apply, they are included in the relevant chapter.

3.1.2 The Definitions

Most of the more commonly used definitions can be found in the Road Traffic Act 1988 but many are duplicated in other legislation (e.g. the Road Vehicles (Construction and Use) Regulations 1986 (SI 1986/1078) as amended).

3.1.2.1 Vehicle, Mechanically Propelled Vehicle and Motor Vehicle

Vehicle

A 'vehicle' is not, of itself, defined in the Road Traffic Act 1988. The *Oxford English Dictionary* defines 'vehicle' as a 'carriage or conveyance of any kind used on land'. It follows that virtually anything may be capable of amounting to a 'vehicle' under the right circumstances, even a chicken shed on wheels (see *Garner v Burr* [1951] 1 KB 31) or a hut (*Horn v Dobson* 1933 JC 1). Road traffic legislation almost always qualifies the word 'vehicle' in some particular way and so it is important to understand the different ways in which the legislation defines different types of vehicle.

Mechanically Propelled Vehicle

A mechanically propelled vehicle is, quite simply, a vehicle that is constructed so that it can be propelled mechanically. If the vehicle is so constructed, it does not cease to be 'mechanically propelled' just because the mechanism is not being used to propel it at the relevant time. Therefore a motor-assisted pedal cycle (but not an *electrically* assisted one; see below) has been held to be a mechanically propelled vehicle even when it is being pedalled (*Floyd* v *Bush* [1953] 1 WLR 242). So the test as to whether a vehicle is 'mechanically propelled' is one of construction rather than use (see *McEachran* v *Hurst* [1978] RTR 462). The prosecution bears the burden of showing that a vehicle meets the requirements of being 'mechanically propelled' (*Reader* v *Bunyard* [1987] RTR 406).

The test will be an objective one which looks at the raison d'être of the vehicle's design; it does not look at the intention of the owner (*Chief Constable of Avon and Somerset* v *Fleming* [1987] RTR 378).

In *Winter* v *DPP* [2002] EWHC 1524, the Administrative Court acknowledged a 'City Bug' conveyance as being a mechanically propelled vehicle. The court went on to uphold the Crown Court's decision that such a contraption could not be made into an 'electrically assisted cycle' simply by the addition of pedals by which the conveyance could not really be propelled and therefore the user required insurance for it when used on a road or other public place.

'Mechanically propelled' generally includes steam and electrically powered vehicles (*Elieson* v *Parker* (1917) 81 JP 265). It does not include electrically assisted *pedal cycles*.

Removing an engine from a vehicle does not stop it from being 'mechanically propelled' if you can show that the engine could easily be replaced (*Newberry* v *Simmonds* [1961] 2 All ER 318) by taking the batteries out. A car with a flat battery is still a mechanically propelled vehicle (*R* v *Paul* [1952] NI 61).

Motor Vehicle

The definition of a 'motor vehicle' which will apply in most cases can be found in s. 185 of the Road Traffic Act 1988. Section 185(1) defines a motor vehicle as a mechanically propelled vehicle intended or adapted for use on roads. (Similar definitions of motor vehicles, motor cars, etc. can be found under s. 136 of the Road Traffic Regulation Act 1984 and the Road Vehicles (Construction and Use) Regulations 1986, reg. 3).

If a vehicle is not intended or adapted for use on a road it will not be a motor vehicle for these purposes. Whether a vehicle is so intended or adapted is a question of fact to be decided in each case.

There are three further definitions of motor vehicle for specific purposes.

The first is a long definition which includes trailers and chassis and is used for the purposes of the Refuse Disposal (Amenity) Act 1978 (for the full definition **see chapter 3.8**). The second definition applies to s. 59 of the Police Reform Act 2002, where motor vehicle means any mechanically propelled vehicle *whether or not it is intended or adapted for use on roads* (s. 59(9)). This is probably because the power itself can be used where there are reasonable grounds for believing that a vehicle has been used in a way that contravenes several specific offences. For a full discussion of the powers under s. 59, **see chapter 3.2**.

The third definition of motor vehicle can be found in the Vehicles (Crime) Act 2001. Motor vehicle here means *any vehicle whose function is or was to be used on roads as a mechanically propelled vehicle*.

The Vehicles (Crime) Act 2001 introduced a new definition, that of 'written-off motor vehicles'. These are motor vehicles in need of substantial repair but in relation to which a decision has been made not to carry out the repairs.

A petrol-driven micro-scooter was held to be a motor vehicle within the definition of the Road Traffic Act 1988 by magistrates. In that case (*Chief Constable of North Yorkshire Police* v *Saddington* [2001] RTR 227) the Divisional Court upheld the magistrates' decision, asking whether a reasonable person would say that one of the 'Go-Ped's' uses would be some general use on the road. Although acknowledging that users would therefore need a driving licence and insurance (as to which, **see chapters 3.10 and 3.6**), the court declined to classify 'Go-Peds' in any particular category.

Note that a motor vehicle continues to be such if it is towed by another vehicle (*Cobb* v *Whorton* [1971] RTR 392), and a car which is rebuilt for off-road racing continues to be 'intended' for use on a road even though those rebuilding it never intended to use it so again (*Nichol* v *Leach* [1972] RTR 476).

Dumper trucks intended for use solely on construction sites will probably not be 'motor vehicles' but, if you are able to adduce evidence that they *are suitable* for use on a road, they may be held to be motor vehicles (*Daley* v *Hargreaves* [1961] 1 All ER 552). They will, of course, still be 'mechanically propelled vehicles' even when used elsewhere than a road.

Section 189 of the Road Traffic Act 1988 specifies which vehicles will *not* be treated as motor vehicles; they include pedestrian controlled vehicles and some implements for cutting grass.

3.1.2.2 Passenger Vehicles

A 'passenger vehicle' is defined under reg. 3(2) of the Road Vehicles (Construction and Use) Regulations 1986 as being a vehicle 'constructed solely for the carriage of passengers and their effects' (**see also para. 3.1.2.6** for Passenger-Carrying Vehicles).

The test to be applied to a vehicle in order to see if it falls within the definition of a 'passenger vehicle' is by asking whether or not at the material time the vehicle was of a type that would ordinarily be used for the carriage of passengers and their effects (*Flower Freight Co. Ltd* v *Hammond* [1963] 1 QB 275). The inclusion of the word 'solely' in the definition means that vehicles ordinarily used for the carriage of goods will not be passenger vehicles even if they also happen ordinarily to be used for the carriage of passengers and their effects as well (*Flower Freight Co. Ltd*).

If a passenger vehicle is constructed or adapted to carry more than 8 but no more than 16 passengers it will be a minibus, and if more than 16 seated passengers it will be a 'large bus' (reg. 3(2)).

References to passengers do not include the driver for this definition.

A large bus as defined above which has a gross weight in excess of 7.5 tonnes and having a maximum speed exceeding 60 mph is a 'coach'.

3.1.2.3 Goods Vehicles

Although some goods vehicles will also fall under the categories above (e.g. motor cars), 'goods vehicles' are themselves defined under s. 192(1) of the Road Traffic Act 1988 as motor vehicles constructed or adapted for use for the carriage of goods or a trailer so constructed or adapted (a further definition is found in the Road Vehicles (Construction and Use) Regulations 1986 as 'a motor vehicle or trailer constructed or adapted for use for the carriage or haulage of goods or burden of any description'). 'Goods' for these purposes includes goods or burden of any description. Goods vehicles are further categorised into 'large' goods vehicles and 'medium-sized' goods vehicles. Medium-sized goods vehicles are defined under s. 108(1) of the 1988 Act as motor vehicles constructed or adapted to carry or haul goods, which are not adapted to carry more than nine persons including the driver and the permissible maximum weight of which exceeds 3.5 tonnes but not 7.5 tonnes (including a combination of such a motor vehicle and a trailer where the relevant maximum weight of the trailer does not exceed 750 kg).

3.1.2.4   Motor Cycles, Motor Bicycles and Mopeds

There are differences in definition between motor cycles, motor bicycles, large motor bicycles and mopeds. In practice, the same machine may fall into a number of these definitions. Again, it is important to identify in what context the definition is used.

Motor Cycle

The general definition of a *motor cycle* can be found under s. 185(1) of the Road Traffic Act 1988. Section 185(1) defines a motor cycle as 'a mechanically propelled vehicle, not being an invalid carriage, with less than four wheels and the weight of which unladen does not exceed 410 kilograms'. This definition would include some three-wheeler cars and pedestrian-controlled vehicles.

For the purposes of part III of the 1988 Act—the part that deals with licensing (**see chapter 3.10**)—s. 108 creates further definitions of:

• a motor bicycle
• a moped.

Motor Bicycle

Under s. 108(1) a motor bicycle is defined as:

> . . . a motor vehicle which—
> (a) has two wheels, and
> (b) has a maximum design speed exceeding 45 kilometres per hour and, if powered by an internal combustion engine, has a cylinder capacity exceeding 50 cubic centimetres,
> and includes a combination of such a motor vehicle and a side-car, . . .

Moped

Also under s. 108(1), a moped is defined as:

> . . . a motor vehicle which has fewer than four wheels and—
> (a) in the case of a vehicle the first use (as defined in regulations made for the purpose of section 97(3)(d) of this Act) of which occurred before 1st August 1977, has a cylinder capacity not exceeding 50 cubic centimetres and is equipped with pedals by means of which the vehicle is capable of being propelled, and
> (b) in any other case, has a maximum design speed not exceeding 50 kilometres per hour and, if propelled by an internal combustion engine, has a cylinder capacity not exceeding 50 cubic centimetres, . . .

These definitions are really sub-divisions of motor cycles and are relevant for the purposes of driver licensing.

Learner Motor Bicycle

Section 97 of the Road Traffic Act 1988 deals with the granting of driving licences (as to which, **see chapter 3.10**). In particular, s. 97 sets out the requirements for, and restrictions on, provisional licences and, in that context, makes reference to *learner* motor bicycles, introducing yet another sub-division of motor cycles. A learner motor bicycle is defined at s. 97(5) as a motor bicycle which is either:

• propelled by electric power; or
• the cylinder capacity of its engine does not exceed 125 cc and the maximum net power output of its engine does not exceed 11 kW.

For the purposes of driving licence categories, learner motor bicycles fall under category A1.

Large Motor Bicycle and Standard Motor Bicycle

The Motor Vehicles (Driving Licences) Regulations 1999 (SI 1999/2864) (as to which, **see chapter 3.10**) create another sub-division, that of 'large' and 'standard' motor cycles.

Large motor bicycles are defined (under reg. 3) as being:

- in the case of a motor bicycle without a sidecar, a bicycle the engine of which has a maximum net power output exceeding 25 kW or which has a power to weight ratio exceeding 0.16 kW per kilogram; or
- in the case of a motor bicycle and sidecar combination, a combination having a power to weight ratio exceeding 0.16 kW per kilogram.

For the purposes of reg. 3, a 'standard' motor bicycle is a motor bicycle that does not fit into the above category (i.e. it is the opposite of a 'large' motor bicycle).

Motor Tricycles and Quadricycles

Finally, there is a classification of motor tricycles and quadricycles. These are mainly relevant for the purposes of registration marks (see the Road Vehicles (Display of Registration Marks) Regulations 2001 (SI 2001/561). Motor tricycles are vehicles having three wheels symmetrically arranged. Quadricycles are four-wheeled vehicles having a net engine power not exceeding 15 kW and an unladen mass not exceeding 400 kilograms (unless a goods vehicle in which case the relevant mass is 550 kg). Basically they are quad bikes.

Summary

So, to summarise, the definition of a motor cycle, which will be of general application, can be found under s. 185 of the Road Traffic Act 1988.

In relation to the *licensing of drivers of vehicles under part III of that Act*, there are further classifications of motor bicycles and mopeds. These are defined at s. 108 of the 1988 Act.

With regard to the *licensing of learner drivers generally*, s. 97 of the 1988 Act refers to a further classification, namely a learner motor bicycle.

In relation to the *minimum ages for holding and obtaining a driving licence*, and *the provisional entitlements of other licences*, the 1999 Regulations make reference to 'large' motor bicycles and their opposites, 'standard' motor bicycles.

And finally, for the purposes of registration plates, there are further categories of motor tricycles and quadricycles which are relevant when considering number plates.

3.1.2.5 Trailer

A 'trailer' is defined, for most purposes, under s. 185(1) of the Road Traffic Act 1988 as a vehicle drawn by a motor vehicle.

When a motor vehicle is towed by another motor vehicle, the latter still falls within the category of motor vehicle but can also be regarded as a 'trailer' (*Milstead* v *Sexton* [1964] Crim LR 474).

3.1.2.6 Other Definitions

Motor Car

Section 185(1) of the Road Traffic Act 1988 also defines a 'motor car':

> . . . 'motor car' means a mechanically propelled vehicle, not being a motor cycle or an invalid carriage, which is constructed itself to carry a load or passengers and the weight of which unladen—

(a) if it is constructed solely for the carriage of passengers and their effects, is adapted to carry not more than seven passengers exclusive of the driver and is fitted with tyres of such type as may be specified in regulations made by the Secretary of State, does not exceed 3050 kilograms,

(b) if it is constructed or adapted for use for the conveyance of goods or burden of any description, does not exceed 3050 kilograms, or 3500 kilograms if the vehicle carries a container or containers for holding for the purposes of its propulsion any fuel which is wholly gaseous at 17.5 degrees Celsius under a pressure of 1.013 bar or plant and materials for producing such fuel,

(c) does not exceed 2540 kilograms in a case not falling within sub-paragraph (a) or (b) above.

This definition, as are others, is also repeated in s. 136 of the Road Traffic Regulation Act 1984.

However, in relation to the law regulating driving instruction (part V of the Road Traffic Act 1988) there is a further definition of a 'motor car'. This definition is a motor vehicle other than an invalid carriage or motor cycle which is not constructed or adapted to carry more than nine persons including the driver and which has a maximum gross weight not exceeding 3.5 tonnes (s. 141A).

Invalid Carriage

An invalid carriage is defined (under s. 185(1)) as being:

> . . . a mechanically propelled vehicle the weight of which unladen does not exceed 254 kilograms and which is specially designed and constructed, and not merely adapted, for the use of a person suffering from some physical defect or disability and is used solely by such a person.

An invalid carriage complying with the regulations under the Chronically Sick and Disabled Persons Act 1970 will not be treated as a motor vehicle under the Road Traffic Act 1988.

Heavy Commercial Vehicle

A 'heavy commercial vehicle' is defined under s. 138 of the Road Traffic Regulation Act 1984 (and also under s. 20 of the Road Traffic Act 1988) as any goods vehicle with an operating weight exceeding 7.5 tonnes.

Large Goods Vehicles

A large goods vehicle (LGV) is defined under s. 121 of the Road Traffic Act 1988 as:

• a motor vehicle (not being a medium-sized goods vehicle)
• which is constructed or adapted
• to carry or haul goods
• having a permissible maximum weight over 7.5 tonnes.

Passenger-Carrying Vehicles

A passenger-carrying vehicle (PCV) is defined under s. 121 as either:

• a vehicle used for carrying passengers
• which is constructed or adapted
• to carry more than 16 passengers (a 'large PCV')
or
• a vehicle used for carrying passengers *for hire or reward*
• which is constructed or adapted
• to carry more than 8 but not more than 16 passengers (a 'small PCV').

3.1.3 Key Concepts

In addition to the statutory and common law definitions, there are some key concepts and classifications that are fundamental to an understanding and application of road traffic law.

3.1.3.1 Accident

'Accidents' are relevant in a number of road traffic offences (e.g. drink driving (**see chapter 3.5**) and notices of intended prosecution (**see chapter 3.3**)).

Apart from 'reportable' accidents (**see chapter 3.4**), there is no single definition of what an accident is. Rather, the courts have warned against creating any hard and fast rule as to what will amount to an 'accident' (*Chief Constable of West Midlands Police* v *Billingham* [1979] RTR 446).

The general test which courts will apply is whether an ordinary person would say that there had been an accident in all the circumstances.

Such an approach will include not only an unintended occurrence or an inadvertent act, but also a deliberate act by a driver such as ramming a gate (*Chief Constable of Staffordshire* v *Lees* [1981] RTR 506).

There is no need for the involvement of another vehicle in an 'accident' (*R* v *Pico* [1971] RTR 500).

3.1.3.2 Driver

It is possible for more than one person to be the 'driver' of a vehicle: s. 192(1) of the Road Traffic Act 1988 makes provision for any person steering a motor vehicle also to be included in the definition of 'driver' (except for the offence of causing death by dangerous driving under s. 1). Where one person sits in the driving seat while another reaches across them and operates the steering wheel, both can be 'drivers' of the vehicle (*Tyler* v *Whatmore* [1976] RTR 83). Similarly, a learner driver and his or her instructor may be the drivers of a vehicle (*Langman* v *Valentine* [1952] 2 All ER 803).

The only situation where the above will not apply is in cases of causing death by dangerous driving under s. 1 of the Road Traffic Act 1988 (**see chapter 3.2**).

Whether a person was actually the driver of a vehicle at a particular time cannot be inferred from the fact that he/she is also the owner; more evidence of his/her actual involvement in the driving of the vehicle will be required (*R* v *Collins* [1994] RTR 216).

For the purposes of many road traffic offences, the person who takes out the vehicle remains the 'driver' of it until he/she has finished that journey. Therefore, even if the vehicle is stationary and has been for some time, a person may still be the 'driver' of it if he/she has not completed the journey (see *Jones* v *Prothero* [1952] 1 All ER 434 where the driver sitting in a parked car opened the offside door causing injury to a passing pedal cyclist). This is particularly relevant in light of the offences involving hand-held mobile phones as simply pulling over to the side of the road can still amount to 'driving' (**see chapter 3.2**).

3.1.3.3 Driving

There are a number of different situations where a person can be said to be 'driving' a vehicle even though they do not conjure up a picture of conventional driving.

Ultimately, whether a person was 'driving' or not at the relevant time will be a question of fact. Although the question will be determined by reference to a number of important factors—such as the extent to which the person had control of both the direction and

7

movement of the vehicle—there must nevertheless be admissible *evidence* of these features. Mere *suspicion* on the part of the arresting or reporting officer will not be sufficient to prove this aspect of the relevant offence (see *R (On the Application of Huntley)* v *DPP* [2004] EWHC 870).

In addition, what the person is actually doing must fall within the ordinary meaning of the word 'driving' (see *McQuaid* v *Anderton* [1980] 3 All ER 540—defendant steering car which was being towed; held to be driving while disqualified).

Other factors which will be considered by the courts will be:

• How long the defendant had control of the movement and direction of the vehicle (*Jones* v *Pratt* [1983] RTR 54—the defendant was a passenger who grabbed the wheel to prevent the driver hitting an animal; held not to be 'driving'). However, the question is one of fact and degree and it is open to the court to find that a defendant had not been 'driving' but merely interfering with the driver (*DPP* v *Hastings* [1993] RTR 205—a front seat passenger saw a friend on the pavement and grabbed the steering wheel, pulling the vehicle over so that the car veered towards the pedestrian, intending to frighten him but in fact hitting him, was not 'driving').
• Whether the defendant set the vehicle in motion deliberately (*Rowan* v *Chief Constable of Merseyside* (1985) *The Times*, 10 December).
• Whether the defendant used the vehicle's controls in order to direct its movement (*Burgoyne* v *Phillips* [1983] RTR 49).

Applying these principles, pushing a car along while steering it has been held not to be driving so far as the law in England and Wales is concerned (*R* v *MacDonagh* [1974] RTR 372).

For the purposes of road traffic law, motor cycles are 'driven' as opposed to being 'ridden'.

Straddling a motorcycle and 'pedalling' it along with the feet can amount to driving (*Gunnell* v *DPP* [1994] RTR 151).

Kneeling up on the driver's seat of a car and releasing the handbrake briefly and then trying to re-apply the handbrake has been held to be 'driving' (see *Rowan* above).

The Divisional Court has accepted a finding that a person sitting in the driver's seat of a car with the engine running had been 'driving' (*Planton* v *DPP* [2002] EWHC 450), and also operating the controls of a car stuck on a grass verge with the wheels spinning but with no movement of the vehicle (*DPP* v *Alderton* [2003] EWHC 2917).

3.1.3.4 Attempting To Drive

Whether a person is 'attempting to drive' is also a question of fact and will usually be determined by the principles applying to attempts generally.

Simply put, these will include acts which are more than merely preparatory to the act of driving (such as opening a car door). The fact that the vehicle is incapable of being driven (say, because the engine is faulty), will not prevent a charge involving an 'attempt' to drive (*R* v *Farrance* [1978] RTR 225).

If a defendant sits in the driver's seat of a car and, being drunk, tries to put his/her house keys in the ignition, that behaviour may be enough to prove a charge of 'attempting to drive' while unfit (*Kelly* v *Hogan* [1982] RTR 352 *obiter*). **See also chapter 3.5.**

3.1.3.5 In Charge

The principles to be applied when considering whether a person is 'in charge' of a vehicle are set out in *DPP* v *Watkins* [1989] 2 WLR 966. Two different situations might arise:

• Where the defendant is the owner of the vehicle or where he/she has recently driven it. In these cases it would be for the defendant to show that he/she was no longer in charge of it and that there was no likelihood of his/her resuming control at the relevant time (e.g. while drunk).

- Where the defendant is not the owner or has not recently driven the vehicle. In these cases the prosecution must show that the defendant was in voluntary control of the vehicle or intended to become so in the immediate future.

In arriving at their decision, courts should consider:

- whether the defendant had the keys for the vehicle;
- where the defendant was in relation to the vehicle at the time;
- what evidence there is of the defendant's intention to take control of the vehicle.

Note that the supervisor of a learner driver can be 'in charge' of the vehicle and can therefore commit an offence if unfit through drink or drugs at the time (*Langman* v *Valentine* [1952] 2 All ER 803) (**see chapter 3.5**).

3.1.3.6 Owner and Keeper

'Owner' in relation to a vehicle subject to a hire purchase agreement is defined under s. 192 of the Road Traffic Act 1988. Section 192 provides that the 'owner' in such circumstances means the person in possession of the vehicle under that agreement. Whether a person is the owner of a vehicle in any other case is a question of fact to be determined by the court in each case. Facts including the way in which the alleged owner treats and uses the vehicle, whether he/she has spent any money on its purchase or upkeep and whether he/she has taken out insurance in relation to it may all be evidence of 'ownership'.

A 'keeper' is different from an owner but again the question will be one of fact for a court. In any enactment relating to the keeping of vehicles on public roads (e.g. vehicle excise offences), a person so 'keeps' a vehicle if he/she causes it to be on such a road for any period, however short, when it is not in use there (Vehicle Excise and Registration Act 1994, s. 62(2)).

An owner remains as such until he/she properly disposes of the vehicle or passes ownership to someone else and an owner will remain a 'keeper' even though he/she has temporarily parted with the vehicle (e.g. leaving it with a garage for repairs) (*R* v *Parking Adjudicator Ex p. Wandsworth LBC* [1998] RTR 51).

3.1.3.7 Automatism

Where a person's movements are beyond his/her control or his/her actions are brought about involuntarily, he/she will not generally be liable at criminal law as the element of *actus reus* is not present (**see Crime, chapter 1.2**).

A notable example of this is *automatism*. Where the defendant is temporarily deprived of his/her ability to control his/her movements, he/she may claim that the resulting consequences (e.g. the car swerving or colliding with something) were beyond his/her control and that the defence of automatism should apply. When this happens to the driver of a vehicle, it may remove his/her liability for certain offences such as driving without due care. This is because there is no willed action or omission by the defendant. It is also highly unlikely that he/she would have the required state of mind (**see chapter 3.2**).

Such a situation might be brought about by a swarm of bees flying in through the open window of a moving car or the driver lapsing into a coma (*Hill* v *Baxter* [1958] 1 All ER 193).

If a defendant is suffering from a particular medical condition or is prone to effects which are likely to impair his/her driving ability (such as dizziness—*R* v *Sibbles* [1959] Crim LR 660), he/she has a duty to take reasonable steps to avoid driving when the symptoms are likely to arise. If a diabetic continues to drive while experiencing the start of a hypoglycae-mic episode, it is unlikely that the defence of automatism would be available to a charge of careless driving; the diabetic should have stopped driving until the episode had passed (see *Moses* v *Winder* [1981] RTR 37).

Similarly, where the loss of voluntary movement or control is brought about by self-induced measures (such as taking/failing to take medication or by drinking), automatism is not generally available as a defence (*R* v *Quick* [1973] QB 910).

Driving in a state of reduced awareness brought on by the continuous focusing on a long, featureless road (sometimes called 'motorway hypnosis') is not enough to raise the defence of automatism (*Attorney-General's Reference (No. 2 of 1992)* [1993] RTR 337).

3.1.3.8 Road

One of the key definitions in road traffic legislation is that of a road. While this word in itself has created a great deal of case law, the position is complicated by the additional consider-ations of whether a 'public place' was involved. This is slightly circular because—as can be seen below—the definition of a road includes a reference to public access. In addition, most key road traffic offences specifically apply to roads *and* public places. Nevertheless, the two definitions are different and even the courts get themselves into difficulties when consider-ing them. A good example is where the defendant collided with a caravan on a camp site and was charged with driving *on a road* while over the prescribed limit (**see para. 3.5.3**). The Divisional Court held that the magistrates had given too much consideration to the public access point and not enough to the overall question of whether the location amounted to a 'road' (*R (On the Application of Dunmill)* v *DPP* [2004] EWHC 1700).

A road is defined under s. 192(1) of the Road Traffic Act 1988 as:

> . . . any highway and any other road to which the public has access, and includes bridges over which a road passes.

This definition (or one very similar to it, e.g. under s. 142(1) of the Road Traffic Regulation Act 1984) is applicable to most occasions where the expression 'road' is used in statutes.

Whether the public has access is a question of fact. If only a restricted section of the public (such as members of a club) has access to a road, that is not enough to make it a 'road' (*Blackmore* v *Chief Constable of Devon and Cornwall* (1984) *The Times*, 6 December).

In one case the Divisional Court accepted the magistrates' finding that Trafalgar Square was a 'road' for the purpose of ss. 67 and 69 of the Road Traffic Act 1988 (*Sadiku* v *DPP* [2000] RTR 155).

Any access enjoyed by the public must be with the agreement of the landowner. As Lord Sands put it in *Blackmore*, the members of the public must not have obtained access 'either by overcoming a physical obstruction or in defiance of prohibition, express or implied'. Therefore roads are capable of being closed or cordoned off in a way that alters their status as such.

In two further cases, both involving car parks, the Court of Appeal took a very broad approach to the construction of the definition of a 'road' in relation to the requirements for compulsory insurance (**see chapter 3.6**). The first case, *Clarke* v *Kato* [1998] 1 WLR 1647, involved a person being struck by an uninsured driver while in the car park behind a parade of shops. The second case, *Cutter* v *Eagle Star Insurance Co. Ltd* [1997] 2 All ER 311, involved a passenger being injured while in a vehicle in a multi-storey car park. On appeal to the House of Lords, the plaintiffs in both cases argued that the Road Traffic Act 1988 already made provision for the distinction between roads and car parks and that there was no justification for extending the meaning of the definition of a road beyond its normal meaning. In each of the cases before the House, the car parks were provided solely for the parking of vehicles. The House of Lords accepted the plaintiffs' arguments and overturned the earlier decisions of the Court of Appeal. Whether a particular location falls within the definition under s. 192 of the Road Traffic Act 1988 will ultimately be one of fact for the court to decide, having reference to the character and function of the land in question. Their lordships held that, on that construction, it would only be in exceptional circumstances that a car park would be deemed to fall within the definition of a road. Their lordships held that, in the first case, the mere presence of an alleyway which joined onto the car park did not change the ultimate character or purpose of the land while, in the second case, the parking bays within a multi-storey car park could not be regarded as an integral part of the carriageway which led into the car park itself (*Cutter* v *Eagle Star Insurance Co. Ltd, Clarke* v *Kato* [1998] 1 WLR 1647).

In practical terms, the effect of these decisions was limited to offences and regulations which are confined to 'roads'. However, some changes in legislation were needed such as the requirement for compulsory insurance under s. 143(1)(a) of the Road Traffic Act 1988 (**see chapter 3.6**) and the duty to report accidents under s. 170 of the 1988 Act (**see chapter 3.4**). Many of the more common or more serious road traffic provisions related to roads *or* 'public places' without the need for amendment (see below) and may still be committed in the sorts of places considered by the House of Lords in the above cases.

Car parks and forecourts may, *in exceptional cases*, be shown to be roads (see *Baxter* v *Middlesex County Council* [1956] Crim LR 561) but the prosecution would need to show that they fell squarely within the definition under s. 192 in the light of *Clarke* v *Kato* above. As well as showing them to be roads, you can also show some pub car parks to be 'public places'—at least during licensing hours—for the purposes of drink/drive offences (*Sandy* v *Martin* [1974] Crim LR 258).

Generally a road stretches to the boundary fences or grass verges adjacent to it, including any pavements (*Worth* v *Brooks* [1959] Crim LR 885).

If a vehicle is partly on a road and partly on some other privately owned land it can be treated as being 'on a road' for the purposes of road traffic legislation (*Randall* v *Motor Insurers' Bureau* [1969] 1 All ER 21).

'Public roads' which are referred to in the Vehicle Excise and Registration Act 1994 are those roads which are repairable at the public expense. Clearly this is a much more restrictive definition than that under the Road Traffic Act 1988.

3.1.3.9 Public Place

In order to prove that a place is in fact a 'public place' for the purposes of road traffic offences, it must be shown by the prosecution that:

- those people who are admitted to the place in question are members of the public and are admitted as such, not as members of some special or particular *class* of the public (e.g. people belonging to an exclusive club) or as a result of some special characteristic that is not shared by the public at large; *and*
- those people are so admitted with the permission, express or implied, of the owner of the land in question.

(*DPP* v *Vivier* [1991] RTR 205)

Whether a place is a 'public place' will be a question of fact for the court. This means that different magistrates' courts can arrive at different decisions when presented with the same facts. Some examples of places which have been held to qualify as 'public places' are:

- a privately owned caravan site open to campers (*DPP* v *Vivier* above);

- a school playground used outside school hours as a leisure park by members of the public (*Rodger* v *Normand* 1995 SLT 411);
- the 'Inward Freight Immigration Lanes' at Dover Eastern Docks (*DPP* v *Coulman* [1993] RTR 230);
- a field used in connection with an agricultural show (*Paterson* v *Ogilvy* 1957 SLT 354);
- a multi-storey car park (*Bowman* v *DPP* [1991] RTR 263);
- a car park attached to commercial premises intended only for the use of customers but accessible *from* a public place and with no restrictions placed on people entering the car park (*May* v *DPP* [2005] EWHC 1280).

A case in Essex involving a causeway between the mainland and an island provides a good illustration of the process that a court will go through in arriving at its decision in this area. In this case—which involved a motorist sitting in his car with the engine running on the causeway—the Divisional Court held that:

- the use of the causeway by members of the public was extremely limited;
- those visitors were limited to a 'special class of public' as discussed in *DPP* v *Vivier* (above);
- no invitation or permission was given to the general public and there was no evidence of general public access to the island;
- the only real access applied to residents and people with purposes connected to those residents.

Therefore, on these facts, the causeway was held not to be a 'public place' within the meaning of s. 5(1)(a) of the Road Traffic Act 1988 (e.g. for the purposes of drink driving—**see chapter 3.5**)—*Planton* v *DPP* [2001] EWHC Admin 450. The court accepted, however, that, by sitting in the car with the engine running, the defendant had been 'driving' (see above).

These requirements should not be confused with the test for whether a piece of land amounts to 'a road' (see above). The importance of police officers providing enough evidence to show that a particular location amounted to a public place was highlighted in *R* v *DPP, ex parte Taussik* [2001] ACD 10. In that case the defendant was stopped as she drove out of an access road leading from a block of flats. The road was a cul-de-sac leading off a highway and was maintained by the local housing department. At the entrance to it there was a large sign saying 'Private Residents Only'. Following her conviction under s. 5(1)(b) of the Road Traffic Act 1988 (as to which, **see chapter 3.5**), the defendant appealed, alleging that the sign on the access road excluded anyone other than residents from using it and therefore it was not a 'public place'. The Divisional Court took the view that the evidence of the police officers as to the actual use of the road by other people was very thin. As there was no evidence from the officers themselves that they had seen motorists (other than residents) using the road, the court was unable to conclude that the road was anything other than a private one. The court held that, as the issue of whether a place is a 'public place' or not is largely a question of fact, it is essential that the prosecution present clear evidence showing who uses the road, when and for what purpose. However, in a case involving a motorist stopped in a pub car park, the police witness did not adduce specific evidence that the car park was in fact a public place at the time of the offence. Nevertheless, the Divisional Court went on to hold that it was clear from previous authorities that a car park was certainly *capable* of being a public place and this was more likely when its use was not restricted to a particular group of people. Therefore it could properly be inferred that the car park—attached as it was to a pub to which members of the public were generally invited by the landlord—was in fact a public place. The court held that it was not necessary for the prosecution to adduce evidence to show that the car park was a public place and that the magistrates were entitled to reach the decision that they had—*R (On the Application of Lewis) v DPP* [2004] EWHC 3081.

For a place which is ostensibly *public* in its nature to become a *private* place, either permanently or temporarily, there needs to be some form of physical obstruction to be overcome in order to enter that place (*R v Waters* (1963) 107 SJ 275). Therefore a pub landlord, by ordering people to leave the car park of his pub, had not done enough to turn what was a public place (the car park during opening hours) into a private place.

In deciding whether or not a place is in fact a 'public place', magistrates may use their own local knowledge, but must be circumspect in doing so (*Clift v Long* [1961] Crim LR 121).

3.1.3.10 Highway

A 'highway' is a way over which the public has a right to pass and re-pass by foot, horse or vehicle, or with animals (*Lang v Hindhaugh* [1986] RTR 271).

For a highway to exist, there must be some form of 'dedication' of the relevant land to the public and, once so dedicated, it is unlikely that the public status of a highway can be changed.

Unlike a road, a highway does not cease to be such when it is temporarily roped off or closed (*McCrone v J and L Rigby (Wigan) Ltd* (1950) 50 LGR 115).

Highways will include public bridleways and footways; they also include public bridges over which they pass. Broadly, footways are the bits of a highway that you walk on and carriageways are the bits that you drive on. Bridleways, as the name suggests, are highways where the public have a right to ride or lead horses (and related animals) or to pass on foot. Some of these definitions have been reclassified by the Countryside and Rights of Way Act 2000 which creates a number of different types of byway with differing rights of access on foot, horseback or with vehicles that are not mechanically propelled. These definitions are relevant when considering issues of obstruction and off-road driving (see **chapter 3.8**).

3.1.3.11 Use, Cause or Permit?

The concepts of using, causing or permitting are central to many road traffic offences, particularly in relation to construction and use (see **chapter 3.9**). They are also relevant in the fixed penalty system which is not available for offences of 'causing or permitting' (**see chapter 3.11**).

3.1.3.12 Use

One of the difficulties with 'using' as a concept is that it is contextual. In deciding the many cases that have grown up around the word 'use', the courts have often interpreted the expression in a way that is specific to its statutory context. This means that there is no hard and fast 'definition' that can be applied to every circumstance. 'Using' a motor vehicle in relation to an insurance offence will be interpreted differently from the same expression in a construction and use offence.

'Using' has been held to involve an element of 'controlling, managing or operating the vehicle as a vehicle' (*Thomas v Hooper* [1986] RTR 1).

The 'using' of a vehicle is generally, though not exclusively, restricted to:

- the driver;
- the driver's employer (when the driver is driving the vehicle on the employer's business).

In the *West Yorkshire Trading Standards* case (below) the Court of Appeal restricted the meaning of the word 'use' when it appears alongside 'cause' and 'permit' (see below). A good example of this can be found in the numerous construction and use offences (as to which, **see chapter 3.9**).

In such circumstances 'using' is restricted to the driver or owner of the vehicle and, in the case of the owner, only if he/she employed the driver under a contract of service and at the material time the vehicle was being driven on the owner's business. Where the expression 'use' does not appear alongside 'cause' and 'permit' the concept is wider. Practically, if there is any doubt as to the appropriate wording of a charge/summons, the advice of the CPS should be sought.

If a person driving a vehicle is doing so in the ordinary course of his/her employer's business, the employer is *using* the vehicle (see e.g. *West Yorkshire Trading Standards Service* v *Lex Vehicle Leasing Ltd* [1996] RTR 70). In such a case you must prove that:

- the defendant (employer) actually owned the vehicle;
- at the relevant time, the driver was employed by the defendant; and
- the driver was driving the vehicle in the ordinary course of his/her employment

(Jones v *DPP* [1999] RTR 1).

It is immaterial that the employer has not specifically authorised the employee to use the vehicle in such a way (*Richardson* v *Baker* [1976] RTR 56).

If the driver is not an employee then the employer is not using the vehicle, even if that driver is a partner of the firm or has been asked to drive the vehicle by the employer (*Crawford* v *Haughton* [1972] 1 WLR 572). The employer may, however, be shown to be 'causing' or 'permitting' (see below).

If a garage lends one of its vehicles to a customer and the customer then uses the vehicle on his/her own business, the garage cannot be said to be 'using' the vehicle (see *Dove* (*LF*) v *Tarvin* (1964) 108 SJ 404).

If a vehicle is shown to be a 'motor vehicle' and on a 'road', it may be said to be in 'use' even if it is in such a state that it cannot be driven (*Pumbien* v *Vines* [1996] RTR 37). There is now no longer a need to show some element of control or operation of the vehicle by the owner in order to prove 'use'.

The *intention* of the owner is irrelevant in determining whether or not a vehicle was being 'used' at the time of an offence; what matters is that the defendant can be shown to have 'had the use of' that vehicle (*Eden* v *Mitchell* [1975] RTR 425).

Therefore, if a vehicle is not in a roadworthy condition it can still be available for the owner's use even though the owner has no intention of utilising it while it remains in that state.

For the owner of a vehicle to be convicted of 'using' a vehicle without insurance when it is being driven by someone else, you must prove that the defendant was in fact the owner *and* that the driver was his/her employee acting in the course of their employment (*Jones* v *DPP* [1999] RTR 1).

It should be noted that the Divisional Court has applied a broader interpretation to the meaning of 'use' when considering offences involving *trailers*. The court held that the owner of a defective trailer who is responsible for putting it on a road should not be able to escape liability for its condition simply by arguing that it was being drawn—and therefore 'used'—by someone else (*NFC Forwarding Ltd* v *DPP* [1989] RTR 239).

3.1.3.13 Passengers as Users

A pillion passenger on a motor cycle or a passenger in a car does not generally 'use' the vehicle (see e.g. *Hatton* v *Hall* [1997] RTR 212). However, if a passenger arranges to travel in or on a vehicle for his/her own benefit, he/she will 'use' the vehicle (*Cobb* v *Williams* [1973] RTR 113). A passenger can also 'use' the vehicle if there is an element of 'joint enterprise' (*O'Mahoney* v *Joliffe and Motor Insurers' Bureau* [1999] RTR 245).

3.1.3.14 Cause

'Causing' will involve some degree of 'control' or 'dominance' by, or some express mandate from, the *causer*.

Causing requires both positive action and knowledge by the defendant (*Price* v *Cromack* [1975] 1 WLR 988). If the owner of a vehicle is to be shown to have 'caused' an offence to be committed, he/she must be shown to have done something to contribute to it (e.g. by instructing another to drive it) *and also* to have known of any relevant facts (e.g. that it was overloaded) (*Ross Hillman Ltd* v *Bond* [1974] QB 435).

In cases involving employers' vehicles it may be easier to prove 'use' of the vehicle (see above).

Wilful blindness by employers to their employees' unlawful actions (e.g. not completing drivers' records) is not enough to amount to 'causing' the offence (*Redhead Freight Ltd* v *Shulman* [1989] RTR 1).

3.1.3.15 Permit

Permitting is less direct or explicit than causing. Permitting involves giving leave or licence to do something (see *Houston* v *Buchanan* [1940] 2 All ER 179). The relevant permission (e.g. to use a vehicle in a certain way or subject to some proviso) can be express or it can be inferred by the relevant person (such as where someone is given the use of a friend's car without any conditions being stipulated by the friend).

Generally, in order to prove an offence of 'permitting', you will need to show knowledge by the defendant of the vehicle's *use*, and the *unlawful nature* of that use. However, it is necessary to consider the relevant piece of legislation in each case, together with its intended purpose. (For the situation regarding insurance, **see chapter 3.6**.)

You cannot 'permit' yourself to do something (*Keene* v *Muncaster* [1980] RTR 377).

If there is any doubt as to which offence is appropriate it is acceptable to charge 'using' *or* 'causing' *or* 'permitting' as alternatives (see *Ross Hillman Ltd* above) but the advice of the local CPS should be sought.

<table>
<tr><td>

3.2

</td><td>

Offences Involving Standards of Driving

</td></tr>
</table>

3.2.1 Introduction

This chapter deals with the main offences involving driving below the required standard or in a way which presents a danger to others including the newly created offences of causing death by careless driving or causing death whilst driving unlicensed, uninsured or disqualified.

3.2.2 Causing Death by Dangerous Driving

OFFENCE: **Causing Death by Dangerous Driving—*Road Traffic Act 1988, s. 1***
 • Triable on indictment • Fourteen years' imprisonment • Obligatory disqualification—minimum two years • Compulsory re-test

The Road Traffic Act 1988, s. 1 states:

> A person who causes the death of another person by driving a mechanically propelled vehicle dangerously on a road or other public place is guilty of an offence.

KEYNOTE

This offence applies to a 'mechanically propelled vehicle'—a wider term than 'motor vehicle' and one which includes dumper trucks, cranes, trials and quad bikes.

It can be committed on a road or in other public places which again give it a wider effect.

Provided the basic elements (mechanically propelled vehicle on a road/public place) are met, you must prove that:

• the defendant caused the death of another person
• the defendant drove dangerously.

Where the defendant is charged under s. 1, evidence of drink will be admissible where the quantity of it may have adversely affected the quality of his/her driving (*R* v *Woodward* [1995] RTR 130).

Section 36 of the Road Traffic Offenders Act 1988 (requiring the court to disqualify a person convicted of certain offences until they have passed the relevant test) applies to this offence (see para. 3.10.8.1). This means that, if convicted of this offence, the defendant will have to take an extended driving test before he/she can get his/her licence back.

3.2.2.1 Causing Death of Another

The death must be that of a person other than the defendant. This would include a foetus which was later born alive but which subsequently died.

In deciding an extradition case, the House of Lords held that the offence under s. 1 had not repealed the common law offence of manslaughter and, as such, a driver causing the death of another in this way could still be indicted for homicide (*R* v *Governor of Holloway Prison, ex parte Jennings* [1983] 1 AC 624). However, a charge of manslaughter will rarely be brought in such cases.

The driving by the defendant must be shown to have been *a* cause of the death; it is not necessary to show that it was the sole or even a substantial cause of death (*R* v *Hennigan* [1971] 3 All ER 133). Therefore it is irrelevant whether or not the person killed contributed to the incident which resulted in his/her death.

3.2.2.2 Dangerous Driving

The Road Traffic Act 1988, s. 2A states:

(1) For the purposes of sections 1 and 2 above a person is to be regarded as driving dangerously if (and, subject to subsection (2) below, only if)—
   (a) the way he drives falls far below what would be expected of a competent and careful driver, and
   (b) it would be obvious to a competent and careful driver that driving in that way would be dangerous.
(2) A person is also to be regarded as driving dangerously for the purposes of sections 1 and 2 above if it would be obvious to a competent and careful driver that driving the vehicle in its current state would be dangerous.
(3) In subsections (1) and (2) above 'dangerous' refers to danger either of injury to any person or of serious damage to property; and in determining for the purposes of those subsections what would be expected of, or obvious to, a competent and careful driver in a particular case, regard shall be had not only to the circumstances of which he could be expected to be aware but also to any circumstances shown to have been within the knowledge of the accused.
(4) In determining for the purposes of subsection (2) above the state of a vehicle, regard may be had to anything attached to or carried on or in it and to the manner in which it is attached or carried.

KEYNOTE

This is clearly an *objective* test which focuses, at s. 2A(1)(a), on the manner of driving rather than the defendant's state of mind and, at s. 2A(1)(b), on what would have been obvious to a hypothetical 'competent and careful driver'. An example is where a diabetic driver drives on a road in the knowledge that he/she is likely to suffer a hypoglycaemic episode (*R* v *Marison* [1997] RTR 457).

In *Attorney-General's Reference (No. 4 of 2000)* [2001] EWCA Crim 780, the Court of Appeal reviewed the requirements of s. 2A. That case involved a bus driver who had inadvertently pressed the accelerator pedal instead of the brake, killing two pedestrians. The court held that under s. 2A the test is an objective one and there is no requirement to show any specific intent to drive dangerously. It is for the jury to determine what constituted dangerous driving. The court held that the relevant *actus reus* is the act of driving in a manner which was either dangerous (in the case of a dangerous driving charge) or without due care and attention in the case of the alternative offence. Where, as in this case, the driver had been conscious of the act he was performing, it was no defence to claim that he had not intended to press the accelerator. That was more a matter for mitigation than guilt.

The standard of driving must be shown to have fallen far below that expected of a competent and careful driver; minor driver errors would not amount to such behaviour (but contrast offences under s. 3 below).

In *R* v *Bannister* [2009] EWCA 1571, the Court of Appeal (overruling the previous authority of *Milton* v *CPS* [2007] EWHC 532) held that the fact that the defendant was a highly skilled advanced police driver was not a relevant circumstance that could be taken into account pursuant to s. 2A(3)—i.e. in determining whether or not the driving fell far below the required standard. In determining whether or not driving is dangerous, the standard to be considered is simply that of the competent and careful driver, *not* the competent and careful driver who has any particular skill or ability (**see also para. 3.2.12**).

In determining what would have been obvious to a competent and careful driver, s. 2A(3) and (4) introduces a *subjective* element by taking account of circumstances known to the defendant. This unusual mixture of tests means that, although a defendant's behaviour will be judged against the ordinary standards of competent and careful drivers, the defendant's conduct will also be assessed in the light of facts personally known to him/her (such as knowledge of the risk of a load falling off the vehicle (*R* v *Crossman* [1986] RTR 49)). However, the test is a high one—as confirmed in *R* v *Conteh (Kondeh)* [2003] EWCA Crim 962. In that case the defendant had caused the death of a pedestrian who was crossing the road at a pelican crossing. The lights were red for pedestrians and green for the defendant who was driving at 20 mph in a bus lane. It was shown that the driver of a vehicle in the outside lane had indicated to the pedestrian that she could cross the road. Quashing his conviction under s. 1, the Court of Appeal held that the threshold in s. 2A was a high one and it could not be said that the defendant's driving fell 'far below' the required standard, nor would it have been 'obvious' to a competent and careful driver that it was dangerous. Further, it was good practice expressly to remind a jury that breach of the Highway Code did not necessarily mean that an offence had been committed; however there could be no criticism of the judge in the instant case in this regard.

If the vehicle involved was in a dangerous condition it is important that you prove either:

- that the dangerous condition would itself have been obvious to a competent or careful driver; or
- that the defendant actually *knew* of its dangerous condition

(see *R* v *Strong* [1995] Crim LR 428).

In some circumstances the condition of the *driver* will be relevant. There are specific offences involving driving while under the influence of drink and/or drugs (**see para. 3.2.7**) and there are several generic road policing offences dealing with drink and drugs (**see chapter 3.5**). However, the mere presence of a controlled drug (such as cocaine) in a driver's blood may of itself be relevant to the issue of whether a person drove dangerously—even if there is no specific evidence as to the drug's effect on the person's driving (see *R* v *Pleydell* [2005] EWCA Crim 1447).

The defendant's belief, however honestly held, as to the conditions surrounding his/her driving at the time are not relevant to the issue of whether he/she drove competently and carefully (see *R* v *Collins* [1997] RTR 439). In *Collins* a police driver went through a red traffic light at almost 100 mph colliding with another vehicle and killing two people. His belief that the traffic at the lights was being operated by other officers was not a relevant factor for the jury in considering whether or not his driving had been dangerous.

The dangers presented by dangerous driving mean that there will be many occasions where significant injury is caused to another person by the driving of the vehicle. The Court of Appeal has held that there is nothing wrong in principle in charging a driver with causing grievous bodily harm as well as dangerous driving in appropriate circumstances and that to do so did not amount to an abuse of process (*R* v *Bain* (2005) 149 SJLB 113). However, where a driver was charged with both offences, a court could not impose consecutive terms of imprisonment for both offences arising out of the same incident.

3.2.2.3 Meaning of Dangerous 'Current State'

The Court of Appeal has considered the meaning of the term 'current state' of the vehicle. In *R* v *Marchant and Muntz* [2003] EWCA Crim 2099, the court held that the term implied a state different from the original state of the vehicle. In that particular case the vehicle involved had been a tractor fitted with a boom and grab for moving bales. The grab comprised a set of forward-pointing spikes on an upper and lower jaw. With the boom and grab set in the position recommended by the manufacturer, the defendant manoeuvred the tractor to make a turn and, while he waited to do so, a motorcyclist rode into the spikes and later died from his injuries. The defendants were charged with causing death by dangerous driving with the prosecution relying on the s. 2A(2) provision that it would have been obvious to a competent and careful driver that driving the vehicle in its current state would have been dangerous. The defendants argued that the vehicle was an agricultural vehicle specially authorised by the Secretary of State under s. 44 of the Road Traffic Act 1988. The Court of Appeal held that there would be cases where, even though a vehicle was authorised in this way, its condition would allow a prosecution under ss. 1 or 2. However, such cases would almost always involve allegations that the driver had created the danger by manoeuvring the vehicle, rather than simply relying on any danger caused by the vehicle's presence on a road (or other public place). Clearly if the vehicle had been used in a built-up area, or had been altered, allowed to deteriorate or used in a way that contravened the manufacturer's recommendations, the s. 2A argument would have had more force. In the circumstances of the particular case however, the defendants' convictions were quashed.

In a further case involving another tractor the Court of Appeal clarified the extent to which the practice of piling bales of straw onto a trailer would give rise to liability under s. 2. In that case the defendant had been towing a semi-trailer with some 22 bales of straw on it, one of which fell off and seriously injured a pedestrian. The defendant maintained that this 'system of work' had been employed for 25 years without incident and that he had never been warned that it might be unsafe. On the evidence, the court held that it would be perverse to find that the system of carrying bales in this way was inherently 'dangerous' (*R v Few* [2005] EWCA Crim 728).

3.2.3 Dangerous Driving

OFFENCE: **Dangerous Driving—*Road Traffic Act 1988, s. 2***
- Triable either way • Two years' imprisonment and/or a fine on indictment
- Six months' imprisonment and/or statutory maximum summarily • Obligatory disqualification • Compulsory re-test

The Road Traffic Act 1988, s. 2 states:

A person who drives a mechanically propelled vehicle dangerously on a road or other public place is guilty of an offence.

KEYNOTE

The elements of this offence are the same as those for s. 1.

Evidence showing how the particular vehicle was being driven before the incident itself may be given in support of the charge of dangerous driving. Where the dangerous driving leads to an accident, the court may allow a police officer who is an expert in the investigation of accidents to give evidence of opinion as to the cause of that accident (*R v Oakley* [1979] RTR 417).

In addition, there is a rarely used offence of causing bodily harm by wanton or furious driving or racing (Offences Against the Person Act 1861, s. 35) and a further offence of furious driving under the Town Police Clauses Act 1847. The offence applies to any vehicle or carriage and is not restricted to roads.

Section 36 of the Road Traffic Offenders Act 1988 (requiring the court to disqualify a person convicted of certain offences until they have passed the relevant test) applies to this offence (see para. 3.10.8.1).

This means that, if convicted of this offence, the defendant will have to take an extended driving test before he/she can get his/her licence back.

3.2.4 Careless and Inconsiderate Driving

OFFENCE: **Careless and Inconsiderate Driving—*Road Traffic Act 1988, s. 3***
  • Triable summarily • Fine • Discretionary disqualification

The Road Traffic Act 1988, s. 3 states:

> If a person drives a mechanically propelled vehicle on a road or other public place without due care and attention, or without reasonable consideration for other persons using the road or place, he is guilty of an offence.

KEYNOTE

Like the offences under ss. 1 and 2, this offence also applies to a mechanically propelled vehicle and to public places as well as roads.

Where a constable in uniform has reasonable grounds for believing that a mechanically propelled vehicle is being used or has been used on any occasion in a manner which contravenes ss. 3 or 34 (off-road driving—see chapter 3.8) and is causing (or is likely to cause) alarm, distress or annoyance to members of the public, he/she has the powers set out in the Police Reform Act 2002, s. 59 (as to which, see para. 3.2.4.2).

A person is to be regarded as driving without due care and attention if (and only if) the way he/she drives falls below what would be expected of a competent and careful driver (s. 3ZA(2)).

As with dangerous driving, the test is entirely objective in nature and focuses on the manner of driving rather than the defendant's state of mind. The element that distinguishes dangerous driving from careless driving is that the dangerous driver falls *far* below the required standard whilst the careless driver merely falls below the required standard (see para. 3.2.2.2 above, keynote).

Note also that if the defendant is alleged to have driven without reasonable consideration for another road user, then that other road user must *actually* be inconvenienced by the defendant's driving; it is not enough that there was potential for inconvenience (s. 3ZA(4)).

There is one *objective* standard of driving which is expected of all drivers—even learner drivers (*McCrone v Riding* [1938] 1 All ER 157) (see para. 3.10.9.5). Once you have proved that a defendant departed from that standard of driving, and that his/her actions were 'voluntary', then the offence is complete. There is no need to prove any *knowledge* or *awareness* by the defendant that his/her driving fell below that standard (*R v Lawrence* [1981] RTR 217).

The standard of driving that would be expected of a competent and careful driver will be a question of fact for the court to decide and, in so deciding, the magistrate(s) may take into account local factors such as the expected level of traffic, the time of day, peculiar hazards, etc. (*Walker v Tolhurst* [1976] RTR 513).

The Administrative Court has accepted that a distraction (such as children on the carriageway) can amount to a defence to a charge of careless driving (*Plunkett v DPP* [2004] EWHC 1937). However, each case will turn on its own facts and a court may nevertheless find that the nature or extent of the distraction does not absolve the driver from the consequences of not paying sufficient attention (e.g. by concentrating for too long on the distraction itself when considered in light of the speed of the vehicle and the nature of other hazards on the road).

Other persons using the road/public place can include pedestrians who are deliberately sprayed with water from a puddle or passengers in a vehicle (see *Pawley v Wharldall* [1965] 2 All ER 757).

3.2.4.1 Factors Affecting Offence of Careless Driving

There is a considerable overlap between the criminal and civil law in the area of careless driving, mainly because of the relevant civil duty of care owed by drivers to other road users and also because claims for damages against drivers are involved in many accidents and collisions. For this reason many of the authorities cited in identifying the principles of 'due care and attention' are civil ones.

Evidence of earlier incidents involving careless or inconsiderate driving around the same time as the offence charged may be admissible to support that charge under some circumstances (*Hallett* v *Warren* (1926) 93 JP 225) as it may if the offence is charged as one continuing offence (*Horrix* v *Malam* [1984] RTR 112).

If a witness reports the driver of an unidentified vehicle as having committed a driving offence, it is critical that the witness provides direct evidence of what he/she actually saw. It would not be enough to produce evidence from the police to show that they had received details of the vehicle which they subsequently traced back to the driver. Both vehicle *and* driver must be linked by admissible and relevant evidence (*Ahmed* v *DPP* [1998] RTR 90).

If a driver falls asleep at the wheel he/she will be guilty of careless driving (*Henderson* v *Jones* (1955) 119 JP 304) but evidence of this fact from the driver alone will not be enough to support a charge under s. 3 (*Edwards* v *Clarke* (1951) 115 JPN 426). A graphic example of what can happen in such cases can be seen from the circumstances and consequences of the Selby train crash in 2002.

Responding to an Emergency Situation

If a motorist takes action in response to an emergency situation, his/her actions are to be judged against what was a 'reasonable' course of action in those circumstances in assessing whether or not the driving amounted to an offence (*Jones* v *Crown Court* [1986] RTR 259).

Relevance of Breaching Road Traffic Regulations

Breaching certain road traffic regulations will always be potentially relevant evidence of poor driving but will not always be conclusive of the issue. For instance, although colliding with another vehicle has been held not to amount to sufficient evidence in itself of careless driving, crossing a central white line without explanation has (*Mundi* v *Warwickshire Police* [2001] EWHC Admin 448). (See also *Bensley* v *Smith* [1972] Crim LR 239.) However, simply breaching the regulations at a pedestrian crossing (**see chapter 3.8**) is not of itself proof that the person's driving fell below the required standard (*Gibbons* v *Kahl* [1956] 1 QB 59). On the other hand, just because a traffic signal is showing a green light does not mean that a driver is entitled to assume that no other person or vehicle might be proceeding from another direction and it may be that, in the circumstances, a reasonably careful driver would have anticipated that a pedestrian or other road user might still move into his/her path (see *Goddard and Walker* v *Greenwood* [2002] EWCA Civ 1590).

3.2.4.2 Vehicles Used for Causing Harassment etc.

The Police Reform Act 2002, s. 59 states:

(1) Where a constable in uniform has reasonable grounds for believing that a motor vehicle is being used on any occasion in a manner which—
   (a) contravenes section 3 or 34 of the Road Traffic Act 1988 (c. 52) (careless and inconsiderate driving and prohibition of off-road driving), and
   (b) is causing, or is likely to cause, alarm, distress or annoyance to members of the public he shall have the powers set out in subsection (3).

(2) A constable in uniform shall also have the powers set out in subsection (3) where he has reasonable grounds for believing that a motor vehicle has been used on any occasion in a manner falling within subsection (1).

KEYNOTE

This legislation gives uniformed police officers additional powers to deal with motor vehicles being used in the unlawful, anti-social or just plain annoying ways described.

A point to note here is the definition of a motor vehicle which is *not* that under s. 185 of the Road Traffic Act 1988. For the purposes of these powers above, 'motor vehicle' means any mechanically propelled vehicle *whether or not it is intended or adapted for use on roads* (s. 59(9)). The definition of motor vehicle here will cover everything from go-karts and home-made trials bikes to dumper trucks and building site vehicles.

The requirement for the constable to have 'reasonable grounds for believing' in the facts set out above is greater than mere suspicion or even belief. He/she must be able to point to the existence of *reasonable grounds* giving rise to a belief that the motor vehicle is being or has been used in one of the ways described.

The powers available in these circumstances are listed in s. 59(3):

(a) power, if the motor vehicle is moving, to order the person driving it to stop the vehicle;

(b) power to seize and remove the motor vehicle;

(c) power, for the purposes of exercising a power falling within paragraph (a) or (b), to enter any premises on which he has reasonable grounds for believing the motor vehicle to be;

(d) power to use reasonable force, if necessary, in the exercise of any power conferred by any of paragraphs (a) to (c).

Although the power of entry excludes entry into a 'private dwelling house' (see s. 59(7)), that definition does not include garages or other structures occupied with the dwelling, nor driveways or other land related to the property (see s. 59(9)). This means that the above power is available in relation to garages and driveways of houses.

The powers under s. 59(3) above are among those that can be conferred on a Community Support Officer (CSO) designated under sch. 4 to the Police Reform Act 2002. However, a designated CSO cannot enter any premises in the exercise of those powers unless he/she is in the company *and* under the supervision of a constable (sch. 4, para. 9(2)).

A vehicle cannot be seized under the s. 59 power unless the officer:

- has warned the person appearing to the officer to be the person whose use falls within subsection (1) that he/she will seize it, if that use continues or is repeated; and

- it appears to the officer that the use has continued or been repeated after the warning (s. 59(4)).

However, a warning is not required if:

- the circumstances make it impracticable for the officer to give a warning;

- the officer has already on that occasion given such a warning in respect of any use of that motor vehicle or of another motor vehicle by that person or any other person;

- the officer has reasonable grounds for believing that such a warning has been given on that occasion otherwise than by him/her; or

- the officer has reasonable grounds for believing that the person whose use of that motor vehicle on that occasion would justify the seizure is a person to whom a warning under that subsection has been given (whether or not by that officer or in respect of the same vehicle or the same or a similar use) on a previous occasion in the previous 12 months (s. 59(5)).

Reference to warning the person 'using' the vehicle here makes the requirements broader than simply warning the relevant *driver*.

The above conditions where a warning will not be needed are alternatives and any one of them will suffice. The sensible provision that a warning is not needed where it would be impracticable to give one is also fairly wide and does not mean the officer has to show it was *impossible* to do so, or even very difficult.

Given the provisions in relation to earlier warnings that may have been given by that or other officers, it will be important from a practical point of view to maintain accurate records of any warnings given.

OFFENCE: **Failing to Stop—*Police Reform Act 2002, s. 59(6)***
- Triable summarily • Fine

The Police Reform Act 2002, s. 59 states:

(6) A person who fails to comply with an order under subsection (3)(a) is guilty of an offence . . .

KEYNOTE

The power under s. 59(3)(a) is to order the person *driving* the motor vehicle in the relevant circumstances to stop. 'Driving' has the same meaning as in the Road Traffic Act 1988. If you are going to prosecute someone for failing to comply with the order, you will first need to prove that the order was properly given (e.g. that the person giving it had the authority to do so under the circumstances) and that the order was both heard and understood. The first of those matters will be of particular importance to CSOs. In the context of the general power to stop vehicles on roads, 'stop' has been held to mean bringing the vehicle to a halt and remaining at rest for long enough for the officer to exercise whatever additional powers are appropriate (see *Lodwick* v *Sanders* [1985] 1 All ER 577). If the same interpretation is given to the power here, 'stopping' must be at least long enough to allow the officer to deliver the statutory warning if appropriate, or perhaps to check whether any such warning has already been given. Although the power does not extend to demanding the keys from the driver, the section clearly gives uniformed officers powers of enforcement, including a power to use reasonable force if necessary.

Interestingly, there is no requirement that any failure to comply be without reasonable excuse or anything of that nature.

The Police (Retention and Disposal of Motor Vehicles) Regulations 2002 (SI 2002/3049) (as amended) provide detailed regulation over the seizing and retention of vehicles under the above power, including the steps which must be taken to serve seizure notices and the time limits for doing so.

Under reg. 4, the relevant authority having custody of the vehicle must take steps to give a notice to the person who owns the vehicle. The date specified in the seizure notice, on or before which the person must claim the vehicle, must be a date not less than seven working days from the day on which the notice was given to that person (see reg. 4). The notice must indicate that charges may be payable by that person and that the vehicle may be retained until these charges are paid. The level of the charges is set out in reg. 6.

If, before a vehicle is disposed of by an authority, a person satisfies the authority that he/she is the owner and pays the relevant fee in respect of its removal and retention, the authority must permit him/her to remove the vehicle (reg. 5).

If a person can prove that:

- the use of the vehicle causing it to be seized under s. 59 was not a use by him/her

- he/she did not know of the use of the vehicle in the manner which led to its seizure

- he/she had not consented to its use in that manner and could not, by the taking of reasonable steps, have prevented its use in that manner

then no charge is payable by that person (reg. 5(3)).

Where the authority is unable to serve a notice on the owner of the vehicle, or that person fails to remove the vehicle from their custody, the authority must take further steps to identify the owner of the vehicle. Where the person appearing to be the owner of the vehicle fails to comply with a seizure notice under reg. 4(1) or where the authority has not been able, having taken such steps as are reasonably practicable, to give a seizure notice to that person, the relevant authority can (subject to the time limits specified) dispose of the vehicle (reg. 7). Where a vehicle is sold, the net proceeds of sale are payable to the owner of a vehicle, if he/she makes a claim within a year of the sale (reg. 8).

3.2.4.3 National Driver Improvement Scheme

Most forces in England and Wales now use the Driver Improvement Scheme whereby the police offer a course of retraining to drivers who meet the relevant criteria as an alternative to prosecution for offences of careless and inconsiderate driving.

3.2.5 Aiding and Abetting

It is possible for someone to aid and abet another to commit an offence under ss. 1–3 of the Road Traffic Act 1988. The supervisor of a learner driver may commit such an offence if he/she fails to supervise the other person properly (*Rubie* v *Faulkner* [1940] 1 All ER 285). (For the supervision of learner drivers generally, **see chapter 3.10**.) A driving test examiner however is in the vehicle for a different purpose and will not generally be liable for the driver's behaviour (*British School of Motoring Ltd* v *Simms* [1971] 1 All ER 317).

However, although driving test examiners are not 'supervisors' or instructors, there are occasions where the driving of the examinee may be so incompetent that it would be a danger to other road users to allow it to continue. As such, the examiner may be liable as an accessory to any relevant offence. Support for this view can be found in an unreported appeal to the Crown Court at Burnley (*R* v *Charles Hoyle* (1980) unreported) where the judge upheld the examiner's conviction of aiding and abetting the offence of driving without due care and attention.

3.2.6 Dangerous, Careless and Inconsiderate Cycling

There are similar offences which regulate the standard of cycling *on roads*. These are found under ss. 28 and 29 of the Road Traffic Act 1988 and are summary offences punishable with a fine. The offence of causing bodily injury by 'furious driving' also applies to pedal cycles.

'Cycles' will include tricycles and any cycle having four or more wheels (s. 192 of the 1988 Act).

OFFENCE: **Refusing to Give, or Giving False Details after Allegation of Dangerous or Careless Driving or Cycling—*Road Traffic Act 1988, s. 168***
• Triable summarily • Fine

The Road Traffic Act 1988, s. 168 states:

Any of the following persons—
(a) the driver of a mechanically propelled vehicle who is alleged to have committed an offence under section 2 or 3 of this Act, or

(b) the rider of a cycle who is alleged to have committed an offence under section 28 or 29 of this Act,

who refuses, on being so required by any person having reasonable ground for so requiring, to give his name or address, or gives a false name or address, is guilty of an offence.

KEYNOTE

This requirement arises where the driver (or rider) is alleged to have committed an offence of dangerous or careless driving or cycling.

There is no requirement for an accident of any sort to have occurred.

The section uses the word 'refuses' but makes no mention of a *failure* to provide the required details. Although s. 11(2) of the 1988 Act makes provision for a 'failure' to include a 'refusal' (in relation to drink driving offences), the Act says nothing about a *vice versa* situation. Given that omission, together with the fact that the courts have held (albeit in an employment law case) that 'failure' is not synonymous with 'refusal' (see *Lowson* v *Percy Main & District Social Club and Institute Ltd* [1979] ICR 568), it would seem that a mere *failure* to provide the details required under s. 168 will not amount to the offence above.

Section 154 of the Road Traffic Act 1988 imposes a duty on any person against whom a claim under s. 145 is made to state whether he/she was insured and to give relevant particulars of that insurance. Failure to do so is a summary offence.

3.2.7 Causing Death by Careless Driving when under the Influence of Drink or Drugs

OFFENCE: **Causing Death by Careless Driving when under the Influence of Drink or Drugs—Road Traffic Act 1988, s. 3A**

• Triable on indictment • Fourteen years' imprisonment • Obligatory disqualification—minimum two years

The Road Traffic Act 1988, s. 3A states:

(1) If a person causes the death of another person by driving a mechanically propelled vehicle on a road or other public place without due care and attention, or without reasonable consideration for other persons using the road or place, and—

(a) he is, at the time when he is driving, unfit to drive through drink or drugs, or

(b) he has consumed so much alcohol that the proportion of it in his breath, blood or urine at that time exceeds the prescribed limit, or

(c) he is, within 18 hours after that time, required to provide a specimen in pursuance of section 7 of this Act, but without reasonable excuse fails to provide it, or

(d) he is required by a constable to give his permission for a laboratory test of a specimen of blood taken from him under section 7A of this Act, but without reasonable excuse fails to do so,

he is guilty of an offence.

(2) For the purposes of this section a person shall be taken to be unfit to drive at any time when his ability to drive properly is impaired.

(3) Subsection (1)(b) (c) and (d) above shall not apply in relation to a person driving a mechanically propelled vehicle other than a motor vehicle.

KEYNOTE

The elements in relation to the 'causing' of death and 'another person' are the same as those under s. 1.

The elements relating to 'due care and attention' and 'reasonable consideration' are the same as those under s. 3.

The elements relating to 'unfitness to drive' and the consumption of alcohol should be read in conjunction with those discussed in **chapter 3.5**.

Although the offence under s. 3A applies to a road or other public place, note that s. 3A(1)(b), (c) and (d) can *only* be committed by a driver of a *motor vehicle*.

The requirement under s. 3A(1)(c) is for the provision of a specimen for *analysis* under s. 7 of the Road Traffic Act 1988 and not a screening breath test under s. 6.

It would appear that the request must be made within 18 hours *after the driving which caused the death* and not after the death itself.

Section 36 of the Road Traffic Offenders Act 1988 (requiring the court to disqualify a person convicted of certain offences until they have passed the relevant test) applies to this offence (see para. 3.10.8.1). This means that, if convicted of this offence, the defendant will have to take an extended driving test before he/she can get his/her licence back.

3.2.8 Causing Death by Careless, or Inconsiderate, Driving

OFFENCE: **Causing Death by Careless or Inconsiderate Driving—*Road Traffic Act 1988, s. 2B***

- Triable either way • Five years' imprisonment and/or a fine on indictment
- Twelve months' imprisonment (six months in Scotland) and/or statutory maximum summarily • Obligatory disqualification

The Road Traffic Act 1988, s. 2B states:

> 2B A person who causes the death of another person by driving a mechanically propelled vehicle on a road or other public place without due care and attention, or without reasonable consideration for other persons using the road or place, is guilty of an offence.

KEYNOTE

The elements in relation to the 'causing' of death and 'another person' are the same as those under s. 1.

The elements relating to 'due care and attention' and 'reasonable consideration' are the same as those under s. 3.

3.2.9 Causing Death by Driving: Unlicensed, Disqualified or Uninsured Drivers

OFFENCE: **Causing Death by Driving: Unlicensed, Disqualified or Uninsured Drivers—*Road Traffic Act 1988, s. 3ZB***

- Triable either way • Two years' imprisonment and/or a fine on indictment • Twelve months' imprisonment (six months in Scotland) and/or statutory maximum summarily • Obligatory disqualification

The Road Traffic Act 1988, s. 3ZB states:

> 3ZB A person is guilty of an offence under this section if he causes the death of another person by driving a motor vehicle on a road and, at the time when he is driving, the circumstances are such that he is committing an offence under—
>
> (a) section 87(1) of this Act (driving otherwise than in accordance with a licence),

(b) section 103(1)(b) of this Act (driving while disqualified), or

(c) section 143 of this Act (using motor vehicle while uninsured or unsecured against third party risks).

KEYNOTE

The elements in relation to the 'causing' of death and 'another person' are the same as those under s. 1 but note, there does *not* need to be any improper *standard* of driving for the offence to be committed. An uninsured, unlicensed or disqualified driver may commit this offence notwithstanding that the quality of his driving is otherwise excellent.

This offence may only be committed by the driver of a *motor vehicle* (not a mechanically propelled vehicle unlike ss. 2, 2B and 3).

3.2.10 The Highway Code

One way of illustrating the standard of driving expected of a prudent and competent driver is through the Highway Code. Section 38 of the Road Traffic Act 1988 states:

(7) A failure on the part of a person to observe a provision of the Highway Code shall not of itself render that person liable to criminal proceedings of any kind but any such failure may in any proceedings (whether civil or criminal, and including proceedings for an offence under the Traffic Acts, the Public Passenger Vehicles Act 1981 or sections 18 to 23 of the Transport Act 1985) be relied upon by any party to the proceedings as tending to establish or negative any liability which is in question in those proceedings.

KEYNOTE

The Highway Code gives motorists and road users guidance on all manner of practical and safety issues, and in particular advice in relation to considerate driving and the proper use of headlights, horns and indicators. The Code also gives advice on police stopping procedures.

However, as the Court of Appeal has reminded us, breach of the Highway Code does not necessarily mean that an offence has been committed (*R v Conteh (Kondeh)* [2003] EWCA Crim 962).

The braking distances shown in the Highway Code however are not admissible in proving speeding cases as they amount to hearsay (*R v Chadwick* [1975] Crim LR 105).

3.2.10.1 Driving a Motor Vehicle on Road while using Hand-Held Phone

OFFENCE: **Driving a Motor Vehicle on Road while using Hand-Held Phone—Road Vehicles (Construction and Use) Regulations 1986 (SI 1986/1078) and Road Traffic Act 1988, s. 41D**
• Triable summarily • Fine • Discretionary disqualification • Endorseable—3 points

Regulation 110 states:

(1) No person shall drive a motor vehicle on a road if he is using—
(a) a hand-held mobile telephone; or
(b) a hand-held device of a kind specified in paragraph (4).
(2) No person shall cause or permit any other person to drive a motor vehicle on a road while that other person is using—
(a) a hand-held mobile telephone; or
(b) a hand-held device of a kind specified in paragraph (4).

(3) No person shall supervise a holder of a provisional licence if the person supervising is using—

    (a) a hand-held mobile telephone; or

    (b) a hand-held device of a kind specified in paragraph (4),

at a time when the provisional licence holder is driving a motor vehicle on a road.

KEYNOTE

This piece of legislation sets out three specific offences (which will be prosecuted under s. 41D of the Road Traffic Act 1988) involving the use of a hand-held mobile telephone or specified hand-held device. This means a device (other than a two-way radio operating at a specified frequency) which performs an interactive communication function by transmitting and receiving data (reg. 110(4)).

A device will be hand-held if it is, or must be, held at some point during the course of making or receiving a call or performing any other interactive communication function (reg. 110(6)(a))—therefore even the use of some hands-free attachments or earpieces may still amount to offences under this legislation.

'Interactive communication function' includes the sending and receiving of oral or written messages, faxes, still or moving images and access to the internet (reg. 110(6)(c)). Therefore it covers text messages and photographs sent or received by mobile phones.

The first offence relates to 'driving' a motor vehicle on a road. The second offence concerns using or permitting and is most likely to be encountered where employers are requiring or expecting their drivers to make or receive communications using a hand-held mobile phone or other relevant device while driving.

The third offence is committed where a person supervising a learner driver who is driving a motor vehicle on a road uses a hand-held mobile phone or other relevant device. For the general duties of supervisors, **see chapter 3.10.**

The regulations provide for a specific defence under very limited circumstances. These circumstances are where the person:

- is using the telephone or other device to call the police, fire, ambulance or other emergency service on 112 or 999;

- is acting in response to a genuine emergency; and

- it is unsafe or impracticable for him or her to cease driving in order to make the call (or, in the case of the third offence, for the provisional licence holder to cease driving while the call was being made)

(reg. 110(5)).

All three features must be present if the defence is to apply.

Note also that the offence is now endorseable with 3 points and offenders are also subject to discretionary disqualification.

3.2.10.2 Continuing Requirement to Exercise Proper Control

While many of the rules relating to the use of vehicles on roads are concerned with the condition of the vehicle itself (see the Road Vehicles (Construction and Use) Regulations 1986 (SI 1986/1078) (as amended)—**see para. 3.9.4**), some are aimed at the driving or control of the vehicle. One such regulation (reg. 104) requires the driver to maintain proper control over the vehicle at all times and to maintain a full view of the road.

It is worth noting two further things about this offence. The first is that, even though other in-car activities are not specifically rendered unlawful (such as lighting a cigarette, checking your appearance in the mirror or turning round and shouting at the kids), these are all activities which might amount to an offence (e.g. driving without due care and attention).

The second thing is that, even if a driver or supervisor is complying with the specific regulations regarding the use of mobile phones and devices above, they may still have impaired control of their vehicle and therefore commit the other offences referred to. As the Highway Code puts it:

> You MUST exercise proper control of your vehicle at all times. Never use a hand held mobile phone or microphone when driving. Using hands free equipment is also likely to distract your attention from the road. It is far safer not to use any telephone while you are driving—find a safe place to stop first.

3.2.11 Identity of Drivers

The Road Traffic Act 1988, s. 172 states:

(1) This section applies—
    (a) to any offence under the preceding provisions of this Act except—
        (i) an offence under Part V, or
        (ii) an offence under section 13, 16, 51(2), 61(4), 67(9), 68(4), 96 or 120,
    and to an offence under section 178 of this Act,
    (b) to any offence under sections 25, 26 or 27 of the Road Traffic Offenders Act 1988,
    (c) to any offence against any other enactment relating to the use of vehicles on roads, and
    (d) to manslaughter, or in Scotland culpable homicide, by the driver of a motor vehicle.
(2) Where the driver of a vehicle is alleged to be guilty of an offence to which this section applies—
    (a) the person keeping the vehicle shall give such information as to the identity of the driver as he may be required to give by or on behalf of a chief officer of police, and
    (b) any other person shall if required as stated above give any information which it is in his power to give and may lead to identification of the driver.
(3) Subject to the following provisions, a person who fails to comply with a requirement under subsection (2) above shall be guilty of an offence.

KEYNOTE

Section 172 applies to offences other than those listed at s. 172(1)(a)–(d). The excepted offences listed at s. 172(1)(a) and (b) are offences relating to:

- driving instructors
- motoring events on public highways
- protective headgear
- testing of goods vehicles
- regulations for 'type approval'
- obstruction of a vehicle examiner
- requirements to proceed to a place of vehicle inspection
- uncorrected eyesight
- regulations for licensing of large goods vehicle/passenger carrying vehicle drivers
- unlawful vehicle taking in Scotland, and
- post-conviction offences under the Road Traffic Offenders Act 1988.

Therefore s. 172 will apply to regulations made under the applicable sections (e.g. the Road Vehicles (Construction and Use) Regulations 1986; see chapter 3.9).

The requirement under s. 172 applies to the person *keeping* the vehicle and will apply to a person who is the keeper of the vehicle at the time the requirement is made even if he/she was not the keeper at the time of the alleged offence (*Hateley* v *Greenough* [1962] Crim LR 329). The second part of the power (s. 172(2)(b)) applies to *any other person*. Failing to give the information is a summary offence punishable by a fine and, in some circumstances, carrying a power for discretionary disqualification. Although it applies to both parts of the power set out above, the relevant offence (under s. 172(3)) creates one single offence (*Mohindra* v *DPP* [2004] EWHC 490).

There is no particular form of words to be used when making the requirement. It must be shown that the person making the requirement did so by, or on behalf of, the chief officer of police. A computerised form stating that the author is so acting has been held by the Divisional Court to be sufficient for this purpose (*Arnold* v *DPP* [1999] RTR 99).

Registered keepers of vehicles captured on roadside speed cameras are frequently served with a statutory notice under s. 172, along with a standard form. The form provides for details of the actual driver to be entered where the recipient of the form was not the driver at the time. If the recipient is unable to provide details of the driver, the form asks for reasons for that inability. Where a registered keeper returned the form with a covering letter stating that he had not completed the form because on the day of the alleged offence more than one person had used the vehicle, he was convicted of failing to comply with the requirement under s. 172. The defendant argued that he had complied with s. 172 because the form only required him to provide details of the actual driver, not a *potential* driver. The Divisional Court disagreed with him, holding that a notice issued pursuant to s. 172 requires an accurate response and not an inaccurate or misleading statement. That requirement under the notice is carried over to the form. The defendant's claim that he was only required to give details of an actual driver and not a potential driver was clearly contrary to the legislative intention as it would frequently be the case that the registered owner of a vehicle would at least suspect who the driver was, even if they did not know for certain (for example where they lent the vehicle to a friend but were not in the vehicle at the time of the alleged offence)—*R (On the Application of Flegg)* v *Southampton and New Forest Justices* [2006] EWHC 396.

The information must be provided within a reasonable time which may, in the prevailing circumstances, mean immediately (see *Lowe* v *Lester* [1987] RTR 30).

Note that is not necessary for the person to provide the required information on the specific form sent out by the police—it is enough that they give relevant information in writing (*Jones* v *DPP* [2004] EWHC 236).

A flaw in the s. 172 process, which is relied upon in thousands of speeding cases each month, was exposed in the case involving footballer Dwight Yorke. Briefly, the defendants had completed and returned the s. 172 forms but had not signed them. The defendants pointed out that evidence from the s. 172 forms was only admissible if it met the requirements of s. 12 of the Road Traffic Offenders Act 1988, namely being a statement in writing purporting to be signed by the accused. As the s. 172 forms had not been signed the evidence was not admissible in the circumstances and the conviction was set aside (*Mawdesley and Yorke* v *Chief Constable of Cheshire Constabulary* [2004] 1 All ER 58). The evidential loophole only remained open for a short while until the Divisional Court ruled that a chief officer is entitled to require the person providing the information to sign the relevant s. 172 form (*Francis* v *DPP* [2004] EWHC 591).

Where the requirement is made in writing and served by post, it shall have effect as a requirement to provide the information within 28 days beginning with the day on which it is served (s. 172(7)(a) (see the defence below)).

If a person falsely claims to have been the driver, an offence of perverting the course of justice may be appropriate.

Where the defendant is a company or corporate body, any director, secretary, manager or other officer of the company may also be prosecuted for the offence if it can be shown that the offence was committed with his/her 'consent or connivance' (s. 172(5)).

3.2.11.1 Does s. 172 Infringe Human Rights?

The power under s. 172, which is extremely useful in a number of aspects of police work, was subject to legal challenge in the run up to the Human Rights Act 1998. It was argued by some that the requirements of s. 172 infringed a defendant's right against self-incrimination under Article 6 of the European Convention on Human Rights. The issue was addressed by the House of Lords in *Brown* v *Stott* (*Procurator Fiscal, Dunfermline*) [2001] 2 WLR 817, where their Lordships held that the crucial issues were whether s. 172:

- represented a disproportionate response to the high incidence of death and injury on the roads by reason of the misuse of cars; and/or
- undermined the right to a fair trial when the driver's admission was relied on at trial.

Their Lordships held that the European Convention had to be read as balancing community rights with individual rights. The answer to both issues above was 'no' because (among other things):

- The answer required of a keeper by s. 172 could not of itself incriminate the suspect since it was not an offence merely to drive a car.
- All those who owned or drove cars had subjected themselves to a regulatory regime of which s. 172 was a part.

Although this was a Scottish case and some of the arguments turned on the need for corroboration, the Divisional Court for England and Wales has confirmed that an admission to being the driver of a particular vehicle given in response to a s. 172 requirement does not breach the defendant's privilege against self-incrimination under Article 6 of the European Convention (*DPP* v *Wilson* [2001] EWHC Admin 198). The court went on to say that, where a defendant disputed the reliability of any such admission, a judge (or magistrate) ought to exercise his/her general discretion to exclude the written evidence and require the prosecution to adduce oral evidence which could then be tested by cross-examination. The court also held that there was no difference, so far as the effect of the Human Rights Act 1998 was concerned, between s. 172(2)(a) and (b).

3.2.11.2 Defence

Section 172(4) provides that a person shall not be convicted of an offence under s. 172(3) if that person can show that he/she did not know *and* could not have ascertained with reasonable diligence who the driver of the vehicle was.

Section 172(7)(b) provides that, where the requirement is made in writing by post, the person shall not be guilty of an offence if that person can show that either he/she gave the information as soon as reasonably practicable after the end of the 28 day period *or* that it has not been reasonably practicable for him/her to give it.

In both of these cases the evidential burden of proof lies on the defendant.

3.2.12 Police Drivers

Police drivers will be judged against the same standard of care as other drivers (*Wood* v *Richards* [1977] RTR 201) and there is no special exemption for them or any other emergency crews (*R* v *O'Toole* (1971) 55 Cr App R 206). The growth in use of roadside cameras for detecting and prosecuting drivers for exceeding the applicable speed limit and passing through red lights has resulted in a significant increase in the number of emergency services vehicles being reported. As the vast majority of such cases fall within the legal parameters either for speed limits (as to which **see para. 3.7.4.5**) or for passing through lights at red (see below), the government and ACPO (along with others) have signed up to a protocol. Part of the protocol operates by making assumptions where the photograph shows flashing lights being displayed on the vehicle, that the relevant exemption applied (in the absence of evidence to the contrary). This protocol is of practical effect in reducing the bureaucratic burden on the system of roadside cameras; it does not affect the substantive law which the rest of this paragraph addresses. However, police drivers are granted some exemptions from specific traffic regulation and there are several cases—both civil and criminal—that help in identifying the relevant features that will be applied in determining the driver's liability.

It is also worth bearing in mind that, while the particular circumstances under which the police driver found himself/herself driving may not provide a specific defence, they may nevertheless provide significant mitigation and, where appropriate, special reasons for not disqualifying the driver (see, for example, *Agnew* v *DPP* [1991] RTR 144).

In *R* v *Bannister* [2009] EWCA Crim 1571, the Court of Appeal overruled the previous authority of *Milton* v *CPS* [2007] EWHC 532 and held that an advanced police driver with highly developed driving skills was *not* entitled to have that ability taken into account when deciding whether or not the driving in question was dangerous. The statutory test is based simply on the standard of the competent and careful driver, who is not to be vested with any particular level of skill or ability not found in the ordinary motorist.

The Court of Appeal's review of the issues of civil liability arising from police drivers (*Keyse* v *Commissioner of the Metropolitan Police* [2001] EWCA Civ 715) held that:

• Speed alone was not decisive of negligence by a police driver.
• Emergency service vehicles on duty were expressly exempted from the statutory rules for speed limits, keep left signs and traffic lights (s. 87 of the Road Traffic Regulation Act 1984 and regs 15(2) and 33(2) of the Traffic Signs Regulations and General Directions 1994 (SI 1994/1519)) (note the relevant regulation is now reg. 36(1)(b) of the Traffic Signs Regulations and General Directions 2002 (SI 2002/3113)).
• Police and other emergency service drivers were entitled to expect other road users to take note of the signs of their approach (e.g. sirens and flashing lights) and, where appropriate, react accordingly.

Consequently, the court held that a police driver who had accelerated through a green light at a road junction with the vehicle's visual and audible warning equipment in operation, was not liable for the injuries to a pedestrian who stepped off the pavement into the path of the vehicle.

Appropriately trained drivers employed by the Serious Organised Crime Agency will also be covered by emergency drivers' exemptions.

Regulation 33 (now reg. 36(1)(b) of the Traffic Signs Regulations and General Directions 2002) referred to above makes allowances for emergency services drivers to pass through red traffic lights under certain circumstances. The regulations set out the conditions under which a driver may proceed through a red light and failure to meet those conditions will render the driver liable to a charge under s. 2 or 3 of the 1988 Act. Consequently, the driver of a police surveillance vehicle following suspects to the scene of an intended armed robbery could not rely on the fact that he was required by the seriousness of the circumstances to go through a red light when he did so in a way which was not covered by the regulations (*DPP* v *Harris* [1995] RTR 100). See also *R* v *Collins* [1997] RTR 439 at **para. 3.2.2.2, keynote**.

In *Harris*, the Divisional Court held that the wording of the regulation meant that there was no scope for the defence of necessity where police drivers went through red traffic lights. It was held that the exemption for drivers of police vehicles in such circumstances was restricted to the extent that another driver should not be obliged to change speed or course to avoid a collision. The court held that all the driver in *Harris* need have done to avoid the accident was to have stopped for a couple of seconds or to have edged forward slowly.

This view was followed in the civil case of *Griffin* v *Merseyside Regional Ambulance* [1998] PIQR P34, where the Court of Appeal held that the duty of care required of a driver of any emergency vehicle is not to proceed 'in a manner likely to endanger any person' or cause them to change their speed or course of direction (per reg. 33(1)(b), now reg. 36(1)(b) of the Traffic Signs Regulations and General Directions 2002). It is the *manner* of the police officer's driving that must not cause the other driver to be endangered or to change speed or direction. The whole purpose of the audible and visual warning systems on emergency vehicles ('blues and twos') is to alert other drivers and, if necessary, to get them to change speed and/ or direction. Similarly, rule 219 of the Highway Code tells drivers to look and listen for emergency vehicles and to make room for them, pulling over and stopping where necessary provided that does not endanger other road users.

For the provisions relating to emergency service vehicles at pedestrian crossings, **see chapter 3.8**.

It is perhaps worth noting that, if a person drives in a way which creates a need for police officers to pursue him/her and an officer is subsequently injured in that pursuit, that person may owe a duty of care to the police officer and may therefore be sued for damages by the injured officer (*Langley* v *Dray* [1998] PIQR P8/314). This decision suggests that there are times when the police can be placed under an obligation by a driver to pursue him/her.

3.2.13 Defences

The very narrow defence(s) of *duress* and *necessity* have given practitioners and academics a great deal of food for thought. Basically these common law defences apply where the defendant has been compelled to commit an offence, either by a direct threat from another person or by the prevailing circumstances. Whatever the particular arguments for and against the defences, it is clear that they will generally apply to cases of dangerous, careless and inconsiderate driving (they also apply to the offences of driving while disqualified (*R* v *Martin* [1989] RTR 63 and confirmed in *R* v *Backshall* [1998] 1 WLR 1506)). Practically speaking, the defences will apply only where the driver was forced to commit the offence in order to avoid death or serious injury (*R* v *Conway* [1989] RTR 35). It is clear from *DPP* v *Harris* (**see para. 3.2.12**), however, that the defence is not available to police officers driving through red traffic lights in an emergency situation.

In *DPP* v *Bell* [1992] RTR 335, the defence of duress of circumstances was upheld where the defendant had needed to drive a vehicle in order to escape serious physical harm, even though he had drunk a considerable amount of alcohol. However, where the defendant had driven a far greater distance than was necessary to escape the relevant danger, the Divisional Court were not prepared to accept the defence in answer to a charge of driving while over the prescribed limit (*DPP* v *Tomkinson* [2001] EWHC Admin 182).

In *DPP* v *Hicks* [2002] EWHC 1638—a case arising out of driving while over the prescribed limit—the Administrative Court set out the following guidelines to be applied before the defence of necessity will generally be available to drivers:

- the defence is only available if the driving was undertaken to avoid consequences that could not otherwise have been avoided;
- those consequences must have both been inevitable and involved the risk of serious harm to the driver or someone else for whom he/she was responsible;
- the driver must do no more than is reasonably necessary to avoid the harm;
- the danger of so driving must not be disproportionate to the harm threatened.

The defence of 'self-defence' also appears to be available, where appropriate, to offences involving driving standards. This was made clear by the Court of Appeal in *R v Symonds* [1998] Crim LR 280 where the defendant was approached by a drunken pedestrian who tried to drag him from his car. It was held that, to allow the defence of 'self-defence' in relation to an *assault* caused by driving a vehicle (in this case, by driving off while the pedestrian had his arm through the driver's window), but not to allow it in relation to an offence such as dangerous driving arising from the same incident, was an anomaly. Therefore the defence of 'self-defence' should, where the circumstances require it, be open to someone who is charged with an offence involving the standard of their driving.

The defence afforded by the Criminal Law Act 1967, s. 3(1) which allows the use of reasonable force in arresting offenders and preventing crime—may apply to cases of dangerous, careless or inconsiderate driving (*R v Renouf* [1986] 2 All ER 449). See also the 'defence' of automatism in **chapter 3.1**.

3.2.13.1 **Mechanical Defect**

If an unforeseen mechanical defect suddenly deprives the driver of control of the vehicle, he/she may have a defence similar to 'automatism'. The reasoning for this seems to be that there is little distinction between a totally unexpected aberration in the bodily functions of a driver and a similar eventuality affecting the workings of his/her vehicle. In each case the driver has been deprived suddenly and unexpectedly of proper control of the vehicle and ought to be afforded the same 'defence' (*R v Spurge* [1961] 2 QB 205). As with automatism, if the possibility of such a defect ought to have been foreseeable by reasonable prudence, the defence will not be available.

The possibility of raising 'mechanical defect' as a defence has given rise to a number of calls from the higher courts for a procedure whereby vehicles involved in accidents cannot be scrapped without the permission of the police (see, e.g., *R v Thind* (1999) 19 WRTLB 12).

Notices of Intended Prosecution

This chapter is only tested in the Sergeants' examination—Inspectors' examination candidates should not study this material.

3.3.1 | Introduction

Under s. 1 of the Road Traffic Offenders Act 1988, before certain offences can be prosecuted:

- the defendant must have been warned of the possibility of that prosecution at the time of the offence (s. 1(1)(a)); or
- the defendant must have been served with a summons (or charged) within 14 days of the offence (s. 1(1)(b)); or
- a notice setting out the possibility of that prosecution must have been sent to the driver or registered keeper of the vehicle within 14 days of the offence (s. 1(1)(c)).

The notice or warning must be given by the 'prosecutor' which will ordinarily be the police. If the person giving it is not empowered to make a decision whether or not to prosecute (such as a vehicle examiner employed by the vehicle inspectorate), the warning or notice will not be deemed to have been served (*Swan* v *Vehicle Inspectorate* [1997] RTR 187).

The notice referred to is a Notice of Intended Prosecution (NIP). If a verbal warning is given at the time it must be shown that the defendant understood it (*Gibson* v *Dalton* [1980] RTR 410). Proof that they understood it will lie on the prosecution and, for that reason, it is common practice to send an NIP whether a verbal warning was given or not.

Where an offence is committed partly within the jurisdiction of one court and partly within that of another, either court may try the case. Consider the following scenario. A person whose home address is in county A commits a traffic offence in county B. Later, at his/her home address, that person is required to provide details of the driver at the time of the original traffic offence. The person fails to provide the details as required. The fact that the original offence was in county B does not stop the court in county A from hearing the case as the person's subsequent offence—failure to provide the details required—occurred within the jurisdiction of county A (*Kennet DC* v *Young* [1999] RTR 235).

3.3.2 | Relevant Offences

The offences which require an NIP are listed in sch. 1 to the Road Traffic Offenders Act 1988 and include:

- Dangerous, careless or inconsiderate driving.
- Dangerous, careless or inconsiderate cycling.

- Failing to comply with traffic signs and directions.
- Leaving a vehicle in a dangerous position.
- Speeding offences under ss. 16 and 17 of the Road Traffic Regulation Act 1984.

The list of offences in sch. 1 is exhaustive; other offences, even if similar in nature to those in the list, will not be covered by the requirements of s. 1(1) (*Sulston* v *Hammond* [1970] 1 WLR 1164).

3.3.3 | **Exceptions**

Section 2(1) of the Road Traffic Offenders Act 1988 states that the requirement to serve an NIP does not apply in relation to an offence if:

- at the time or
- immediately afterwards and
- owing to the presence of the vehicle concerned
- on a road
- an accident occurred.

Each of these features must be present to remove the need for an NIP to be served or a warning given.

'Accident' is defined at **para. 3.1.3** and is broader than the expression used under s. 170 of the Road Traffic Act 1988. However, although such 'reportable' accidents now extend to public places as well as roads, the exemption under s. 2(1) above is limited to an accident that occurs on *a road* at the time or immediately after the offence.

Whether the accident occurred 'at the time' is a matter of fact and degree (*R* v *Okike* [1978] RTR 489).

If the driver is unaware that the accident has taken place because it is so minor, there *will* be a need to serve an NIP (*Bentley* v *Dickinson* [1983] RTR 356). The thinking behind this ruling is that the warning or NIP will allow the driver to gather evidence to answer any charge arising from the accident.

Where the accident is so severe that the driver has no recollection of it, there is no need to serve an NIP and the ruling in *Bentley* (above) will not apply (*DPP* v *Pidhajeckyj* [1991] RTR 136).

There must be some causal connection between the presence of the vehicle concerned and the accident (*Quelch* v *Phipps* [1955] 2 All ER 302).

The vehicle must have been on a 'road'.

Section 2 goes on to say:

(2) The requirement of section 1(1) of this Act does not apply in relation to an offence in respect of which—

(a) a fixed penalty notice (within the meaning of Part III of this Act) has been given or fixed under any provision of that Part, or

(b) a notice has been given under section 54(4) of this Act.

(3) Failure to comply with the requirement of section 1(1) of this Act is not a bar to the conviction of the accused in a case where the court is satisfied—

(a) that neither the name and address of the accused nor the name and address of the registered keeper, if any, could with reasonable diligence have been ascertained in time for a summons or, as the case may be, a complaint to be served or for a notice to be served or sent in compliance with the requirement, or

(b) that the accused by his own conduct contributed to the failure.

3.3.4 Presumption

The Road Traffic Offenders Act 1988, s. 1 states:

> (3) The requirement of subsection (1) above shall in every case be deemed to have been complied with unless and until the contrary is proved.

3.3.5 Proof

The Road Traffic Offenders Act 1988, s. 1 states:

> (1A) A notice required by this section to be served on any person may be served on that person—
>   (a) by delivering it to him;
>   (b) by addressing it to him and leaving it at his last known address; or
>   (c) by sending it by registered post, recorded delivery service or first class post addressed to him at his last known address.
> (2) A notice shall be deemed for the purposes of subsection (1)(c) above to have been served on a person if it was sent by registered post or recorded delivery service addressed to him at his last known address, notwithstanding that the notice was returned as undelivered or was for any other reason not received by him.
> (3) The requirement of subsection (1) above shall in every case be deemed to have been complied with unless and until the contrary is proved.

Although any of the methods of posting set out at s. 1(1A)(c) will suffice, if the question of posting is challenged, evidence of posting may be required. There is an irrebuttable presumption that if an NIP is sent by registered post or recorded delivery then it has been served within two days. However it is a rebuttable presumption if the notice is sent by first class post if the defence can give evidence that the notice was received after the 14 day period (*Gidden v Chief Constable of Humberside* [2010] 2 All ER 75).

As the purpose of the warning or notice is to alert the defendant to the likelihood of prosecution, it is not necessary to specify exactly which offence is being considered; it is enough that the defendant is made aware of the *nature* of the offence (*Pope* v *Clarke* [1953] 2 All ER 704).

3.4 Accidents and Collisions

3.4.1 Introduction

There are certain provisions that relate to accidents and collisions and these, rather than the causes of accidents, are the subject of this chapter.

Although there are many types of event involving vehicles which can be described as an 'accident'—including those brought about deliberately—there are specific circumstances where that 'accident' imposes duties on certain people involved. This chapter is primarily concerned with these 'reportable' accidents.

3.4.2 Reportable Accidents

The Road Traffic Act 1988, s. 170 states:

(1) This section applies in a case where, owing to the presence of a mechanically propelled vehicle on a road or other public place, an accident occurs by which—
    (a) personal injury is caused to a person other than the driver of that mechanically propelled vehicle, or
    (b) damage is caused—
        (i) to a vehicle other than that mechanically propelled vehicle or a trailer drawn by that mechanically propelled vehicle, or
        (ii) to an animal other than an animal in or on that mechanically propelled vehicle or a trailer drawn by that mechanically propelled vehicle, or
        (iii) to any other property constructed on, fixed to, growing in or otherwise forming part of the land on which the road or place in question is situated or land adjacent to such land.
(2) The driver of the mechanically propelled vehicle must stop and, if required to do so by any person having reasonable grounds for so requiring, give his name and address and also the name and address of the owner and the identification marks of the vehicle.
(3) If for any reason the driver of the mechanically propelled vehicle does not give his name and address under subsection (2) above, he must report the accident.
(4) . . .
(5) If, in a case where this section applies by virtue of subsection (1)(a) above, the driver of a motor vehicle does not at the time of the accident produce such a certificate of insurance or security, or other evidence, as is mentioned in section 165(2)(a) of this Act—
    (a) to a constable, or
    (b) to some person who, having reasonable grounds for so doing, has required him to produce it, the driver must report the accident and produce such a certificate or other evidence.
    This subsection does not apply to the driver of an invalid carriage.
(6) To comply with a duty under this section to report an accident or to produce such a certificate of insurance or security, or other evidence, as is mentioned in section 165(2)(a) of this Act, the driver—
    (a) must do so at a police station or to a constable, and
    (b) must do so as soon as is reasonably practicable and, in any case, within twenty-four hours of the occurrence of the accident.

(7) . . .

(8) In this section 'animal' means horse, cattle, ass, mule, sheep, pig, goat or dog.

KEYNOTE

Accidents as defined under s. 170(1)(a) and (b) above are generally referred to as 'reportable' accidents. These should be distinguished from the wider definition of 'accident' used elsewhere in the Act (**see para. 3.1.3**).

Following the decision of the House of Lords in *Cutter* v *Eagle Star Insurance Co. Ltd* [1998] 4 All ER 417, the requirements under s. 170 were extended to cover accidents occurring in 'other public places' as well as roads (Motor Vehicles (Compulsory Insurance) Regulations 2000 (SI 2000/726)).

Note that the duty upon the driver under s. 170(2) is to stop *and* give his/her name and address (and name and address of the owner) (*DPP* v *Bennett* [1993] RTR 175).

However, it has been held that, as the reason for this requirement to 'exchange details' is to allow future communications between interested parties, the address of the driver's solicitor would be enough to discharge the duty at s. 170(2) (*DPP* v *McCarthy* [1999] RTR 323).

No mention is made of who may have been to blame for the accident. A driver will attract the duties imposed by s. 170 even if he/she is not at fault. In order to attract those duties, however, the driver must know of the accident (see *Harding* v *Price* [1948] 1 All ER 283).

Even though there may be a break in the actual driving of the vehicle, the driver may still be under the obligations imposed by s. 170 if an accident occurs while he/she is away from the vehicle. Therefore, where a driver left his vehicle on a road with its hazard warning lights on while he ran to a post box and the vehicle coasted downhill into a wall, the driver still had a duty to report the accident under s. 170 (*Cawthorn* v *DPP* [2000] RTR 45). In *Cawthorn*, even though a passenger may have been directly responsible for the accident (by letting off the handbrake), it was held that the circumstances met the requirements of s. 170 and that the driver attracted the relevant statutory duties. The Divisional Court held that the offence under s. 170(4) is not a 'driving offence' as such and does not require that the person be 'driving' at the time.

In proving the offence you would not have to show that the driver was so aware; once the damage or injury is proved it is for the driver to show (on the balance of probabilities) that he/she was unaware of its occurrence (*Selby* v *Chief Constable of Avon and Somerset* [1988] RTR 216).

Damage caused under the circumstances set out at s. 170(1)(b) applies to any vehicle (such as bicycles and trailers) and not just one which is mechanically propelled.

If the only damage caused is to the vehicle concerned or an animal in it then the accident will not fall within the criteria of being 'reportable'. Similarly if the only person injured is the driver of the vehicle concerned, the accident will not be reportable; it will, however, be reportable if a passenger in that vehicle is injured.

Where a bus driver braked hard, causing injury to one of his passengers, the Divisional Court held that he had a duty to stop at the place and the time that the passenger was caused to be injured. It was not open to the driver to claim that the bus itself was the scene of the accident. The fact that the driver failed to stop immediately meant that he was guilty of an offence under s. 170(4) (*Hallinan* v *DPP* [1998] Crim LR 754).

The list of animals under s. 170(8) does not include one of the most common 'victims' of road traffic accidents—cats.

The accident must have been brought about owing to the vehicle's presence on a 'road' or other public place; therefore s. 170 does not apply to accidents which occur on private premises.

In order to determine whether the motor vehicle was being driven without insurance (**see chapter 3.6**), s. 171 of the Road Traffic Act 1988 places a requirement on the *owner* of the vehicle to give such information as required by the police. Failure to comply with such a requirement is a summary offence.

Where it appears to a constable that, by reason of *any* accident having occurred owing to the presence of the vehicle on a road, it is requisite that a test should be carried out forthwith, he/she may require it to be so carried out and, if the officer does not carry out the test himself/herself, he/she can require that the vehicle is not taken away until the test has been carried out (s. 67(7) of the Road Traffic Act 1988). For testing of vehicles generally, **see chapter 3.9**.

3.4.2.1 Stop

Stop under s. 170(2) means to stop safely and remain at the scene for such a time as would allow anyone having a right or reason for doing so to ask for information from the driver (*Lee* v *Knapp* [1967] 2 QB 442); it does not require the driver to make enquiries of his/her own to try and find such a person (see *Mutton* v *Bates* [1984] RTR 256).

This duty also appears to require the driver to stay with his/her vehicle for a reasonable time (*Ward* v *Rawson* [1978] RTR 498).

3.4.2.2 Injury

Injury under s. 170 has been held to include shock and, given the developments in the area of assaults (e.g. *R* v *Ireland* [1997] 3 WLR 534; *R* v *Chan-Fook* [1994] 1 WLR 689), it would appear that psychological harm may well amount to an 'injury' for these purposes.

3.4.2.3 Duty to Report

If the driver does not give his/her name and address, he/she must report the accident to a police officer or at a police station. It does *not* matter what the reason for non-provision of the information is. If there are no other persons in the vicinity to whom the information may be given, then the matter *must* be reported to a police officer or at a police station. The report must be made as soon as reasonably practicable (which will be a question of fact for the court to decide in each circumstance) and in any case within 24 hours of the occurrence of the incident. This latter requirement does not give the driver up to 24 hours to report the accident; that report must be made as soon as is reasonably practicable. The report to the police within 24 hours appears to apply even if it is not practicable—or even possible?—to do so within that time limit (see *Bulman* v *Lakin* [1981] RTR 1).

That duty is probably not discharged if the driver waits until the police call at his/her house and then tells them (see *Dawson* v *Winter* (1932) 49 TLR 128 *obiter*); neither is it discharged if the driver tells a friend who happens to be a police officer (*Mutton* v *Bates* [1984] RTR 256).

Any report must be made in person; telephoning (and presumably sending a fax or e-mail to) a police station is not enough (*Wisdom* v *McDonald* [1983] RTR 186).

3.4.3 The Offences

OFFENCE: **Failing to Stop or Report an Accident—*Road Traffic Act 1988, s. 170(4)***
• Triable summarily • Six months' imprisonment and/or a fine • Discretionary disqualification

The Road Traffic Act 1988, s. 170 states:

(4) A person who fails to comply with subsections (2) or (3) above is guilty of an offence.

OFFENCE: **Failing to Produce Proof of Insurance after Injury Accident—*Road Traffic Act 1988, s. 170(7)***
• Triable summarily • Fine

The Road Traffic Act 1988, s. 170 states:

(7) A person who fails to comply with a duty under subsection (5) . . . is guilty of an offence, but he shall not be convicted by reason only of a failure to produce a certificate or other evidence if, within seven days after the occurrence of the accident, the certificate or other evidence is produced at a police station that was specified by him at the time when the accident was reported.

KEYNOTE

This is not a 'driving' offence and s. 170 is not limited to situations where the accident is caused by 'driving' the vehicle concerned (see *Cawthorn* above). Whether a defendant was the driver of a relevant vehicle at the relevant time is a question of fact for the court to determine. In doing so, the court may take into account facts such as those in *Cawthorn*, e.g. that the defendant had been driving the vehicle before the accident, that he had parked the vehicle—returning to it immediately after the accident—and that he had left his hazard warning lights on indicating that his journey was not finished.

If a driver fails to stop *and* fails to report an accident he/she commits *two* offences (*Roper* v *Sullivan* [1978] RTR 181). For the additional obligations with regard to insurance claims made against drivers or vehicle owners see para. 3.6.2.

Section 170 imposes a clear obligation on the driver of a vehicle involved in an accident resulting in damage or injury to report the accident to the police. That requirement is not negated either by police attendance at the accident or by the driver being taken to hospital—*DPP* v *Hay* [2005] EWHC 1395.

The Court of Appeal refused to accept that a driver who failed to stop and report an accident for fear of being breathalysed did not, without more, commit an offence of perverting the course of justice (*R* v *Clark* [2003] EWCA Crim 991). While it is true that driving home and remaining there allowed the passage of time to dissipate the level of alcohol in the driver's body and thereby avoid conviction for a drink driving offence (as to which, see chapter 3.5), the court was not convinced that this was enough to justify being charged with such a serious offence. The *failure* to report the accident could not amount to an offence of perverting the course of justice as that offence required a positive *act* by the defendant.

3.5 Drink, Drugs and Driving

3.5.1 Introduction

Identified by ACPO and the government as being one of the four most significant dimensions of unlawful, disorderly and dangerous road and vehicle use, drink and drug influenced driving is a significant issue in effective road policing.

The law regulating drinking and driving is contained in the Road Traffic Act 1988 and the Road Traffic Offenders Act 1988. It has been substantially developed by common law and entire books could be devoted to the cases which the subject has generated since its introduction over 30 years ago.

Although what follows in this chapter is a discussion of some of the relevant law and powers of enforcement, there is an increasing emphasis on judicial action to prevent re-offending. The Road Traffic Offenders Act 1988 contains a series of measures designed to allow for driver retraining and to offer reduced periods of disqualification for drivers who undergo the prescribed courses. The initial period of disqualification must be at least 12 months; any reduction cannot be less than three months or more than a quarter of the whole period (see s. 34A). Drivers must be at least 17 years old to take part in the scheme and must generally pay for the course. Full details of the courses are set out in the various regulations made under s. 34C.

A further scheme designed to emphasise the safety considerations in driving while unfit or over the prescribed limit is the High Risk Offender (HRO) scheme. This scheme generally applies to offenders who are convicted of relevant offences and at the time were either more than two and a half times the prescribed limit or for whom the conviction is their second (or more) in ten years. Under the scheme, these offenders will be required to take a medical test before being allowed to regain their drivers' licence at the end of their period of disqualification and they must effectively satisfy the licensing authority that they do not have a serious alcohol problem.

3.5.2 Unfit through Drink or Drugs

OFFENCE: **Driving or Attempting to Drive a Mechanically Propelled Vehicle when Unfit through Drink or Drugs—*Road Traffic Act 1988, s. 4(1)***
> • Triable summarily • Six months' imprisonment and/or a fine • Obligatory disqualification

The Road Traffic Act 1988, s. 4 states:

> (1) A person who, when driving or attempting to drive a mechanically propelled vehicle on a road or other public place, is unfit to drive through drink or drugs is guilty of an offence.

43

OFFENCE: **Being in Charge of a Mechanically Propelled Vehicle when Unfit through Drink or Drugs—*Road Traffic Act 1988, s. 4(2)***
- Triable summarily • Three months' imprisonment and/or a fine • Discretionary disqualification

The Road Traffic Act 1988, s. 4 states:

(2) Without prejudice to subsection (1) above, a person who, when in charge of a mechanically propelled vehicle which is on a road or other public place, is unfit to drive through drink or drugs is guilty of an offence.

KEYNOTE

Section 4 creates three separate offences. For the definitions of 'driving', 'attempting to drive' and 'in charge', see chapter 3.1.

The likelihood of driving is not an element of the offence itself; the intention of the defendant is material only to the statutory defence, which he/she is required to prove on a balance of probabilities—*CPS* v *Bate* [2004] EWHC 2811.

Although many of the so-called 'drink driving' offences carry police powers based on reasonable suspicion, it will not be enough to rely on a suspicion *that the defendant had been driving* in order to prove the relevant offence. Suspicion may be enough to trigger powers to require preliminary tests or powers of entry; it will not however be enough to prove the required element of *driving/attempting to drive/being in charge* for the purposes of prosecuting the relevant offence (see *R (On the Application of Huntley)* v *DPP* [2004] EWHC 870).

The power of entry in connection with an offence under s. 4 is found in s. 17(1)(c)(iiia) of the Police and Criminal Evidence Act 1984 which states:

Subject to the following provisions of this section, and without prejudice to any other enactment, a constable may enter and search any premises for the purpose of

. . .

(iiia) section 4 (driving etc. when under influence of drink or drugs) or s. 163 (failure to stop when required to do so by constable in uniform) of the Road Traffic Act 1988.

Under s. 4:

(3) . . . a person shall be deemed not to have been in charge of a mechanically propelled vehicle if he proves that at the material time the circumstances were such that there was no likelihood of his driving it so long as he remained unfit to drive through drink or drugs.

KEYNOTE

The onus is on the defendant to prove this fact. However, in determining whether the defendant was likely to drive the vehicle while unfit a court *may* disregard any injury to the defendant or damage to the vehicle (s. 4(4)).

Although the wording of the above defence means the issues are slightly different here from those under s. 5(1)(b), the requirements and standards of proof involved are the same (see para. 3.5.3.1).

3.5.2.1 Evidence of Impairment

Evidence of impairment must be produced by the prosecution. That evidence may be given by any 'lay' witness and does not require expert testimony (*R* v *Lanfear* [1968] 2 QB 77). Such a witness cannot, however, give evidence as to the defendant's ability to drive.

It is not necessary to show what quantity of alcohol or drug the defendant had in his/her system for this offence. Therefore there is no need for any form of breath test. However, the police powers under s. 4 do not 'fall away' if you do embark on the procedure under s. 6 (e.g. requiring a breath sample: **see para. 3.5.4**). This was made clear in the decision of the Administrative Court in *DPP* v *Robertson* [2002] EWHC 542. In that case, the officers had breathalysed the defendant who produced a negative result. However, on talking to the officers further, the defendant slurred his speech when giving the name of his solicitor. The officers then arrested the defendant under s. 4 (above) and took him to a police station where he provided an evidential sample of breath which was over the prescribed limit. The magistrates held that the defendant had been unlawfully arrested and the prosecutor appealed on a number of grounds. The Administrative Court held that it was quite conceivable to have a case where, notwithstanding that a driver had given a negative screening breath test, he/she was seen moments later staggering in a way that gave rise to a suspicion of unfitness. In such a case the law (s. 4) clearly gave a constable a power to arrest if what he/she had witnessed amounted to reasonable cause to suspect that the person was impaired.

'Drugs' will include any intoxicant other than alcohol (s. 11); toluene found in some glues will amount to such a drug (*Bradford* v *Wilson* (1983) 78 Cr App R 77).

3.5.3 Over Prescribed Limit

OFFENCE: **Driving or Attempting to Drive a Motor Vehicle while Over the Prescribed Limit—*Road Traffic Act 1988, s. 5(1)(a)***
  • Triable summarily • Six months' imprisonment and/or a fine • Obligatory disqualification

The Road Traffic Act 1988, s. 5 states:

(1) If a person—
  (a) drives or attempts to drive a motor vehicle on a road or other public place . . . after consuming so much alcohol that the proportion of it in his breath, blood or urine exceeds the prescribed limit he is guilty of an offence.

OFFENCE: **Being in Charge of a Motor Vehicle while Over the Prescribed Limit—*Road Traffic Act 1988, s. 5(1)(b)***
  • Triable summarily • Three months' imprisonment and/or a fine • Discretionary disqualification

The Road Traffic Act 1988, s. 5 states:

(1) If a person—
  (a) . . .
  (b) is in charge of a motor vehicle on a road or other public place,
  after consuming so much alcohol that the proportion of it in his breath, blood or urine exceeds the prescribed limit he is guilty of an offence.

KEYNOTE

These offences apply to *motor vehicles* as defined in **para. 3.1.2.1**.

'Consuming' is not restricted to drinking and will encompass other methods of getting alcohol into the bloodstream (*DPP* v *Johnson* [1995] RTR 9).

Where a person is charged under s. 5(1)(a), the charge should specify whether the person was 'driving' or 'attempting to drive' (*R* v *Bolton Justices, ex parte Zafer Alli Khan* [1999] Crim LR 912).

The prescribed limit is:

- 35 microgrammes of alcohol in 100 millilitres of breath
- 80 milligrammes of alcohol in 100 millilitres of blood
- 107 milligrammes of alcohol in 100 millilitres of urine.

Section 11(2) which sets out these limits also allows for the levels to be changed.

The prosecution have to establish that the defendant's breath-alcohol content exceeded the permitted maximum; it does not have to establish a specific figure (*Gordon* v *Thorpe* [1986] RTR 358). In proving the content of breath-alcohol there is no requirement to make a distinction between 'deep lung' air and 'mouth alcohol' (see *Zafar* v *DPP* [2004] EWHC 2468).

When dealing with the offence under s. 5(1)(b) it will be important to remember the statutory defence (see para. 3.5.3.1). The effect of this is that police officers investigating offences of being 'in charge' will have to ensure that a defendant is interviewed properly and fully as to all the circumstances, taking particular care to establish that he/she is fully sober at the time of interview and that there was a real risk of his/her driving the vehicle while still over the prescribed limit.

The Divisional Court has held that there is some positive duty on a person to enquire whether a drink contains alcohol before drinking it if that person intends to drive afterwards (see *Robinson* v *DPP* [2004] EWHC 2718).

3.5.3.1 Defence

The Road Traffic Act 1988, s. 5 goes on to state:

(2) It is a defence for a person charged with an offence under subsection (1)(b) above to prove that at the time he is alleged to have committed the offence the circumstances were such that there was no likelihood of his driving the vehicle whilst the proportion of alcohol in his breath, blood or urine remained likely to exceed the prescribed limit.

(3) The court may, in determining whether there was such a likelihood as is mentioned in subsection (2) above, disregard any injury to him and any damage to the vehicle.

KEYNOTE

A good practical example of this defence in operation is the case of *CPS* v *Bate* [2004] EWHC 2811. In that case the defendant had been found in a car with the keys to the ignition in his hand. Following a positive breath test, he appeared at court charged under s. 5(1)(b) above. The defendant argued that he had only been in the car for the purpose of retrieving a disabled permit (as to which see para. 3.8.4.4) before ringing his wife to arrange a taxi for him to get home. Although the magistrates' court accepted this account, the CPS argued that they were wrong to do so. The Divisional Court held that the magistrates had treated the likelihood of driving as an element of the offence itself. The court held that this was the wrong approach; that the defendant had manifestly been 'in charge' of the vehicle and had also been over the prescribed limit. Therefore the likelihood of the defendant's driving the vehicle while still over the limit was only relevant if and when he raised the statutory defence. If he chose to rely on that defence, the usual considerations with regard to standards of proof (set out below) would then apply.

This defence was subjected to considerable scrutiny in a case where a defendant was found asleep in a van and, on being breathalysed, provided a reading that showed his alcohol to breath ratio to be four times the legal limit. The defendant claimed that there had been no likelihood of his driving while over the prescribed limit but the magistrates did not accept that he had proved the point sufficiently. The defendant then argued that the application of s. 5(2) above was contrary to Article 6(2) of the European Convention on Human Rights (presumption of innocence, see **General Police Duties, chapter 4.5**). Although the Divisional Court failed to agree at the first hearing and were still not unanimous on the second occasion, the majority decision was that the defence could be read as follows: 'It is a defence for a person charged with an offence under s. 5(1)(b) above to *demonstrate from the evidence an arguable case that* at the time he is alleged to have committed the offence etc.' (emphasis added). Therefore, once the prosecution prove the elements of the offence beyond a reasonable doubt, the defendant must demonstrate an arguable case that there was no likelihood of his/her driving the vehicle while still over the prescribed limit. Once the defendant does this, the prosecution must then prove beyond a reasonable doubt that there *was* such a likelihood (*Sheldrake* v *DPP* [2003] EWHC 273). This case came before the House of Lords as *Attorney-General's Reference (No. 4 of 2002) Sheldrake v DPP* [2004] UKHL 43. There it was held that, although the subsection did in fact infringe the presumption of innocence under Article 6, the burden placed on the defendant was reasonable because it was in pursuance of a legitimate aim. The likelihood of the defendant's driving was a matter that was so closely linked to his/her own knowledge at the relevant time that it made it much more appropriate for the defendant to prove—on the balance of probabilities—that he/she would not have been likely to drive (as opposed to requiring the prosecution to prove the opposite, beyond a reasonable doubt).

3.5.4 Preliminary Tests

The relevant police powers now provide for three different types of preliminary test, set out under ss. 6A, 6B and 6C of the Road Traffic Act 1988.

The Road Traffic Act 1988, s. 6 states:

(1) If any of subsections (2) to (5) applies a constable may require a person to co-operate with any one or more preliminary tests administered to the person by that constable or another constable.

(2) This subsection applies if a constable reasonably suspects that the person—
(a) is driving, is attempting to drive or is in charge of a motor vehicle on a road or other public place, and
(b) has alcohol or a drug in his body or is under the influence of a drug.

(3) This subsection applies if a constable reasonably suspects that the person—
(a) has been driving, attempting to drive or in charge of a motor vehicle on a road or other public place while having alcohol or a drug in his body or while unfit to drive because of a drug, and
(b) still has alcohol or a drug in his body or is still under the influence of a drug.

(4) This subsection applies if a constable reasonably suspects that the person—
(a) is or has been driving, attempting to drive or in charge of a motor vehicle on a road or other public place, and
(b) has committed a traffic offence while the vehicle was in motion.

KEYNOTE

These powers allow the police to administer three preliminary tests—a breathalyser test, a test indicating whether a person is unfit to drive due to drink or drugs, and a test to detect the presence of drugs in the person's body.

Section 6 allows a constable to require a person to co-operate with one or more of the preliminary tests under certain circumstances. Although the police officer *making the requirement* does not have to be in uniform, the officer *administering* a preliminary test under s. 6(2)–(4) must be in uniform (s. 6(7)).

The circumstances fall into the three main categories set out at s. 6(2)–(4) above, with the final category (under s. 6(5)) relating to accidents (see para. 3.5.4.3). It can be seen from the categories above that they involve:

• the present—someone who is reasonably suspected to be driving, attempting to drive or being in charge of a motor vehicle on a road or other public place, and of having alcohol or a drug in their body or being under the influence of a drug;

- the past—someone reasonably suspected of having been driving, attempting to drive or in charge of a motor vehicle on a road or other public place while having alcohol or a drug in their body or while unfit to drive because of a drug, and who still has alcohol or a drug in their body or is still under the influence of a drug; and
- a combination of the past and present—someone who it is reasonably suspected is or has been driving, attempting to drive or in charge of a motor vehicle on a road or other public place, and who is reasonably suspected to have committed a traffic offence while the vehicle was in motion. 'Traffic offence' here means an offence under any provision of the Road Traffic Act 1988 (other than part V—driving instruction), the Road Traffic Offenders Act 1988 (other than part III—the fixed penalty system), the Road Traffic Regulation Act 1984 and part II of the Public Passenger Vehicles Act 1981. Such offences, which include offences under any regulations made under those Acts, must have been committed while the vehicle was moving.

Random Tests

Although the police can use their powers to stop vehicles at random (see below) the law in England and Wales does not permit entirely random testing of drivers for drink or drugs.

The courts have accepted that the police are empowered to stop vehicles at random (under the Road Traffic Act 1988, s. 163), whether to establish the identity of the driver, to enquire whether the driver has been drinking or to train newly appointed officers in traffic procedures (see *Chief Constable of Gwent* v *Dash* [1986] RTR 41). That does not empower officers to conduct random preliminary tests but, having randomly stopped a vehicle, they may carry out preliminary tests provided they follow the procedure set out above. It has been held that the only limit on the power under s. 163 is that it should not be used capriciously or oppressively (*Stewart* v *Crowe* 1999 SLT 899).

3.5.4.1 'Reasonably Suspects'

There is a distinction between 'reasonably suspects' and 'reasonably believes' (see s. 6(5)).

Whether the constable reasonably suspected or believed a fact in issue will be determined in the light of all the available evidence. The distinction between the two expressions has, however, been held to be a significant one, intended by Parliament (*Baker* v *Oxford* [1980] RTR 315). In that case it was held that the deliberate use of the word 'believe' in the Act imposed a requirement for a greater degree of certainty in the mind of the officers concerned. While an officer might reasonably suspect someone has been drinking or taking drugs, a single error of judgment or carelessness on the part of a driver will not necessarily justify such a suspicion (see e.g. *Williams* v *Jones* [1972] RTR 4).

The importance of whether such suspicion or belief existed or not lies not only in triggering the relevant powers; it also affects the nature of any conversation that might take place between the officer and a suspected driver. A good example of this can be seen in *Ortega* v *DPP* [2001] EWHC 143. In that case the officers were held not to have had reasonable grounds to suspect that any offence had been committed at the time they questioned the defendant about his ownership and driving of a particular car. The absence of such reasonable grounds to suspect an offence meant that the doorstep conversation, which was not contemporaneously recorded and some of which took place without caution, was nevertheless admissible. This distinction is not as straightforward as it seems and has arisen a number of times before the courts. The difficulty arises because having grounds to suspect someone of an offence not only gives rise to the power to require a specimen; it also triggers the requirement (under PACE, Code C) to caution the person as a suspect before asking any questions about an offence (**see Evidence and Procedure, appendix 2.1**). The approach of the courts is slightly confusing when comparing the authorities. For instance, the Divisional Court has held that a 'roadside confession' before any caution was given is admissible where it was made prior to the driver being given a breath test (*Whelehan* v *DPP* [1995] RTR 177). In that case the defendant was found sitting in the driver's seat of a car at the roadside with the keys in the ignition. On being approached by a police officer, he admitted that he had been drinking and was then asked if he had driven to that location. The driver replied that he had and was required to provide a roadside screening breath test which was positive. The driver was convicted of driving while over the prescribed limit. Dismissing his appeal, the court held that the time, place and circumstances in which he had been found afforded sufficient evidence to infer that he had driven to the scene, quite apart from the admission. The magistrates' court had been entitled to find that it was only *after* the roadside breath test that the police officer suspected an offence had been committed and therefore it was only then the need to caution arose. The problem with this approach is that, as can be seen above, the power to require a breath test in this situation requires suspicion of an offence. A further example can be seen in *Ridehalgh* v *DPP* [2005] EWHC 1100. In that case the defendant (a police officer) was called to a police station to deal with a prisoner. Other officers noticed that the defendant smelled of intoxicants and asked him whether he had been drinking and also whether he had driven to the police station. He confirmed both. Subsequent breath tests showed the defendant to have been over the prescribed limit. At the magistrates' court the defendant argued that the questions asked of him prior to caution constituted an 'interview' and that, as such, Code C of the PACE Codes of Practice (paras 10.1 and 11.1A) (**see Evidence and Procedure, appendix 2.1**) had been breached. The magistrates held that no interview had taken place prior to the caution and that there had been no breach of Code C. The magistrates held that the questions regarding driving and having had a drink first were merely preliminary and had been made with the intention of finding the possibility of whether an offence had been committed. They also held that such questions were analogous to the police stopping a driver and asking whether he had been drinking, prior to administering a caution and proceeding to require a breath specimen. On appeal by the defendant the Divisional Court held that a 'necessary precondition' for the giving of a caution was that there had to be grounds for the suspicion of a criminal offence. Whether or not there were grounds to suspect an offence was essentially a decision for the magistrates. In the instant case the magistrates had been entitled to reach their decision for the reasons that they had given. All that the police officers had prior to the questions posed to R was a smell of alcohol on his breath; they had no indication as to how much alcohol R had consumed or whether he had driven.

In addition to first-hand observation of a driver's behaviour, reasonable suspicion may arise from the observations of another officer (*Erskine* v *Hollin* [1971] RTR 199) and this is clearly provided for now in the extended wording of s. 6. Reasonable suspicion may even arise from information provided by a member of the public (see *DPP* v *Wilson* [1991] RTR 284). An officer receiving a radio message that a driver had been seen driving erratically may thereby acquire enough reasonable suspicion to require the administering of one of the three preliminary tests on that basis (for an example in relation to alcohol consumption see *R* v *Evans* [1974] RTR 232).

3.5.4.2 The Tests

The Road Traffic Act 1988 states:

6A Preliminary breath test

(1) A preliminary breath test is a procedure whereby the person to whom the test is administered provides a specimen of breath to be used for the purpose of obtaining, by means of a device of a

type approved by the Secretary of State, an indication whether the proportion of alcohol in the person's breath or blood is likely to exceed the prescribed limit.

(2) A preliminary breath test administered in reliance on section 6(2) to (4) may be administered only at or near the place where the requirement to co-operate with the test is imposed.

6B Preliminary impairment test

(1) A preliminary impairment test is a procedure whereby the constable administering the test—
   (a) observes the person to whom the test is administered in his performance of tasks specified by the constable, and
   (b) makes such other observations of the person's physical state as the constable thinks expedient.

. . .

(4) A preliminary impairment test may be administered—
   (a) at or near the place where the requirement to co-operate with the test is imposed, or
   (b) if the constable who imposes the requirement thinks it expedient, at a police station specified by him.

6C Preliminary drug test

(1) A preliminary drug test is a procedure by which a specimen of sweat or saliva is—
   (a) obtained, and
   (b) used for the purpose of obtaining, by means of a device of a type approved by the Secretary of State, an indication whether the person to whom the test is administered has a drug in his body.

(2) A preliminary drug test may be administered—
   (a) at or near the place where the requirement to co-operate with the test is imposed, or
   (b) if the constable who imposes the requirement thinks it expedient, at a police station specified by him.

KEYNOTE

The officer *administering* any of the tests above must be in uniform (s. 6(7)). This requirement does not apply in the case of preliminary tests following an accident (as to which **see para. 3.5.4.3**). Whether the constable (which includes an officer of any rank, including special constables) was in uniform at the time is a matter of fact for a court to determine in each case. What counts as uniform is unclear but, if the constable can be easily identified from his/her manner of dress as a police officer, the requirement has probably been met (*Wallwork v Giles* [1970] RTR 117; officer without helmet on held to be 'in uniform').

The tests referred to at ss. 6A and 6C are for the purpose of obtaining, by means of a device of a type approved by the Secretary of State, an indication whether either the proportion of alcohol in a person's breath or blood is likely to exceed the prescribed limit, or the person has a drug in their body. This is an important distinction as the preliminary test is undertaken only to give an indication to the officer administering it of the likelihood of the offence, not for proving the relevant offence. However, under s. 7, an evidential breath test can be carried out at or near a place where a preliminary breath test has been administered to that person or would have been but for their failure to co-operate with it (**see para. 3.5.5.1**).

Under the previous legislation, evidence of a roadside breath test was held to be admissible on the issue of the defendant's veracity, i.e. to prove whether he/she is telling the truth or not (see *DPP* v *Brown and Teixeira* [2001] EWHC Admin 931). In the case of a person required to give a roadside breath specimen under s. 6A, their attitude and conduct may be sufficient to make out the offence of refusing to co-operate (**see para. 3.5.4.4**) even before the officer produces a breath test device (*DPP* v *Swan* [2004] EWHC 2432).

Failure to comply with the manufacturer's instructions on the use of approved devices has always raised contentious points and will no doubt continue to do so. Generally, failing to follow key instructions of the manufacturer such as assembling the tube on a breathalyser or allowing the driver to smoke immediately before taking the test, has meant that the person has not provided a preliminary test and they may be asked to provide another; refusing to do so will be an offence (see below) (*DPP* v *Carey* [1969] 3 All ER 1662).

The Divisional Court also decided that an innocent failure by a police officer to follow the manufacturer's instructions should not be deemed to render either the test or any subsequent arrest unlawful (*DPP* v *Kay* [1999] RTR 109).

Note that, under the legislation for preliminary breath tests, drivers have been prevented from claiming an extra 20 minutes' grace by pretending that they have just had a drink (see *Grant* v *DPP* [2003] EWHC 130). Similar efforts to manipulate the circumstances in light of the relevant manufacturer's instructions for the other tests can be expected to receive similar treatment from the courts.

A preliminary breath test under s. 6A may only be administered at or near the place where the requirement to co-operate with the test is imposed unless it is made under the provisions relating to accidents (**see para. 3.5.4.3**). The other two tests, under ss. 6B and 6C may be administered at or near the place where the requirement to co-operate is imposed, or if the constable imposing it thinks it expedient, at a police station specified by him or her. In the *Oxford English Dictionary*, expedient is defined as 'advantageous . . . suitable to the circumstances of the case'.

A preliminary impairment test under s. 6B is a completely different procedure from the other two and involves an appropriately trained and authorised police officer observing the person performing specified tasks and that officer making such other observations of the person's physical state as he/she thinks 'expedient' (see above). The types of tests are set out in a Code of Practice published by the Secretary of State and include pupillary examination, walk-and-turn tests and finger-to-nose tests. Officers administering these tests must be specifically trained and authorised for this purpose by their chief officer. The police officer administering a preliminary impairment test must have regard to the Code of Practice (s. 6B(5)) and he/she can only administer such a test if approved for that purpose by his/her chief officer (s. 6B(6)).

3.5.4.3

Procedure Following an Accident

The Road Traffic Act 1988, s. 6 states:

> (5) This subsection applies if—
>   (a) an accident occurs owing to the presence of a motor vehicle on a road or other public place, and
>   (b) a constable reasonably believes that the person was driving, attempting to drive or in charge of the vehicle at the time of the accident.

KEYNOTE

As discussed above, reasonable *belief* requires something more than suspicion (*R* v *Forsyth* [1997] Crim LR 589).

The power under s. 6(5) is expressly subject to the provisions of s. 9 which deals with hospital patients (**see para. 3.5.9**). In relying on this section you must show that an accident had taken place, not simply that you believed that to be the case (*Chief Constable of West Midlands Police* v *Billingham* [1979] RTR 446). For the definition of 'accident' in this context, **see para. 3.1.3.1**. The meaning is not restricted to that given to a 'reportable' accident under s. 170 (**see para. 3.4.2**). The requirement here is for the officer to have a 'reasonable belief' that the person was driving, attempting to drive or in charge of a relevant vehicle at the time of an accident (for further requirements in this regard see *Johnson* v *Whitehouse* [1984] RTR 38).

There is no need for the police officer making the requirement to believe or even suspect that the person has been drinking, or that they have committed any offence; reasonable belief in his/her involvement (as a person driving, attempting to drive or being in charge of a vehicle) in the accident is enough. *Nor is there a need for the officer making the requirement to be in uniform.*

A preliminary *breath test* (under s. 6A) administered under the above provisions may be administered:

(a) at or near the place where the requirement to co-operate with the test is imposed, or

(b) if the constable who imposes the requirement thinks it expedient, at a police station specified by him/her (s. 6A(3)).

Note that there is no general power of entry in order to administer preliminary breath tests, however there is a specific power of entry in relation to the above subsection (see para. 3.5.4.6).

Where an officer has imposed a requirement to co-operate with a preliminary breath test in circumstances where s. 6(5) above applies, he/she may also require an evidential breath specimen under s. 7 (as to which see para. 3.5.5.1) at or near the place where the preliminary breath test has been administered or would have been but for the person's failure to co-operate.

Where a constable imposes a requirement to co-operate with a preliminary breath test at any place, he/she is entitled to remain at or near that place in order to impose on the person a requirement for an evidential specimen under s. 7 (s. 7(2C)) there.

3.5.4.4 Failure to Co-operate with Preliminary Test

OFFENCE: **Failing to Co-operate with a Preliminary Test—*Road Traffic Act 1988, s. 6(6)***

- Triable summarily • Fine • Discretionary disqualification

The Road Traffic Act 1988, s. 6 states:

(6) A person commits an offence if without reasonable excuse he fails to co-operate with a preliminary test in pursuance of a requirement imposed under this section.

KEYNOTE

As with any requirement carrying a sanction for failure to comply, you must show that the requirement for the preliminary test was properly made in accordance with the relevant conditions set out earlier in this paragraph. It will also need to be shown that the person both heard and understood the requirement.

An example of 'reasonable excuse' would be where the defendant is physically unable to co-operate with the requirement or where to do so would entail a substantial risk to his/her health (see e.g. *R* v *Lennard* [1973] 2 All ER 831).

Failing includes a refusal (s. 11(2)).

A person does not co-operate with a preliminary test or provide a specimen of breath for analysis unless his/her co-operation or the specimen:

(a) is sufficient to allow the test or the analysis to be carried out, and

(b) is provided in such a way as to enable the objective of the test or analysis to be satisfactorily achieved (s. 11(3)).

Therefore, if the person does not follow the instructions given or does something which purports to fulfil the requirement made by the officer but which does not meet the criteria in s. 11(3), he/she has 'failed' to co-operate. However, it is not necessary for the officer to produce a breath test device before this offence can be committed. The person's attitude and conduct after being required to give a breath specimen under s. 6A may be sufficient to make out the offence above and the evidence of the officer witnessing this attitude or conduct may suffice as proof that it amounted to a failure or refusal. In the event that a person clearly does something which amounts to a refusal to provide a preliminary breath test, the offence will be made out even though the officer did not produce a device for doing so (*DPP* v *Swan* [2004] EWHC 2432).

Having been required to provide a specimen of breath, a person may also be required to wait until a device is brought to the scene; failing to wait for a reasonable time, or doing anything which demonstrates an intention not to provide the specimen can amount to a 'failure' (see *R* v *Wagner* [1970] Crim LR 535).

Simply producing enough breath to enable the device to give a positive reading does not necessarily mean the defendant has 'provided a specimen'; he/she must produce sufficient breath in the manner required to enable the device to give a reliable reading—positive or negative (*DPP* v *Heywood* [1998] RTR 1).

3.5.4.5 Powers of Arrest

The Road Traffic Act 1988, s. 6D states:

(1) A constable may arrest a person without warrant if as a result of a preliminary breath test the constable reasonably suspects that the proportion of alcohol in the person's breath or blood exceeds the prescribed limit.

(1A) . . .

(2) A constable may arrest a person without warrant if—

   (a) the person fails to co-operate with a preliminary test in pursuance of a requirement imposed under section 6, and

   (b) the constable reasonably suspects that the person has alcohol or a drug in his body or is under the influence of a drug.

(2A) A person arrested under this section may, instead of being taken to a police station, be detained at or near the place where the preliminary test was, or would have been, administered, with a view to imposing on him there a requirement under section 7 of this Act.

(3) A person may not be arrested under this section while at a hospital as a patient.

KEYNOTE

The power of arrest is divided into two parts, neither of which requires the officer to be in uniform. The first part relates to the situation where an officer (not necessarily the arresting officer) has administered a preliminary breath test under s. 6A. If any officer reasonably suspects, as a result of that preliminary test, that the proportion of alcohol in the person's breath or blood exceeds the prescribed limit, he/she may arrest the person without warrant. However, there is no obligation to do so.

Note that even where evidential specimens of breath have been provided under s. 7 this does not prevent the power of arrest under s. 6D(1) above from having effect (see para. 3.5.5.1).

The second part of the section allows any officer to arrest a person who fails to co-operate with *any* preliminary test imposed under s. 6 provided the officer reasonably suspects that the person has alcohol or a drug in his/her body or is under the influence of a drug. Without this reasonable suspicion, s. 6D(2) provides no power of arrest for failing to co-operate with a preliminary test.

Instead of being taken to a police station, a person who is arrested under this section may be detained at or near the place where the preliminary test was, or would have been, administered, with a view to imposing a requirement for an evidential specimen under s. 7 there.

3.5.4.6 Powers of Entry

There is a specific power of entry provided by the Road Traffic Act 1988, s. 6E as follows:

(1) A constable may enter any place (using reasonable force if necessary) for the purpose of—

   (a) imposing a requirement by virtue of section 6(5) following an accident in a case where the constable reasonably suspects that the accident involved injury of any person, or

   (b) arresting a person under section 6D following an accident in a case where the constable reasonably suspects that the accident involved injury of any person.

> **KEYNOTE**
>
> The wording of this subsection limits the purposes of entry to:
>
> - imposing a requirement for a preliminary test;
>
> - arresting the person if, as a result of a preliminary breath test, the officer reasonably suspects that the proportion of alcohol in the person's breath or blood exceeds the prescribed limit;
>
> - arresting the person for failing to co-operate with a preliminary test where the officer reasonably suspects that the person has alcohol or a drug in their body or is under the influence of a drug.
>
> In order for this power to apply you must show that:
>
> - there was an accident (mere suspicion or belief by the officer, however strong, is not enough);
>
> - the officer reasonably believed that the person had been driving, attempting to drive or in charge of the vehicle concerned (suspicion is not enough);
>
> - the officer reasonably suspected that the accident involved injury to any person—including the driver (for this part suspicion is enough provided it is reasonable).

3.5.4.7 Trespassing

Many legal arguments have raged over the legitimacy of a breath test carried out or requested where the officers concerned are in fact trespassing on the property of another. The results of these deliberations are:

- If police officers are trespassing *on the defendant's property* they are not entitled to require a breath test (*R* v *Fox* [1986] AC 281).
- If the officers are trespassing at the time they make the requirement, any subsequent arrest made by them is unlawful (*Clowser* v *Chaplin* [1981] RTR 317).
- Although the entry and the arrest may be unlawful, this will only affect the offence under s. 6(4) and not any other offences detected at the police station (see below).
- Any requirement for a sample of breath properly made, and any subsequent arrest remains lawful *until* the officers become trespassers. A police officer, like any other member of the public, has an implied licence to go onto certain parts of someone's property (e.g. the front doorstep) unless and until that licence is withdrawn. If a police officer goes onto such a part of the defendant's property, he/she is not trespassing until told to leave and any requirement for a breath test, or any arrest made before this happens will be lawful. (See *Pamplin* v *Fraser* [1981] RTR 494 where the defendant drove onto his own land and locked himself in his car. It was held that the officers' licence to enter the land had not been withdrawn at that stage.) Telling officers to 'fuck off' is not necessarily enough to withdraw this implied licence (*Snook* v *Mannion* [1982] RTR 321).
- A person cannot seek refuge on someone else's land as a trespasser themselves; a requirement for a breath test and any subsequent arrest may be lawful if the person is a trespasser (see *Morris* v *Beardmore* [1980] RTR 321).
- If a person has been lawfully arrested on their own land, officers may remain on the land and enter premises to recapture them, even if asked to leave (*Hart* v *Chief Constable of Kent* [1983] Crim LR 117).
- Although the provisions of s. 15(2) of the Road Traffic Offenders Act 1988 may render evidence from a specimen taken after an unlawful arrest admissible (**see para. 3.5.7.3**), any finding that the officer(s) concerned acted in a way that they knew to be unlawful or unwarranted may lead to that evidence being excluded under s. 78 of the Police and Criminal Evidence Act 1984 (see *DPP* v *Godwin* [1991] RTR 303).

- Note that, where a constable imposes a requirement to co-operate with a preliminary breath test at any place, he/she is entitled to remain at or near that place in order to impose on the person a requirement for an *evidential* specimen under s. 7 (s. 7(2C)) there.

3.5.5 Evidential Specimens

Sections 7–9 of the Road Traffic Act 1988 govern the procedure for obtaining specimens for analysis, or evidential specimens. Unlike the preliminary breath tests above, specimens taken under this part of the Act are retained for evidential purposes in subsequent hearings. Such specimens will either be by breath samples taken on an approved machine (e.g. the Lion Intoximeter or the Camic Breath Analyser) or by blood/urine samples.

The printouts from 'approved' machines will generally be admissible in evidence under s. 69 of the Police and Criminal Evidence Act 1984. Minor errors in the printing functions of such machines will not necessarily invalidate the evidence produced by the machine, provided it can be shown that the analytical function of the machine was calibrated and working properly (*Reid* v *DPP* [1999] RTR 357).

Many of the difficulties which have been encountered during the police station process have now been addressed by police forces adopting a national pro-forma and strict adherence to those forms will significantly reduce the likelihood of convictions being quashed (see below).

3.5.5.1 Provision of Specimens for Analysis

The Road Traffic Act 1988, s. 7 states:

(1) In the course of an investigation into whether a person has committed an offence under section 3A, 4 or 5 of this Act a constable may, subject to the following provisions of this section and section 9 of this Act, require him—
   (a) to provide two specimens of breath for analysis by means of a device of a type approved by the Secretary of State, or
   (b) to provide a specimen of blood or urine for a laboratory test.
(2) A requirement under this section to provide specimens of breath can only be made—
   (a) at a police station,
   (b) at a hospital, or
   (c) at or near a place where a relevant breath test has been administered to the person concerned or would have been so administered but for his failure to co-operate with it.
(2A) For the purposes of this section 'a relevant breath test' is a procedure involving the provision by the person concerned of a specimen of breath to be used for the purpose of obtaining an indication whether the proportion of alcohol in his breath or blood is likely to exceed the prescribed limit.
(2B) A requirement under this section to provide specimens of breath may not be made at or near a place mentioned in subsection (2)(c) above unless the constable making it—
   (a) is in uniform, or
   (b) has imposed a requirement on the person concerned to cooperate with a relevant breath test in circumstances in which section 6(5) of this Act applies.
(2C) Where a constable has imposed a requirement on the person concerned to co-operate with a relevant breath test at any place, he is entitled to remain at or near that place in order to impose on him there a requirement under this section.
(2D) If a requirement under subsection (1)(a) above has been made at a place other than at a police station, such a requirement may subsequently be made at a police station if (but only if)—
   (a) a device or a reliable device of the type mentioned in subsection (1)(a) above was not available at that place or it was for any other reason not practicable to use such a device there, or

(b) the constable who made the previous requirement has reasonable cause to believe that the device used there has not produced a reliable indication of the proportion of alcohol in the breath of the person concerned.

(3) A requirement under this section to provide a specimen of blood or urine can only be made at a police station or at a hospital; and it cannot be made at a police station unless—

(a) the constable making the requirement has reasonable cause to believe that for medical reasons a specimen of breath cannot be provided or should not be required, or

(b) specimens of breath have not been provided elsewhere and at the time the requirement is made a device or a reliable device of the type mentioned in subsection (1)(a) above is not available at the police station or it is then for any other reason not practicable to use such a device there, or

(bb) a device of the type mentioned in subsection (1)(a) above has been used (at the police station or elsewhere) but the constable who required the specimens of breath has reasonable cause to believe that the device has not produced a reliable indication of the proportion of alcohol in the breath of the person concerned, or

(bc) as a result of the administration of a preliminary drug test, the constable making the requirement has reasonable cause to believe that the person required to provide a specimen of blood or urine has a drug in his body, or

(c) the suspected offence is one under section 3A or 4 of this Act and the constable making the requirement has been advised by a medical practitioner that the condition of the person required to provide the specimen might be due to some drug;

but may then be made notwithstanding that the person required to provide the specimen has already provided or been required to provide two specimens of breath.

(4) . . .

(5) A specimen of urine shall be provided within one hour of the requirement for its provision being made and after the provision of a previous specimen of urine.

(6) . . .

(7) A constable must, on requiring any person to provide a specimen in pursuance of this section, warn him that a failure to provide it may render him liable to prosecution.

KEYNOTE

As the evidential samples taken will form part of the case against a defendant, a lot of attention is paid to the device that was used and the extent to which its readings can be relied upon.

Although the technical development of approved devices for taking evidential specimens differentiates between 'deep lung' air and 'mouth alcohol', the wording of the offence under s. 5(1)(a) makes no such distinction. The Divisional Court has therefore held that, using the dictionary definition of 'breath', there is no justification for limiting the offence to 'deep lung air' readings and that, even if a driver's specimen may have come from a reflux of his or her stomach content or from mouth alcohol, both met the ordinary definition of 'breath' and were enough to support a conviction for the offence (*Zafar* v *DPP* [2004] EWHC 2468).

While the reliability of a reading made by any device in any particular case is always open to challenge by way of admissible evidence, a defendant does not have an automatic right to challenge the Secretary of State's approval of devices every time they are used (see *DPP* v *Memery* [2002] EWHC 1720).

In the case of a breath specimen it is presumed that the machine used was reliable; if that presumption is challenged by relevant evidence, the magistrates will have to be satisfied that the machine had provided a reading on which they could rely before they make the assumption (*DPP* v *Brown and Teixeira* [2001] EWHC Admin 931; *Cracknell* v *Willis* [1987] 3 WLR 1082). This is not however the same as the statutory presumption under s. 15(2) of the Road Traffic Act 1988 (as to which, see below). Where there are reasons to believe that a type of device is generally unreliable (as opposed to the specific device used in a particular case), representations should be made to the Secretary of State (see *R* v *Skegness Magistrates' Court, ex parte Cardy* [1985] RTR 49); it is not open to magistrates to consider whether the type of device should be on the list of 'approved devices' because of some alleged general design flaw (*DPP* v *Brown and Teixeira*, above).

The fact that specimens of breath have been provided under s. 7 above does not prevent the power of arrest (under s. 6D(1)—see para. 3.5.4.5) having effect if the constable who imposed the requirement to provide the specimens has reasonable cause to believe that the device used to analyse the specimens has not produced a reliable indication of the proportion of alcohol in the breath of the person (s. 6D(1A)).

Note that where the defendant has provided an alternative specimen of blood or urine (see paras 3.5.5.2 to 3.5.6.1) there is no requirement on the prosecution to prove that the device used was either reliable or of an approved type (*Wright* v *DPP* [2005] EWHC 1211).

3.5.5.2 The Requirement

Unlike the requirement for specimens of blood or urine, a requirement under s. 7 to provide evidential *breath* specimens can be made:

(a) at a police station,
(b) at a hospital, or
(c) at or near a place where a preliminary breath test has been administered to that person or would have been but for their failure to co-operate with it.

That requirement can be made of more than one person in respect of the same vehicle (e.g. if it is believed that one of three defendants was driving the vehicle) (*Pearson* v *Metropolitan Police Commissioner* [1988] RTR 276). A requirement under s. 7 to provide specimens of breath cannot be made at or near the place where a preliminary breath test has been administered to the person (or would have been but for their failure to co-operate) unless the constable making it:

* is in uniform, or
* has imposed a requirement on the person concerned to co-operate with a preliminary breath test in circumstances where s. 6(5) applies (i.e. following an accident; **see para. 3.5.4.3**).

Note that where a constable has imposed a requirement on the person concerned to co-operate with a preliminary breath test at any place, he/she is entitled to remain at or near that place in order to impose on the person a requirement for an evidential specimen under s. 7 there (s. 7(2C)).

If a requirement for an evidential breath specimen is made under s. 7(1)(a) at a place other than at a police station, such a requirement can still be made later *at* a police station but only if:

* a device or a reliable device was not available at that place or it was for any other reason not practicable to use such a device there, or
* the constable who made the previous requirement has reasonable cause to believe that the device used there has not produced a reliable indication of the proportion of alcohol in the breath of the person concerned (s. 7(2D)).

For further discussion of these issues **see para. 3.5.5.4**.

A requirement for blood or urine can only be made at a police station if the conditions under s. 7(3)(a) to (c) are met.

3.5.5.3 Medical Reasons

For the officer making the requirement to have 'reasonable cause to *believe*' that medical reasons exist, there is no need to seek medical advice first (see *Dempsey* v *Catton* [1986] RTR 194). It is the objective *cause* of that belief which will be considered by the courts, not whether the officer actually did believe that a medical reason existed (*Davis* v *DPP* [1988] RTR 156).

In *Kinsall* v *DPP* [2002] EWHC 545, the Divisional Court held that, just because the defendant had a mouth spray (for angina) and tablets at the time of arrest, that did not of itself impose an obligation on the relevant police officer to consult a doctor before deciding that any specimen to be provided would be blood. In that case the officer had asked the defendant if there were any medical reasons why blood should not be taken and he had said that there were not.

Where an officer specifically asks whether there are any medical reasons for not taking a blood sample, he/she is entitled to rely on the answer given unless it is obvious that such reasons exist (*Jubb* v *DPP* [2002] EWHC 2317).

If a person is too drunk to provide a breath specimen, that may be regarded as a 'medical' reason for requiring a sample of blood/urine (*Young* v *DPP* [1992] RTR 328).

3.5.5.4 Device 'Available'?

If the relevant machine at a police station will not calibrate or is in some other way unreliable, this would appear to make it 'unavailable'. In such a case, however, the driver may be taken to another police station where such a machine is 'available'; this may be done *even if the driver has already provided two samples on the inaccurate machine* (*Denny* v *DPP* [1990] RTR 417).

Whether a machine is 'available' if it produces an accurate reading of the analysis of the driver's breath but cannot, for some reason, produce a hard copy printout of that reading is open to some doubt. In one case (*Morgan* v *Lee* [1985] RTR 409) where the officer did not know of the machine's defect, his subsequent request for a blood sample was held to have been unlawful. However, in a later case the Divisional Court held that, if the officer knew at the time that the machine had any form of malfunction, he/she could require a specimen of blood/urine under s. 7(3)(b) (*Thompson* v *Thynne* [1986] Crim LR 629) and this *subjective* approach has been followed and approved many times since.

Where the requirement for blood/urine is made under s. 7(3)(b), that sample must be used and the prosecution cannot revert to evidence produced by the breath sample (*Badkin* v *Chief Constable of South Yorkshire* [1988] RTR 401).

If the option to provide a blood sample is chosen, then, again, the driver may be taken to another police station where a doctor is available (*Chief Constable of Kent* v *Berry* [1986] Crim LR 748). (The general law relating to doctors' involvement has changed since this case, **see para. 3.5.5.7.**)

Section 7(3)(b) also allows the officer (see below) the option of a blood/urine specimen when, 'for any other reason' it is not practicable to use a breath-testing device at the police station. This would clearly include the situation where no trained operator is available to work the machine (*Chief Constable of Avon and Somerset* v *Kelliher* [1986] Crim LR 635).

3.5.5.5 Drugs

In contrast to the condition at s. 7(3)(a), the advice of a medical practitioner *must* be sought before the power to request blood/urine can be made under s. 7(3)(c); even then, it can only be exercised in cases of being unfit (**see para. 3.5.2**) or causing death by careless driving when under the influence of drink or drugs (**see para. 3.2.7**). When such medical advice is sought, the doctor must give the officer a clear verbal statement to the effect that the driver's condition was due to some drug before the power arises (*Cole* v *DPP* [1988] RTR 224).

3.5.5.6 Warning

The warning required by s. 7(7) is critical to a successful prosecution for failing to provide a specimen when required under s. 7(3). It is not needed when a driver elects to give an alternative sample under s. 8 below (see *Hayes* v *DPP* [1993] Crim LR 966 and also *DPP* v *Jackson; Stanley* v *DPP* [1998] 3 WLR 514 below).

3.5.5.7 Choice by Officer

The Road Traffic Act 1988, s. 7 states:

> (4) If the provision of a specimen other than a specimen of breath may be required in pursuance of this section the question whether it is to be a specimen of blood or a specimen of urine and, in the case of a specimen of blood, the question who is to be asked to take it shall be decided (subject to subsection (4A)) by the constable making the requirement.
>
> (4A) Where a constable decides for the purposes of subsection (4) to require the provision of a specimen of blood, there shall be no requirement to provide such a specimen if—
>
>   (a) the medical practitioner who is asked to take the specimen is of the opinion that, for medical reasons, it cannot or should not be taken; or
>
>   (b) the registered health care professional who is asked to take it is of that opinion and there is no contrary opinion from a medical practitioner;
>
> and, where by virtue of this subsection there can be no requirement to provide a specimen of blood, the constable may require a specimen of urine instead.

KEYNOTE

In exercising the power under s. 7(3) and s. 8 below, the decision as to whether the specimen will be blood or urine will be made by the officer. The line of decided cases which allowed a 'driver's preference' was ended by the House of Lords' ruling in *DPP* v *Warren* [1993] AC 319 where their lordships stated unequivocally that the decision, in both situations, is to be made by the officer. However, that is not to say that the officer can simply assume that blood should be taken unless medical reasons prevent it, nor that the officer should take no notice of any information given by the driver. The statutory discretion given to the officer by s. 7(4), although wide, has to be exercised reasonably (*Joseph* v *DPP* [2003] EWHC 3078). In Joseph the driver told the officer that he was a Rastafarian and therefore could not give blood. The officer's insistence that the driver give blood anyway, even though there was no reason not to take urine instead, was held to be so unreasonable as to make it unlawful.

Following the decision in *DPP* v *Warren*, many forces adapted their pro-formas once again in order to close what Lord Bridge called *a variety of wholly unmeritorious avenues of escape from conviction*. For a while it was believed that Lord Bridge's *dicta* in *Warren* would avoid any further appeals based on the procedure followed by police officers when obtaining evidential specimens in line with their respective force forms. However, there have been several more cases where the defendants have argued that the *Warren* formula, as laid down by Lord Bridge, has not been followed. Most of those cases have concerned what information must be given, and when it must be given to a defendant when explaining the choices available under s. 7(4) above and s. 8(2) below. In the first case, *Fraser* v *DPP* [1997] RTR 373, Lord Bingham CJ examined many of the other authorities since *Warren*. In his judgment he endorsed the pro-forma used by the Northumbria police and said that there was a danger of putting *a new and heretical gloss* on the statute itself. His lordship held that there were many things which drivers ought to be told, but they need not be told them all at once. His lordship went on to say that there was no requirement for an officer to explain to a defendant *at the time of making a decision under s. 7(4)* that any blood sample taken would only be so taken by a doctor.

In the second case, *DPP* v *Jackson; Stanley* v *DPP* [1998] 3 WLR 514, the House of Lords stressed the distinction between the roles of the police officer and the doctor. The police officer decides *which* evidential sample(s) should be obtained and the medical practitioner decides *on the validity of the reasons put forward by the defendant* as to why a specimen of blood should not be taken. Their lordships held that, with three exceptions, the rules laid down in *Warren* were not mandatory elements of the procedure for taking evidential specimens but were guidelines indicating matters which should be brought to a defendant's attention before he/she exercised any choice that might be available.

The three elements that are mandatory are:

- in a s. 7(3) case (see above), the warning required under s. 7(7) above;
- a statement as to why, in a case under s. 7(3), a breath specimen could not be used; and
- a statement, in a case under s. 8(2) below (**see para. 3.5.6.1**), that the specimen of breath containing the lower proportion of alcohol did not exceed 50 microgrammes in 100 millilitres of breath. In such a case, the police officer should ask whether there are any medical reasons why a particular specimen could not or should not be taken.

Where the person has given a breath specimen which has a reading not exceeding 50 microgrammes in 100 millilitres of breath as described above, they should raise any medical reasons as to why a particular specimen should not be taken at the time. The Divisional Court has held that giving an unequivocal response declining the option of a blood or urine sample cannot later be raised under the guise of a 'medical reason' (see *R (On the Application of Ijaz)* v *DPP* [2004] EWHC 2635).

Note the alteration in the legislation (s. 7(4A) above) which now permits a registered health care professional (as well as a doctor) to take the blood sample where appropriate. The opinion of the health care professional will be sufficient to authorise the taking of a blood sample provided that there is no contrary opinion from a doctor. This does not mean that the health care professional's opinion has to be confirmed by, or routinely referred to, a doctor—in fact this would defeat the whole purpose of the changed legislation. A registered healthcare professional is either a registered nurse or a registered member of another health care profession designated for the purpose by the Secretary of State (Road Traffic Act 1988, s. 11(2)). This provision does not affect the requirements of s. 7A (see below) which still require a medical practitioner's involvement.

It would seem from the Divisional Court's decision in *Bobin* v *DPP* [1999] RTR 375 that, as long as the information set out above is provided by a police officer, it does not matter *which* police officer. Therefore, the warning under s. 7(7) might be given by, for instance, the arresting officer or by the custody officer who makes the requirement for the relevant specimen.

3.5.5.8 What Information Should be Given to a Defendant?

As with other decisions involving when and where to give information to a defendant, there are probably fewer dangers in giving more than is required, sooner than required than vice versa. Many of the cases before and since *Warren* have turned on the fact that drivers claim that they were not given the chance to reveal medical reasons as to why they could not give blood, or that they were not told that it would be a doctor who took the blood rather than a police officer. Although it is now clear from the House of Lords' decisions above that such opportunity and information need not be given out as a general requirement, there seems to be little harm in following an approach that errs on the side of caution.

The officer should explain what the options are and that the decision as to which will be chosen is the officer's; the driver should also be given the opportunity to state any reasons why blood should not be taken so that the officer may take the appropriate advice (*Edge* v *DPP* [1993] RTR 146).

3.5.5.9 Requesting Medical Practitioners to Take a Specimen

The Road Traffic Act 1988, s. 7A states:

(1) A constable may make a request to a medical practitioner for him to take a specimen of blood from a person ('the person concerned') irrespective of whether that person consents if—

    (a) that person is a person from whom the constable would (in the absence of any incapacity of that person and of any objection under section 9) be entitled under section 7 to require the provision of a specimen of blood for a laboratory test;

(b) it appears to that constable that that person has been involved in an accident that constitutes or is comprised in the matter that is under investigation or the circumstances of that matter;

(c) it appears to that constable that that person is or may be incapable (whether or not he has purported to do so) of giving a valid consent to the taking of a specimen of blood; and

(d) it appears to that constable that that person's incapacity is attributable to medical reasons.

(2) A request under this section—

    (a) shall not be made to a medical practitioner who for the time being has any responsibility (apart from the request) for the clinical care of the person concerned; and

    (b) shall not be made to a medical practitioner other than a police medical practitioner unless—

        (i) it is not reasonably practicable for the request to be made to a police medical practitioner; or

        (ii) it is not reasonably practicable for such a medical practitioner (assuming him to be willing to do so) to take the specimen.

(3) It shall be lawful for a medical practitioner to whom a request is made under this section, if he thinks fit—

    (a) to take a specimen of blood from the person concerned irrespective of whether that person consents; and

    (b) to provide the sample to a constable.

KEYNOTE

This addition to the drink driving legislation came about as a result of the procedural difficulties encountered where suspected drivers are injured in an accident and, as a result, are incapable of giving their consent to the taking of a blood sample. In order to prevent such drivers escaping conviction where they would otherwise have had to provide a blood sample, the legislation now allows for the sample to be taken lawfully without consent at the time. Thereafter, the system relies on the driver giving his or her permission for the sample to be tested in a laboratory. It must appear to the constable that the person has been 'involved' in an accident—this is far wider than suspecting that they were driving, attempting to drive or in charge of a vehicle at the time. However, the *reason* for the test will be important in determining the penalty available in the event that the person fails to give their consent (see below).

It must also appear to the officer that the person is or may be *incapable* (as opposed to simply unwilling) of giving valid consent and that this incapacity is attributable to medical reasons (rather than other issues such as language or ethical objections).

As a general rule the doctor approached should be a medical practitioner employed by or contracted to a police force (see s. 7A(7))—e.g. a Force Medical Examiner or Police Surgeon. If it is not reasonably practicable either to make the request to the police doctor, or for him/her to take the sample, another medical practitioner can be approached but not the doctor who has responsibility for the person's clinical care. The doctor is then empowered both to take the sample and to provide it to the officer without the person's consent if the doctor thinks fit—there is, however, no obligation to do so.

Given that most situations where this power will be relevant will concern people in hospital, the provisions covering patients should be considered (see para. 3.5.10).

The Road Traffic Act 1988, s. 7A goes on to state:

(4) If a specimen is taken in pursuance of a request under this section, the specimen shall not be subjected to a laboratory test unless the person from whom it was taken—

    (a) has been informed that it was taken; and

    (b) has been required by a constable to give his permission for a laboratory test of the specimen; and

    (c) has given his permission.

(5) A constable must, on requiring a person to give his permission for the purposes of this section for a laboratory test of a specimen, warn that person that a failure to give the permission may render him liable to prosecution.

KEYNOTE

The above requirements are critical if the analysis of any sample lawfully taken is to be of any evidential value. By implication, the requirement that the person gives his/her permission to the sample being sent to a laboratory means that he/she should only be informed of the above matters and given the statutory warning once capable of understanding what is going on.

3.5.6 Failing to Give Permission for Test or Provide Specimen

OFFENCE: **Failing to Give Permission for Laboratory Test of Specimen—*Road Traffic Act 1988, s. 7A(6)***

- Triable summarily • If the test was for ascertaining ability to drive or the proportion of alcohol at the time the offender was driving or attempting to drive—six months' imprisonment and/or a fine and obligatory disqualification • In any other case, three months' imprisonment and/or a fine and discretionary disqualification

The Road Traffic Act 1988, s. 7A states:

(6) A person who, without reasonable excuse, fails to give his permission for a laboratory test of a specimen of blood taken from him under this section is guilty of an offence.

KEYNOTE

For a discussion of what may amount to reasonable excuse, see para. 3.5.6.1. There should be far fewer opportunities for claiming reasonable excuses here given that there is no technical equipment involved. The permission being given (or not) is for the laboratory analysis, *not* the taking of the specimen. Therefore delaying the giving of permission in order to obtain legal advice may be acceptable, particularly as, once the specimen has been taken and properly stored, there is not the same urgency as there is with the *taking* of a specimen before the alcohol/drugs dissipate. 'Failing' includes refusing (s. 11(2)).

3.5.6.1 Choice by Defendant

The Road Traffic Act 1988, s. 8 states:

(1) Subject to subsection (2) below, of any two specimens of breath provided by any person in pursuance of section 7 of this Act that with the lower proportion of alcohol in the breath shall be used and the other shall be disregarded.
(2) If the specimen with the lower proportion of alcohol contains no more than 50 microgrammes of alcohol in 100 millilitres of breath, the person who provided it may claim that it should be replaced by such specimen as may be required under section 7(4) of this Act and, if he then provides such a specimen, neither specimen of breath shall be used.
(2A) If the person who makes a claim under subsection (2) above was required to provide specimens of breath under section 7 of this Act at or near a place mentioned in subsection (2)(c) of that section, a constable may arrest him without warrant.

KEYNOTE

Under s. 8(2) the driver does have a choice; that being to ask for the specimen of breath to be replaced by an option under s. 7(4) above. As discussed, once that request has been made, the choice as to whether it will be blood or urine will be the officer's.

There are detailed guidelines available to operators conducting evidential tests to ensure the reliability of the results produced. Just as a failure to follow the key requirements by the *defendant* can amount to a failure/refusal to provide, similarly a failure by the *operator* to follow such a requirement can allow the procedure to be challenged. However, in the latter case any failure must be such as to affect the *reliability* of the test. It is common for device manufacturers to issue guidelines that require a 20-minute period free from consumption of alcohol or other substances prior to the administration of the test. In *DPP* v *Carey* [1970] AC 1072, the House of Lords ruled that if an officer has no knowledge or reason to suspect consumption of any substances within the relevant 20-minute period, the test remains valid even if it later transpires that some substance was actually consumed during that 20-minute period. If the officer *does* have knowledge or reason to suspect such consumption, then 20-minutes should be allowed to elapse before administering the test. In *Coulter* v *DPP* [2005] EWHC 1533 the defendant had provided a positive breath specimen during a roadside screening test. During the police station procedure to obtain an evidential specimen the police officer asked if he had eaten anything. The defendant said he might have had a 'tic-tac' sweet. The officer nevertheless continued with the procedure and required a specimen of breath. The defendant refused and was charged under s. 7(6) of the Road Traffic Act 1988 (and the Road Traffic Offenders Act 1988, sch. 2). The police officer had been unaware of the guidelines recommending a 20-minute wait before testing a driver who had eaten recently before continuing with the procedure. The magistrates' court held that there was no case to answer as the officer should have waited 20 minutes before requiring a breath specimen and because the officer had been unable to show that the waiting period was not mandatory. On appeal by the DPP, the Divisional Court held that there was nothing in s. 7 to indicate that a requirement to produce a breath specimen was unlawful if the particular police guidelines were not followed. While it is possible for a failure to follow the guidelines to affect the reliability of a specimen, the court held that was not relevant in the instant case as no specimen of breath was ever provided.

When the driver is told of the option under s. 8(2), he/she *must* be told that the reason for the option is because the breath specimen with the lower proportion of alcohol contains no more than 50 microgrammes. Simply telling the driver that the option exists without giving this reason will amount to one of the fatal procedural failures set out in *Warren* above (**see para. 3.5.5.7**) (*R* v *Bolton Justices, ex parte Zafer Alli Khan* [1999] Crim LR 912).

If a driver elects to give blood and, through no fault of his/her own, the sample then proves unsuitable for evidential use, the original reading from the machine cannot be used in its place (*Archbold* v *Jones* [1985] Crim LR 740). Conversely, once a person has elected to provide a specimen of blood, there is no reliance on the breath specimen and therefore no requirement on the prosecution to prove that the device used was either reliable or of an approved type (*Wright* v *DPP* [2005] EWHC 1211).

Although the choice is to be made by the requesting officer, the possibility of medical reasons for not giving blood must still be considered. An alleged fear of needles by the driver (which has provided the courts with a number of opportunities to explore this area) is a relevant consideration when making a decision as to whether a blood sample should be taken (*DPP* v *Jackson; Stanley* v *DPP* above and also *Johnson* v *West Yorkshire Metropolitan Police* [1986] RTR 167). The driver should be given the opportunity to state any medical reasons why blood should not be taken but failure to give him/her that opportunity will not necessarily be fatal to an ensuing prosecution (*DPP* v *Orchard* [2000] All ER (D) 1457). However, any such reasons should be raised promptly. Where a driver clearly declined the option of replacing the breath specimen with a blood or urine sample, he was not permitted to claim later that a phobia of needles had caused him to decline the opportunity (*R (On the Application of Ijaz)* v *DPP* [2004] EWHC 2635).

The medical advice may be given to the officer over the telephone if appropriate (*Andrews* v *DPP* [1992] RTR 1).

If the person claims that their specimen should be replaced under the above section and they were required to give that specimen at or near a place where a preliminary breath test had been administered to them (or would have been so administered but for their failure to co-operate) a constable may arrest them without warrant.

In assessing a highly unusual and creative defence to s. 7(6), the Divisional Court was not prepared to accept that seeing blood would have sent the defendant—a registered member of the Zimbabwe National Traditional Healers Association—into a trance whereby he could be violent to himself and others. A refusal to provide a blood specimen for such 'spiritual reasons' was not a reasonable excuse on the facts of this case—*DPP* v *Mukandiwa* [2005] EWHC 2977.

OFFENCE: **Failing to Provide Evidential Specimen—*Road Traffic Act 1988, s. 7(6)***
• Triable summarily • Six months' imprisonment and/or a fine • Obligatory disqualification

The Road Traffic Act 1988, s. 7 states:

(6) A person who, without reasonable excuse, fails to provide a specimen when required to do so in pursuance of this section is guilty of an offence.

KEYNOTE

Section 11(3) of the Road Traffic Act 1988 states that a breath specimen must be provided in such a way as to enable the analysis to be carried out. If a driver produces it in any other way, he/she will have 'failed to provide'.

As with preliminary breath tests, 'fail' will include a refusal. If a driver elects to substitute a breath specimen (which gave a reading of no more than 50 microgrammes) with one of blood/urine under s. 8 (above), and subsequently fails or refuses to do so, he/she does not commit an offence under s. 7(6); you revert to the original breath specimen.

A person's general conduct in answer to a lawful requirement to provide a specimen, or a conditional response (e.g. 'I'm only providing a specimen if . . .') can amount to a refusal. The Court of Appeal has held that any such conduct or any such 'condition' does not need to be 'outrageous' (cf. *R* v *Mackey* [1977] RTR 146). The key issue when considering any condition imposed by a driver before compliance is whether it amounted to a reasonable excuse for his or her failure to comply with the test.

Provision of only one specimen of breath is a 'failure to provide' (*Cracknell* v *Willis* [1987] 3 All ER 801).

The issues arising where a defendant claims to have had a 'reasonable excuse' for failing to provide a specimen of breath were reviewed by the Divisional Court in *DPP* v *Falzarano* [2001] RTR 14.

In *Falzarano* magistrates had accepted the defendant's claim that she was physically unable to provide the specimen as she was suffering from a panic attack. The defendant proved that she had a history of such attacks and that she was receiving medical treatment for the condition. Despite evidence from her own doctor that the condition and her failure to take her medication on the day in question should not have prevented her from providing a specimen of breath, the magistrates found that she did in fact have a reasonable excuse. On appeal by way of case stated, the Divisional Court held that:

• The 'reasonable excuse' had to arise out of a physical or mental inability to provide a specimen or a substantial risk to health in its provision (per *R* v *Lennard* [1973] RTR 252).

• The evidence in support of the 'reasonable excuse' normally had to be medical but the defendant could provide it himself/herself.

• There had to be a causative link between the excuse and the failure to provide a specimen (*DPP* v *Pearman* [1992] RTR 407).

• Being drunk or under stress was not in itself enough to provide a 'reasonable excuse' for failing to provide a specimen.

• Having considered the medical evidence, legal advice from their clerk and the demeanour of the defendant when testifying, the magistrates had been entitled on the evidence to find that Falzarano had a reasonable excuse for failing to provide breath specimens.

This decision does *not* mean that shortness of breath caused by panic attacks or stress will always amount to a reasonable excuse; it does, however, provide a useful review of the law in this area.

Reasonable Excuse

What amounts to a 'reasonable excuse' is a matter of law (see *Falzarano* above); whether the defendant actually *had* such an excuse is a question of fact for the court to determine having regard to the particular circumstances in each case. There have been many cases where 'excuses' have been put forward. The following is a brief summary:

Not Reasonable
- Refusal until legal advice has been sought. The incorporation of the European Convention on Human Rights has not altered this position which was established in *DPP* v *Billington* [1988] RTR 231; *Campbell* v *DPP* [2002] EWHC 1314. This was reiterated by the Divisional Court in *Kennedy* v *DPP* [2002] EWHC 2297 where it was held that the public interest required that the obtaining of specimens should not be delayed in this way.
- The absence of an appropriate adult where the defendant is a juvenile (*DPP* v *Evans* [2002] EWHC 2976).
- Refusal until solicitor present.
- Refusal on advice by solicitor.
- Refusal until driver had read the Codes of Practice under PACE.
- Mistaken belief by the defendant.
- Belief that the officer did not have the authority to make the requirement.
- Religious beliefs.
- Self-induced intoxication.
- Mental anguish caused by custody officer's behaviour.

Reasonable
- Mental incapacity.
- Physical incapacity.
- Inability to understand requirement caused by factors other than drink or drugs (e.g. language barrier).

Where any physical or mental incapacity (to provide the specimen or to understand the warning which accompanies it) is put forward, there will need to be clear, independent support for the claim being genuine (e.g. from a medical practitioner).

The courts have warned of the need for caution when accepting a defendant's claim of such incapacity, particularly given the generally stressful nature of the police station procedure, together with the possible effects following an accident or motoring incident leading up to the request.

In *DPP* v *Furby* [2000] RTR 181, it was held that if a police officer required a motorist to provide a breath specimen at the police station and the motorist made no effort at all to blow into the machine, he/she could not subsequently argue that he/she had a reasonable excuse for failing to do so. This principle was re-stated by the Administrative Court in a case where the driver alleged at the roadside that he suffered from bronchitis and therefore could not provide a breath sample. The arresting officer did not tell the custody officer of this alleged condition, neither did the motorist himself. As a result, the court held that no objective observer could say that the custody officer had 'reasonable cause to believe that for medical reasons a specimen of breath should not be required' and therefore the defendant should have been convicted for failing to provide a specimen (*DPP* v *Lonsdale* [2001] EWHC Admin 95).

Where a defendant's mental capacity to understand the warning is impaired by his/her drunkenness, this is not a 'reasonable' excuse (*DPP* v *Beech* [1992] RTR 239).

3.5.7 Admissibility and Use of Specimens

The only point in the police taking evidential specimens in road traffic cases is to establish for the purposes of any relevant proceedings the extent to which any alcohol or other drug in the defendant's body amounted/contributed to an offence. Therefore it is important to understand the rules governing the admissibility and use of specimens.

Note that, unlike alcohol, the mere presence of a controlled drug in a driver's body may of itself be relevant to the issue of whether a person drove dangerously (as to which **see para. 3.2.2.2**). In such cases there is no requirement to prove either evidence of actual impairment (as there is with some offences—**see para. 3.5.2.1**) or evidence of a specific level of the drug (as there is with the 'prescribed limit' offences—**see para. 3.5.3**)—*R* v *Pleydell* [2005] EWCA Crim 1447.

3.5.7.1 Blood

Issues regarding the admissibility of blood specimens will differ depending on whether the specimen was taken under s. 7A (without the person's consent) or in any other case.

Taking the general situations first, s. 11(4) of the Road Traffic Act 1988 provides that a person 'provides a specimen of blood' only if he/she consents and the specimen is taken by a medical practitioner or, if at a police station, a medical practitioner or registered health care professional. Section 15 of the Road Traffic Offenders Act 1988 (see below) states that any sample of blood will be disregarded unless it is so taken. Once consent is given, it is for the doctor to say from which part of the body it will be taken. Any insistence on a different course of action will be a refusal (*Rushton* v *Higgins* [1972] RTR 456).

In the case of specimens taken under s. 7A (see above), there will clearly be no consent. Section 15(5A) of the Road Traffic Offenders Act 1988 makes separate provision for these cases.

3.5.7.2 Urine

Urine samples do not need to be taken by a medical practitioner.

The samples will be admissible as long as they are provided within the time set out under s. 7(5) and there are two distinct samples (as opposed to two samples taken during the same act of urinating) (*Prosser* v *Dickeson* [1982] RTR 96).

The hour within which the specimens must be produced starts from the time the request is made. However, the defendant must be given the opportunity to provide the urine within the one hour period (see *Robertson* v *DPP* [2004] EWHC 517).

3.5.7.3 Use of Specimens

The Road Traffic Offenders Act 1988, s. 15 states:

(1) This section and section 16 of this Act apply in respect of proceedings for an offence under section 3A, 4 or 5 of the Road Traffic Act 1988 (driving offences connected with drink or drugs); and expressions used in this section and section 16 of this Act have the same meaning as in sections 3A to 10 of that Act.

(2) Evidence of the proportion of alcohol or any drug in a specimen of breath, blood or urine provided by or taken from the accused shall, in all cases (including cases where the specimen was not provided or taken in connection with the alleged offence), be taken into account and, subject to subsection (3) below, it shall be assumed that the proportion of alcohol in the accused's breath, blood or urine at the time of the alleged offence was not less than in the specimen.

(3) That assumption shall not be made if the accused proves—

    (a) that he consumed alcohol before he provided the specimen or had it taken from him and—

        (i) in relation to an offence under section 3A, after the time of the alleged offence, and

        (ii) otherwise, after he had ceased to drive, attempt to drive or be in charge of a vehicle on a road or other public place, and

    (b) that had he not done so the proportion of alcohol in his breath, blood or urine would not have exceeded the prescribed limit and, if it is alleged that he was unfit to drive through drink, would not have been such as to impair his ability to drive properly.

(4) A specimen of blood shall be disregarded unless—

    (a) it was taken from the accused with his consent and either—

        (i) in a police station by a medical practitioner or a registered health care professional; or

        (ii) elsewhere by a medical practitioner; or

    (b) it was taken from the accused by a medical practitioner under section 7A of the Road Traffic Act 1988 and the accused subsequently gave his permission for a laboratory test of the specimen.

(5) Where, at the time a specimen of blood or urine was provided by the accused, he asked to be provided with such a specimen, evidence of the proportion of alcohol or any drug found in the specimen is not admissible on behalf of the prosecution unless—

    (a) the specimen in which the alcohol or drug was found is one of two parts into which the specimen provided by the accused was divided at the time it was provided, and

    (b) the other part was supplied to the accused.

(5A) Where a specimen of blood was taken from the accused under section 7A of the Road Traffic Act 1988, evidence of the proportion of alcohol or any drug found in the specimen is not admissible on behalf of the prosecution unless—

    (a) the specimen in which the alcohol or drug was found is one of two parts into which the specimen taken from the accused was divided at the time it was taken; and

    (b) any request to be supplied with the other part which was made by the accused at the time when he gave his permission for a laboratory test of the specimen was complied with.

3.5.8 Evidential Matters

There are some further evidential matters that are really matters for the courts but are still of interest to officers and prosecuting authorities in understanding the system as a whole. These are considered below.

KEYNOTE

Section 15(2) requires the court to:

- take into account evidence of the proportion of alcohol *or any drug* in a specimen of breath, blood or urine *in all cases*; and
- assume that the proportion of alcohol (though apparently not drugs) in the defendant's breath, blood or urine at the time of the alleged offence was *not less* than that found in the specimen, subject to the circumstances in s. 15(3).

As such, s. 15 is a 'legislative interference' with the general presumption of innocence in criminal matters and will therefore be viewed with extreme caution by the courts in light of Article 6(2) of the European Convention on Human Rights (see **General Police Duties, chapter 4.5**). However, the Court of Appeal has held that this section and the 'interference' with the general presumption of innocence by it imposing a persuasive burden on the defendant is both justified and no greater than necessary (*R v Drummond* [2002] EWCA Crim 527). (See also *Parker v DPP* [2001] RTR 240.)

For the arguments relating to 'reverse' burdens of proof generally, see *R v Lambert* [2001] UKHL 37.

The presumption in s. 15(2) is specific to offences where alcohol is a constituent of the offence itself and cannot be extended to other driving offences (*R v Ash* [1999] RTR 347).

Note that the presumption is not an assumption that the relevant approved device (**see para. 3.5.5.1**) was working correctly, but an assumption that the proportion of alcohol in the relevant specimen was not less than the proportion of alcohol at the time of the offence (*DPP v Brown and Teixeira* [2001] EWHC Admin 931).

Where the defendant goes on to provide a specimen of blood or urine, the technical issues relating to the reliability or type-approval of the breath testing device become irrelevant (see *Branagan* v *DPP* [2000] RTR 235; *Wright* v *DPP* [2005] EWHC 1211).

3.5.8.1 Taking Evidence into Account

The first requirement, to take the evidence into account in all cases, was accepted by the House of Lords in *Fox* v *Chief Constable of Gwent* [1986] AC 281 as meaning that evidence obtained following an unlawful arrest was still admissible. However, their lordships did not hold this to be an exception to the general law on the admissibility of improperly or unfairly obtained evidence (as to which, **see Evidence and Procedure, chapter 2.8**). Under the general discretion given to courts by s. 78 of the Police and Criminal Evidence Act 1984 to exclude unfair evidence, evidence of specimens could be so excluded in spite of the provisions of s. 15(2) above.

Where a defendant claimed to have asthma and made several unsuccessful attempts to give a specimen of breath at a police station, magistrates were wrong in law to take into account the partial breath test readings regarding a charge of driving whilst unfit through drink (*Willicott* v *DPP* [2001] EWHC 415).

3.5.8.2 Making the Assumption

Section 15(3) allows the defendant to produce evidence which prevents that presumption from being made. This enables a defendant to prove that the alcohol had been consumed between the time of the alleged offence and the provision of the specimen and, that if the defendant had not consumed it, then he/she would not have been over the limit/unfit. That is, the defendant can prove that the alcohol level at the time of the alleged offence was lower than shown in the analysis. This allows for the 'hip flask defence' which was, for a while, raised frequently by drivers who grabbed a flask from their glove compartment and took a swift drink from it before they were asked to provide a breath sample. The attractiveness of 'post-incident drinking' in order to beat the breathalyser in this way was drastically reduced when the process of 'back calculation' was introduced (see below). Nevertheless, s. 15(3) above allows the defence to show, on the balance of probabilities, that the level of alcohol in the defendant's body at the time of the alleged offence was lower than at the time of the analysis.

In *R v Drummond* [2002] EWCA Crim 527, it was argued that this contravened the presumption of innocence (under Article 6(2) of the European Convention) because it placed the burden of proof on the defendant to prove that he/she had consumed alcohol after the offence but before providing a specimen. The Court of Appeal did not agree. It held that conviction for the relevant drink driving offences followed an exact scientific test; if the defendant chose to drink after the event, it was he/she who defeated the aim of the legislation by making the test potentially unreliable. Furthermore, the relevant scientific evidence which the defendant could use to counter the specimen result was within his/her control rather than the prosecution's. The burden of proof upon the defence in making such a case would, as ever, be 'on the balance of probabilities'.

An example of this in practice can be seen in *DPP* v *Ellery* [2005] EWHC 2513. In that case the defendant, who had been seen to drive after drinking, was required to provide a screening breath test at his home. At trial the magistrates accepted that the defendant had drunk a can of lager after he had driven and held that once a driver proved, on a balance of probabilities, that there was post-driving consumption of alcohol, the burden of proof shifted back to the prosecution to prove, beyond reasonable doubt, that he/she was over the limit at the time of driving. On appeal both parties agreed that the magistrates' court had applied the wrong test but the driver argued against the burden of proof imposed on him under s. 15(3)(b). The Divisional Court held that the case authorities allowed legislative interference with the presumption of innocence provided it was necessary. The court held that it was the defendant's drinking after the event which defeated the aim of the legislature and that he had done something which made a scientific test potentially unreliable. Any relevant scientific evidence to set against the specimen of breath or blood was all within the knowledge (or means of access) of the defendant rather than the Crown. Accordingly in the instant case the magistrates' court had erred in law and on the facts could not have been satisfied (on the balance of probabilities) that his blood alcohol level, at the time of driving, was below the prescribed limit.

The assumption does not prevent the prosecution from adducing evidence to show that the proportion of alcohol in the defendant's body was in fact *higher* than that in the specimen. To do so, however, requires a process of 'back calculation', a process accepted by the House of Lords in *Gumbley* v *Cunningham* [1989] RTR 49. In that case their lordships said that such a process should be used with caution and evidence of back calculation should not be relied upon unless it is easily understood and clearly persuasive. In a later case Lord Lane CJ said that such calculations should be treated with great care and that they would be less helpful in deciding cases involving driving while over the prescribed limit than they would in offences involving the *standard* of driving (**see chapter 3.2**) (*R* v *Downes* [1991] RTR 395).

The validity of a back calculation relies on there being an unbroken period leading up to the relevant event (e.g. the driving of a vehicle or the occurrence of an accident). If the prosecution are unable to remove the real possibility that alcohol had been consumed between the relevant event and the specimen being taken, it will not be safe for a court to convict (*R* v *Hodnitt* [2003] EWCA Crim 441).

The effect of s. 15(2) is to limit any use of back calculation to the *prosecution*. Other than in the context of s. 15(3), a defendant may not adduce back calculation evidence to show that the level of alcohol in his/her body was in fact *below* the amount in the specimen (*Millard* v *DPP* (1990) 91 Cr App R 108).

3.5.8.3 Specimen of Blood

Under s. 15(4) the prosecution must generally prove that the defendant consented to the taking of blood and that burden will only be discharged if this is proved beyond a reasonable doubt (see *Friel* v *Dickson* [1992] RTR 366). This may generally be proved by documentary evidence signed by a medical practitioner, subject to certain provisos (s. 16(2)). However, note the special provisions that apply where the blood specimen was taken under s. 7A (i.e. without consent following an accident).

3.5.8.4 Provision of Specimen to Defendant

Under s. 15(5) and (5A), the prosecution must show that the defendant, if he/she asked for one, was provided with a specimen divided and supplied as set out in the subsection. Although the specimen must be divided 'at the time' it is taken and as part of the same continuing event, there is no need for it to be done in the defendant's presence (*DPP* v *Elstob* [1992] Crim LR 518). Again, although the *division* of the specimen must be made at the time it is taken, there is no requirement that the defendant be *provided* with his/her part 'at the time'—only that it be provided within a reasonable time thereafter (see *R* v *Sharp* [1968] 2 QB 564). The part-specimen must be in such a quantity and of such a quality that it is capable of being analysed (*Smith* v *Cole* [1971] 1 All ER 200). Whether or not this has been done is a question of fact for the court to determine on its own merits.

The Administrative Court has held, however, that there is no free-standing right, either under the 1988 Act or at common law, for the defendant to be informed of his/her entitlement to a part of the sample (see *Campbell* v *DPP* [2002] EWHC 1314). However, the court acknowledged that there might be occasions where the failure to tell a defendant of this entitlement might cause him/her prejudice and thereby allow the admissibility of the sample to be challenged. Therefore, although there is no specific right to be told of this entitlement, it is probably both good sense and good practice to do so.

The Court of Appeal refused to extend the requirements of s. 15(5) to an offence of causing death by dangerous driving (as to which, **see chapter 3.2**) (*R* v *Ash* [1999] RTR 347). In that case a sample of blood was properly taken at a hospital from a driver who had been very seriously injured in a fatal road traffic accident. The driver argued that, as the sample of blood taken from him had not been divided into two parts, evidence of its analysis should not have been allowed at his trial. The court held that s. 15 applied only to the sections of the Road Traffic Act 1988 that were expressly set out, namely ss. 3A, 4 and 5. This restricted nature of s. 15 meant that it could not be extended to other offences such as causing death by dangerous driving and that, had Parliament intended otherwise, it would have said so. The court also held that the admission of that evidence would not therefore be 'unfair' and should not be excluded under s. 78 of the Police and Criminal Evidence Act 1984.

Where a police officer supplied the defendant with a part-specimen but did not follow the local procedure of sealing it inside an envelope and subsequently convinced the defendant that the part-specimen could not then be submitted for analysis, the conviction based on the specimen was quashed (*Perry* v *McGovern* [1986] RTR 240). Although a 'principle' of law grew up around this case to the effect that actions by the police must not mislead or deter a defendant from submitting the part-specimen for analysis, the provisions of s. 78 of the Police and Criminal Evidence Act 1984 would appear to cover any such eventualities (**see Evidence and Procedure, chapter 2.8**).

3.5.8.5   Documentary Evidence

The Road Traffic Offenders Act 1988, s. 16 states:

(1) Evidence of the proportion of alcohol or a drug in a specimen of breath, blood or urine may, subject to subsections (3) and (4) below and to section 15(5) and (5A) of this Act, be given by the production of a document or documents purporting to be whichever of the following is appropriate, that is to say—

   (a) a statement automatically produced by the device by which the proportion of alcohol in a specimen of breath was measured and a certificate signed by a constable (which may but need not be contained in the same document as the statement) that the statement relates to a specimen provided by the accused at the date and time shown in the statement, and

   (b) a certificate signed by an authorised analyst as to the proportion of alcohol or any drug found in a specimen of blood or urine identified in the certificate.

(2) Subject to subsections (3) and (4) below, evidence that a specimen of blood was taken from the accused with his consent by a medical practitioner or a registered health care professional may be given by the production of a document purporting to certify that fact and to be signed by a medical practitioner or a registered health care professional.

(3) Subject to subsection (4) below—

    (a) a document purporting to be such a statement or such a certificate (or both such a statement and such a certificate) as is mentioned in subsection (1)(a) above is admissible in evidence on behalf of the prosecution in pursuance of this section only if a copy of it either has been handed to the accused when the document was produced or has been served on him not later than seven days before the hearing, and

    (b) any other document is so admissible only if a copy of it has been served on the accused not later than seven days before the hearing.

(4) A document purporting to be a certificate (or so much of a document as purports to be a certificate) is not so admissible if the accused, not later than three days before the hearing or within such further time as the court may in special circumstances allow, has served notice on the prosecutor requiring the attendance at the hearing of the person by whom the document purports to be signed.

KEYNOTE

Section 16 sets out the provisions for documentary evidence to be used when proving the proportion of alcohol *or drugs* in specimens of breath, blood or urine. This has proved to be another fertile ground for litigation and there are many case decisions surrounding the interpretation of the provisions of s. 16. In summary, the section allows for proof of the proportion of alcohol or drugs in a specimen to be made by a statement produced by the approved device that measured the specimen together with a certificate as to its truth signed by a police officer (s. 16(1)(a)). It also provides for evidence to be given in the form of a certificate signed by an authorised analyst as to the proportion of alcohol or drug found in a specimen of blood or urine (s. 16(1)(b)).

Sections 16(3) and 16(4) set out the requirements for service of a copy of any such statement and certificate on the defendant before it can become admissible. Any such copy or other document must be served on the defendant not later than seven days before the hearing (s. 16(3)). Certificates will not be admissible if the defendant serves notice not later than three days before the hearing (or longer if the court allows) on the prosecutor requiring the attendance of the person by whom the certificate purports to be signed (s. 16(4)).

It has been held that there is no requirement for the *copy* to be signed by the police officer (*Chief Constable of Surrey* v *Wickens* [1985] RTR 277).

In *McCormack* v *DPP* [2002] EWHC 173, having provided the required specimens of breath, the driver signed the three copies of the printout produced by the EBTI (Evidential Breath Testing Instrument) machine. However, on being offered a copy of the printout, the driver refused to accept it. On appeal against conviction, the driver queried (among other things) whether s. 16(3)(a) had been complied with by simply offering him the printout, rather than showing that any physical transfer had taken place. The driver argued that the document had not been 'handed' to him as required by s. 16(3)(a) and therefore was not admissible. He also argued that a previous authority on the point (*Walton* v *Rimmer* [1986] RTR 31) was wrong and should not be followed, especially since there was higher authority in Scottish case law to support his argument. The Administrative Court disagreed; there does not have to be proof of any physical transfer of the document to the driver before it becomes admissible here (though that would clearly save any argument). The fact that this situation is applied differently in Scottish cases arising from the same statute did not persuade the court.

Failing to prove service of the certificate on the defendant within the relevant time period will render that certificate inadmissible and the court will not accept hearsay as an alternative (*Whyte* v *DPP* [2003] EWHC 358).

The precise effect of failing to serve the certificate on the defendant is that the evidence contained within it is inadmissible *to prove the proportion of alcohol* in question. This does not mean that it is *inadmissible* in relation to any other purpose, such as showing why it was felt necessary by the police officer to require a blood sample (see *Jubb* v *DPP* [2002] EWHC 2317). Similarly, the failure to serve copies on the defendant does not prevent the relevant witnesses—police officer, analysts or medical practitioners—from providing oral evidence in person.

It would appear that oral evidence as to a defendant's breath-alcohol level may be given by the police officer who operated the machine, provided that evidence also proves that the approved device was properly calibrated (*Owen* v *Chesters* [1985] RTR 191).

Where the proceedings involve a magistrates' court inquiring into an offence as examining justices in a drink driving case, s. 16(4) does not apply (see s. 16(6A)).

3.5.9 Hospital Procedure

The Road Traffic Act 1988, s. 9 states:

(1) While a person is at a hospital as a patient he shall not be required to co-operate with a preliminary test or to provide a specimen under section 7 of this Act unless the medical practitioner in immediate charge of his case has been notified of the proposal to make the requirement; and—

  (a) if the requirement is then made, it shall be for the provision of a specimen at the hospital, but

  (b) if the medical practitioner objects on the ground specified in subsection (2) below, the requirement shall not be made.

(1A) While a person is at a hospital as a patient, no specimen of blood shall be taken from him under section 7A of this Act and he shall not be required to give his permission for a laboratory test of a specimen taken under that section unless the medical practitioner in immediate charge of his case—

  (a) has been notified of the proposal to take the specimen or to make the requirement; and

  (b) has not objected on the ground specified in subsection (2).

(2) The ground on which the medical practitioner may object is—

  (a) in a case falling within subsection (1), that the requirement or the provision of the specimen or (if one is required) the warning required by section 7(7) of this Act would be prejudicial to the proper care and treatment of the patient; and

  (b) in a case falling within subsection (1A), that the taking of the specimen, the requirement or the warning required by section 7A(5) of this Act would be so prejudicial.

KEYNOTE

Note that a requirement to provide evidential *breath* specimens can now be made at a hospital (see para. 3.5.5.2).

A 'hospital' will include an institution providing medical treatment for in-patients or out-patients (s. 11(2) of the Road Traffic Act 1988). It will also include anywhere within the precincts of that hospital.

Whether the person is there as a 'patient' or in another capacity will be a question of fact. In assessing this fact the courts will be helped by reference to hospital records which show names of patients, together with their times of admission and discharge (see *Askew* v *DPP* [1988] RTR 303), although these records will not be conclusive.

If a person has been treated and then discharged from the hospital, he/she ceases to be a 'patient' for these purposes even if he/she has to return at a future date for further, related treatment (e.g. to have stitches removed).

Section 9(1A) was inserted in order to deal with the situations where a doctor has taken a blood specimen from the patient without his/her consent (under s. 7A, see para. 3.5.5.9). The overall effect of s. 7A and the above provision is that both the doctor taking the sample and the doctor in immediate charge of the patient need to be two separate people, both of whom will have to agree to the taking of the specimen.

A useful case illustrating this area is *Webber* v *DPP* [1998] RTR 111. In *Webber* the driver of a vehicle involved in an accident was taken to a hospital where she was requested to provide a specimen of breath under s. 6. She refused. While she was still a patient at the hospital, the driver was required to provide a blood specimen for analysis under ss. 7(1)(b) and 9(1). She agreed but, before she was able to provide the specimen, she was discharged. She was then arrested under s. 6(5)(b) as a result of her earlier refusal. The driver was taken to a police station where she provided a specimen of blood on the strength of which she was subsequently convicted of driving while over the prescribed limit. She appealed, by way of case stated, on the ground that s. 9(1)(a) required the blood specimen to be taken *at the hospital*, which in this case it was not. The Divisional Court held that, once the obligation to provide a specimen for analysis has been made, it is not to be discharged simply by an 'irrelevant change' of *locus*. The court went on to say that by making the requirement, the police officer set in train a procedure which carries a sanction (s. 7(6)), a procedure that was not to be altered by the mere fact that the defendant, for whatever reason, had left the hospital before complying with the requirement.

The restriction applies to both preliminary breath tests and evidential tests.

If the patient provides a positive reading or fails to provide a specimen of breath, he/she cannot then be arrested while still a 'patient' (s. 6D(3)).

3.5.10 Detention of Person Affected

The Road Traffic Act 1988, s. 10 states:

(1) Subject to subsections (2) and (3) below, a person required under section 7 or 7A to provide a specimen of breath, blood or urine may afterwards be detained at a police station (or, if the specimen was provided otherwise than at a police station, arrested and taken to and detained at a police station) if a constable has reasonable grounds for believing that, were that person then driving or attempting to drive a mechanically propelled vehicle on a road, he would commit an offence under section 4 or 5 of this Act.

(2) Subsection (1) above does not apply to the person if it ought reasonably to appear to the constable that there is no likelihood of his driving or attempting to drive a mechanically propelled vehicle whilst his ability to drive properly is impaired or whilst the proportion of alcohol in his breath, blood or urine exceeds the prescribed limit.

(2A) A person who is at a hospital as a patient shall not be arrested and taken from there to a police station in pursuance of this section if it would be prejudicial to his proper care and treatment as a patient.

(3) A constable must consult a medical practitioner on any question arising under this section whether a person's ability to drive properly is or might be impaired through drugs and must act on the medical practitioner's advice.

KEYNOTE

The powers considered in the previous paragraph relate to the removal of the driver or person in charge of the vehicle from a road or public place and the powers to obtain evidence in order to bring a prosecution if appropriate. There is then a further practical consideration of whether or not to release the person once these matters have been dealt with. This has always been a fairly controversial area of law since the police have to balance the individual rights of the person detained (who may no longer present a danger to himself/herself or others) and the likelihood of his/her going back out onto the roads and offending again. That situation is further complicated by the introduction of evidential tests at places other than police stations. Section 10—in its revised form—now addresses the situation of the person's continued detention. The person may be detained (or, if the evidential specimen was provided otherwise than at a police station, he/she may be arrested, taken to and detained at a police station) if a constable has *reasonable grounds for believing* that if the person were to drive/attempt to drive a mechanically propelled vehicle on a road, he/she would commit an offence under ss. 4 or 5 of the Road Traffic Act 1988. The wording of this section means that this is a *subjective* test and the officer must be able to point to the 'reasonable grounds' for his/her belief. Clearly a further screening test would provide such grounds but there is no specific requirement or power for this. In addition, it may be that the officer has reasonable grounds to believe, not that the person would commit an offence relating to *alcohol* if he/she were to drive/attempt to drive, but that he/she would commit an offence by being unfit through *drugs*. Where the source of impairment (past, present or future) is believed to be drugs then s. 10(3) imposes a mandatory requirement to consult a doctor.

But the matter does not end there.

If it ought reasonably to appear to the officer (another *subjective* test) that there is no likelihood of the person driving/attempting to drive such a vehicle while impaired or over the prescribed limit, the power to arrest and/or detain under s. 10(1) *does not apply* and the person cannot be further detained under this section.

While effective, the practice of retaining the person's car keys after their release is not authorised by s. 10.

Under s. 10(2A) if the person is at a hospital as a patient, he/she must not be arrested and taken from there to a police station under s. 10 if it would be prejudicial to his/her proper care and treatment as a patient.

<table>
<tr><td>**3.6**</td><td># Insurance</td></tr>
</table>

3.6.1 Introduction

People using or driving vehicles on roads and public places necessarily present an element of risk to others. In addition to the many provisions which minimise that risk so far as is practicable there is a requirement that most road users are insured against third party risk.

3.6.2 Requirement for Insurance

The Road Traffic Act 1988, s. 143 states:

(1) Subject to the provisions of this Part of this Act—
  (a) a person must not use a motor vehicle on a road or other public place unless there is in force in relation to the use of the vehicle by that person such a policy of insurance or such a security in respect of third party risks as complies with the requirements of this Part of this Act, and
  (b) a person must not cause or permit any other person to use a motor vehicle on a road or other public place unless there is in force in relation to the use of the vehicle by that other person such a policy of insurance or such a security in respect of third party risks as complies with the requirements of this Part of this Act.

OFFENCE: **Contravening Requirement for Insurance—*Road Traffic Act 1988, s. 143(2)***
  • Triable summarily • Fine • Discretionary disqualification

The Road Traffic Act 1988, s. 143 states:

(2) If a person acts in contravention of subsection (1) above he is guilty of an offence.

KEYNOTE

The requirement to have insurance was extended to public places as well as roads by the Motor Vehicles (Compulsory Insurance) Regulations 2000 (SI 2000/726). This change came about as a result of the House of Lords' decision in *Cutter* v *Eagle Star Insurance Co. Ltd* [1998] 4 All ER 417 as to the definition of a road (see chapter 3.1).

The policy behind s. 143 is to safeguard road users and pedestrians from uninsured injury from a mechanically powered vehicle, by providing for compulsory insurance (*Winter* v *DPP* [2002] EWHC 1524). Therefore in deciding whether a particular conveyance or contraption needs insurance or not, the court will have this feature firmly in mind.

Unless the insurer of a vehicle delivers a certificate of insurance to the person taking out the policy, the requirements of s. 143(1) will not have been met (s. 147(1)). Therefore, anyone using, or causing or permitting to be used, a motor vehicle on a road or other public place before the delivery of such a certificate, commits this offence.

Delivery may now also take place electronically—so a certificate of insurance transmitted from the insurer to the insured by e-mail or made available for access on a website is sufficient (s. 147(1A)(a) and (b)).

A driver may be required under s. 165 or s. 170 of the Road Traffic Act 1988 to produce a certificate of insurance (or other acceptable form of security). In such cases, in order to determine whether a motor vehicle was being driven in contravention of s. 143 above, s. 171 of the Road Traffic Act 1988 places a requirement on the *owner* of the vehicle to give such information as required by the police. Failure to comply with such a requirement is a summary offence. However, where a defendant is charged with driving without insurance, once the prosecution have proved that the defendant has driven on a public highway, it is for him or her to show that he/she had insurance and there is no obligation on the police to serve any request for production of the relevant documentation (e.g. an HORT/1)—*DPP* v *Hay* [2005] EWHC 1395.

Many insurance companies appear now to issue instant insurance cover over the telephone by creating an 'agency' to which the insurance certificate is delivered on behalf of the insured. As the agency effectively receives the certificate on the insured's behalf, this gets around the requirement of having to deliver the certificate before the insurance becomes effective as referred to above.

Note that if the driver is employed by the vehicle's owner you must prove that the driver was acting in the course of his/her employment before you can convict the owner of using, causing or permitting the use of the vehicle without insurance. The driver's own inadmissible statement to that effect will not suffice (*Jones* v *DPP* [1999] RTR 1).

The risks which must be covered by any insurance policy for the purposes of s. 143 are set out in s. 145(3). These are generally:

- Liability in relation to bodily injury caused to others when the vehicle is on a road in Great Britain.

- Civil liability in relation to the use of a vehicle from another EU Member State in Great Britain.

- Civil liability in relation to the use of a vehicle from Great Britain in another EU Member State.

If a claim is made against a motorist in respect of any such liability required to be covered by a policy of insurance he/she has a number of legal obligations. In essence, he/she must, on demand by or on behalf of the person making the claim:

(a) state whether or not:
    (i) he/she was insured (or had in force a security) having effect for the purpose of the Act or
    (ii) he/she would have been insured (or had in force such a security) if the insurer (or the giver of the security) had not avoided or cancelled the policy or security, and

(b) if he/she was (or would have been) so insured, or had or would have had in force such a security, he/she must:
    (i) give relevant particulars with respect to that policy or security as specified in any certificate of insurance or security delivered in respect of that policy or security under s. 147 above.
    (ii) where no such certificate was delivered under s. 147, give particulars of the registration mark, the number of the insurance policy, the name of the insurer and the period of the insurance cover.

(See s. 154.)

A local authority has the power (under s. 222 of the Local Government Act 1972) to bring a criminal prosecution for the offence of driving without insurance contrary to s. 143 of the Road Traffic Act 1988 (*Middlesbrough Borough Council* v *Safeer* [2001] EWHC Admin 525). (For a list of other offences for which a local authority may prosecute, see s. 4 of the Road Traffic Offenders Act 1988.)

3.6.2.1 Absolute Liability

Generally the offence under s. 143 is one of absolute liability, that is, you need not prove any intent or guilty knowledge by the defendant in order to convict (*Tapsell* v *Maslen* [1967] Crim LR 53).

If, however, a person allows another to use their vehicle on the express condition that the other person insures it first, the lender cannot be convicted of 'permitting' (*Newbury v Davis* [1974] RTR 367).

3.6.2.2 Defence

The Road Traffic Act 1988, s. 143 states:

> (3) A person charged with using a motor vehicle in contravention of this section shall not be convicted if he proves—
>   (a) that the vehicle did not belong to him and was not in his possession under a contract of hiring or of loan,
>   (b) that he was using the vehicle in the course of his employment, and
>   (c) that he neither knew nor had reason to believe that there was not in force in relation to the vehicle such a policy of insurance or security as is mentioned in subsection (1) above.

KEYNOTE

Note that s. 143(3) provides a special defence for employees using their employer's vehicle in the course of their employment.

The burden of proof in such a case is on the defendant and will be judged on the balance of probabilities (*R* v *Carr-Briant* [1943] 2 All ER 156).

3.6.2.3 Check 'This'

When considering vehicle insurance it is useful to ask:

Does

- **This** policy cover
- **This** person to drive/use
- **This** vehicle for
- **This** purpose on
- **This** day?

Each of these elements is considered in turn.

This Policy

The form in which certificates must appear, together with the requirement for insurers to keep and supply copies of records, are contained in the Motor Vehicles (Third Party Risks) Regulations 1972 (SI 1972/1217) as amended.

Cover notes are included, by s. 161(1) of the Road Traffic Act 1988, in the meaning of 'policy of insurance'.

The internationally recognised 'green card scheme' allows for the insurance of British vehicles abroad and overseas vehicles in Great Britain (see the Motor Vehicles (International Motor Insurance Card) Regulations 1971 (SI 1971/792)).

There is a requirement (under s. 145(3)(b) of the 1988 Act) however, for insurance policies to provide cover which extends to other European Union countries, removing the need for the 'green card' scheme within the EU for vehicles from Member States.

This Person

If a policy is restricted to a named person, only that person will generally be covered by it.

If, as often happens, the policy covers any person who holds a current driving licence, that description may include the holder of a provisional licence (see *Rendlesham* v *Dunne* [1964] 1 Lloyd's Rep 192) or even the holder of a licence issued in another country.

If a policy refers to 'agents' or 'employees', you will need to establish whether or not the relevant person fits into those categories. Garage proprietors returning vehicles to the owner after repairing them are not in the owner's employment (*Lyons* v *May* [1948] 2 All ER 1062). However, an employee driving an employer's vehicle in an unauthorised manner will not negate the effect of a policy of insurance (*Marsh* v *Moores* [1949] 2 All ER 27).

Generally, an insurance policy obtained by false representations will be valid for the purposes of s. 143 and will remain so until the contract has been 'avoided' (ended) by the insurer (*Durrant* v *MacLaren* [1956] 2 Lloyd's Rep 70).

This Vehicle

Generally the question of whether or not a policy applies to the particular vehicle will not present a problem. Trailers can create difficulties, both in relation to the vehicles covered by the policy, and the use to which they are being put. Trailers are themselves 'vehicles' (**see para. 3.1.2.5**) at times and may be included in the definition of motor vehicle when charging an offence under s. 143 (see *Rogerson* v *Stephens* [1950] 2 All ER 144).

When motor vehicles are being towed by other vehicles, they remain 'motor vehicles' and, as such, require insurance when used on roads (*Milstead* v *Sexton* [1964] Crim LR 474) and also public places.

This Purpose

Insurance policies will often exclude certain uses (e.g. racing and time trials). The particular wording of each policy is important when determining any purpose that is expressly included or excluded and many policies use the wording 'social and domestic purposes'. Lending vehicles to friends in return for payment reimbursing petrol costs will amount to a social and domestic purpose, as will using the vehicle to help a friend move house (see *Lee* v *Poole* [1954] Crim LR 942).

'Social and domestic' does not include business trips (see *Wood* v *General Accident etc. Assurance Co.* (1948) 65 TLR 53).

Insurance cover in respect of 'the insured's business' does not extend to other businesses of friends or colleagues (see *Passmore* v *Vulcan etc. Insurance Co.* (1935) 154 LT 258).

If employees deviate from the ordinary course of their duties or employment, on what is often termed a 'frolic of their own', they may not be covered by the terms of the employer's policy. Simply taking a two-mile detour in order to give someone a lift has been held not to invalidate the employer's insurance policy (*Ballance* v *Brown* [1955] Crim LR 384) but each case will have to be decided on its own facts.

This Day

Clearly any insurance policy must be shown to have been in force at the relevant time. Many business users have arrangements whereby they pass the risk to their insurers at short notice and it will always be necessary to establish whether a particular policy is actually operative at the time (see e.g. *Samuelson* v *National Insurance etc. Ltd* [1986] 3 All ER 417).

Although many policies exclude use of the particular vehicle for payment or reward, s. 150 of the 1988 Act makes provision for 'car-sharing' agreements, provided that they meet the criteria set out.

3.6.2.4   Exclusions

Section 148(1) of the Road Traffic Act 1988 makes the effects of some restrictions in a policy void in relation to s. 143. This means that, if a policy purports to restrict the extent of its cover by reference to any of these features, breach of them by the insured person will not affect the validity of that policy for the purposes of s. 143.

Those features (under s. 148) are:

(2) ...

    (a) the age or physical or mental condition of persons driving the vehicle,

    (b) the condition of the vehicle,

    (c) the number of persons that the vehicle carries,

    (d) the weight or physical characteristics of the goods that the vehicle carries,

    (e) the time at which or the areas within which the vehicle is used,

    (f) the horsepower or cylinder capacity or value of the vehicle,

    (g) the carrying on the vehicle of any particular apparatus, or

    (h) the carrying on the vehicle of any particular means of identification other than any means of identification required to be carried by or under the Vehicle Excise and Registration Act 1994.

3.6.2.5   Exemptions

Crown vehicles do not appear to require insurance *while being used as such*; if they are being used for some other purpose, they will need insurance on a road or public place.

Section 144 of the 1988 Act sets out other occasions where vehicles will be exempt. Such occasions include police authority vehicles and vehicles being used for police purposes; this will include an off duty police officer using his/her own vehicle for police purposes (*Jones* v *Chief Constable of Bedfordshire* [1987] RTR 332).

3.6.2.6   Registered Keeper of an Uninsured Vehicle

Section 144A of the Road Traffic Act 1988 provides:

(1) If a motor vehicle registered under the Vehicle Excise and Registration Act 1994 does not meet the insurance requirements, the person in whose name the vehicle is registered is guilty of an offence.

(2) For the purposes of this section a vehicle meets the insurance requirements if—

    (a) it is covered by such a policy of insurance or such a security in respect of third party risks as complies with the requirements of this Part of this Act, and

    (b) either of the following conditions is satisfied.

(3) The first condition is that the policy or security, or the certificate of insurance or security which relates to it, identifies the vehicle by its registration mark as a vehicle which is covered by the policy or security.

(4) The second condition is that the vehicle is covered by the policy or security because—

    (a) the policy or security covers any vehicle, or any vehicle of a particular description, the owner of which is a person named in the policy or security or in the certificate of insurance or security which relates to it, and

    (b) the vehicle is owned by that person.

(5) For the purposes of this section a vehicle is covered by a policy of insurance or security if the policy of insurance or security is in force in relation to the use of the vehicle.

The Act then goes on to provide in s. 144B for a number of exceptions to the offence, many of which mirror the exceptions applicable to the s. 143 offence (**see para. 3.6.2.5**). Additionally, registered keepers who, by the relevant time, have supplied a valid SORN declaration are also exempt.

The aim of the provision is to clamp down further on the use or potential use of uninsured vehicles, with the DVLA and the MIB co-operating to identify registered keepers of uninsured vehicles. It is **not** anticipated that police officers will play a primary role in enforcement. The DVLA will initially send a letter to identified keepers of uninsured vehicles warning of the need to insure the vehicle. If insurance is not then obtained, the keeper will be subject to a £100 fixed penalty (reduced to £50 for prompt payment). Ultimately, a persistent offender may find that the vehicle is seized and disposed of.

3.6.2.7 Producing Documents

The Road Traffic Act 1988, s. 165 states:

(1) Any of the following persons—
  (a) a person driving a motor vehicle (other than an invalid carriage) on a road, or
  (b) a person whom a constable or vehicle examiner has reasonable cause to believe to have been the driver of a motor vehicle (other than an invalid carriage) at a time when an accident occurred owing to its presence on a road or other public place, or
  (c) a person whom a constable or vehicle examiner has reasonable cause to believe to have committed an offence in relation to the use on a road of a motor vehicle (other than an invalid carriage),
  must, on being so required by a constable or vehicle examiner, give his name and address and the name and address of the owner of the vehicle and produce the following documents for examination.
(2) Those documents are—
  (a) the relevant certificate of insurance or certificate of security (within the meaning of Part VI of this Act), or such other evidence that the vehicle is not or was not being driven in contravention of section 143 of this Act as may be prescribed by regulations made by the Secretary of State,
  (b) in relation to a vehicle to which section 47 of this Act applies, a test certificate issued in respect of the vehicle as mentioned in subsection (1) of that section, and
  (c) in relation to a goods vehicle the use of which on a road without a plating certificate or goods vehicle test certificate is an offence under section 53(1) or (2) of this Act, any such certificate issued in respect of that vehicle or any trailer drawn by it.
(2A) Subsections (2B) and (2C) below apply where a certificate of insurance is treated as having been delivered to a person under section 147(1) of this Act by virtue of section 147(1A) of this Act.
(2B) In the case of a certificate transmitted to a person as described in section 147(1A)(a) of this Act, the person is to be treated for the purposes of this section as producing the relevant certificate of insurance if—
  (a) using electronic equipment…he provides the constable or examiner with electronic access to a copy of the certificate, or
  (b) he produces a legible printed copy of the certificate.
(2C) In the case of a certificate made available to a person as described in section 147(1A)(b) of this Act, the person is to be treated for the purposes of this section as producing the relevant certificate of insurance if—
  (a) using electronic equipment…he provides the constable or examiner with electronic access on the website in question to a copy of the certificate, or
  (b) he produces a legible printed copy of the certificate.
(2D) Nothing in subsection (2B) or (2C) above requires a constable or examiner to provide a person with electronic equipment for the purpose of compliance with a requirement imposed on the person by this section.
(3) Subject to subsection (4) below, a person who fails to comply with a requirement under subsection (1) above is guilty of an offence.
(4) A person shall not be convicted of an offence under subsection (3) above by reason only of failure to produce any certificate or other evidence…if in proceedings against him for the offence he shows that—
  (a) within seven days after the date on which the production of the certificate or other evidence was required it was produced at a police station that was specified by him at the time when its production was required, or

(b) it was produced there as soon as was reasonably practicable, or

(c) it was not reasonably practicable for it to be produced there before the day on which the proceedings were commenced,

and for the purposes of this subsection the laying of the information. . .shall be treated as the commencement of the proceedings.

(5) A person—

(a) who supervises the holder of a provisional licence granted under Part III of this Act while the holder is driving on a road a motor vehicle (other than an invalid carriage), or

(b) whom a constable or vehicle examiner has reasonable cause to believe was supervising the holder of such a licence while driving, at a time when an accident occurred owing to the presence of the vehicle on a road or at a time when an offence is suspected of having been committed by the holder of the provisional licence in relation to the use of the vehicle on a road,

must, on being so required by a constable or vehicle examiner, give his name and address and the name and address of the owner of the vehicle.

KEYNOTE

The power to require a name and address in s. 165(1) is among the powers that can be conferred on people (e.g. Police Community Support Officers) designated under schs 4 and 5 to the Police Reform Act 2002 where the suspected offence is one under s. 35(1) or (2).

Production of the certificate need not be in person but the certificate must be shown to the officer for long enough to allow proper inspection of it; waving it in front of an officer or snatching it back shortly afterwards will not be enough to comply with s. 165 (see *Tremelling* v *Martin* [1971] RTR 196).

In cases where a requirement has been made under s. 165, s. 171 of the Road Traffic Act 1988 places a requirement on the *owner* of the vehicle to give such information as required by the police in order to determine whether the motor vehicle was being driven without insurance. Failure to comply with such a requirement is a summary offence.

The requirement under s. 165(1)(b) has been extended to 'public places' as well as roads by the Motor Vehicles (Compulsory Insurance) Regulations 2000 (SI 2000/726).

Traffic wardens may also demand a person's name and address under s. 165. They may *not*, however, demand driving documents under these particular circumstances (see Functions of Traffic Wardens Order 1970 (SI 1970/1958)).

3.6.2.8   **Power to Seize Vehicles Driven without Licence or Insurance**

The Road Traffic Act 1988 provides the police with powers in respect of uninsured vehicles. The relevant power and restrictions on it are considered below.

Section 165A states that, if *any* of the specified conditions are satisfied in relation to a vehicle, a constable may:

(a) seize the vehicle (in accordance with s. 165A(6) and (7));

(b) remove the vehicle; and

(c) for the purpose of exercising the power, enter any premises other than a private dwelling house on which he/she has reasonable grounds for believing the vehicle to be (s. 165A(1) and (5)).

Note that the definition of 'private dwelling house' does *not* include any garage or other structure occupied with the dwelling house or land 'appurtenant' (belonging or relating) to it.

The first condition is that:

• a constable *in uniform* requires a person to produce their driving licence and its counterpart for examination (under s. 164),

• the person fails to produce them, and

- the constable has reasonable grounds for believing that:

  > a motor vehicle
  > is or was being driven
  > by that person
  > otherwise than in accordance with a licence (in contravention of s. 87(1)).

The second condition is that:

- a constable *in uniform* requires (under s. 165) a person to produce evidence that a motor vehicle is or was not being driven in contravention of s. 143 (requirement for insurance),
- the person fails to produce such evidence, and
- the constable has reasonable grounds for believing that the vehicle is or was being so driven.

The third condition is that:

- a constable *in uniform* requires a person driving a motor vehicle to stop the vehicle (under s. 163),
- the person fails to stop the vehicle, or to stop the vehicle long enough, for the constable to make such lawful enquiries as he/she considers appropriate,
- and the constable has reasonable grounds for believing that:

  > *that* vehicle
  > is or was
  > being driven
  > otherwise than in accordance with a licence (in contravention of s. 87(1)) or s.143 (requirement for insurance).

In the exercise of any power to seize a vehicle under this provision or to enter relevant premises, a constable may use reasonable force, if necessary (see s. 165A(5)(c)).

However, before seizing the motor vehicle, the constable must warn the person by whom it appears that the vehicle is or was being driven in contravention of s. 87(1) or s. 143 that he/she will seize it:

(a) in the case of s. 87(1) (driving otherwise than in accordance with a licence) if the person does not produce his/her licence *and* its counterpart *immediately*;
(b) in the case of s. 143 (no insurance) if the person does not provide the constable *immediately* with evidence that the vehicle is not or was not being driven in contravention of that section.

But the constable is not required to give such a warning if the circumstances make it impracticable for him/her to do so (see s. 165A(6)).

Section 165A(7) provides that, if the constable is unable to seize the vehicle immediately because the person driving the vehicle has failed to stop as requested or has driven off, he/she may seize it at any time within the period of 24 hours beginning with the time at which the condition in question is first satisfied. The wording of s. 165A(7) suggests (on one view) that the 24 hour 'window' within which to seize the vehicle only applies where the constable has been prevented from seizing the vehicle immediately owing to the person failing to stop or driving away: it does not therefore apply where some other reason prevented the officer from seizing the vehicle (e.g. by their being called away to other duties) in which case there seems to be no restriction on the time during which the vehicle can be seized—ultimately the courts will have to interpret the subsection.

A reference to a motor vehicle does not include an invalid carriage (see s. 165A(9)).

3.6.2.9   Retention etc. of Vehicles Seized under s. 165A

Under s. 165B the Secretary of State may make regulations providing for the removal and retention of motor vehicles seized under s. 165A and for their release or disposal, together with any fees that may be payable. Those regulations may make different provisions for different cases and will apply to local authorities. So far as England is concerned, local authority means:

- a county council
- the council of a district comprised in an area for which there is no county council
- a London borough council
- the Common Council of the City of London, or
- Transport for London.

In relation to Wales it means the council of a county or county borough.

The relevant regulations are the Road Traffic Act 1988 (Retention and Disposal of Seized Motor Vehicles) Regulations 2005 (SI 2005/1606) and they set out the procedures to be followed by the police in exercising the seizure power.

In summary the regulations provide that:

- When a vehicle has been seized the appropriate police officer (or authorised agent) must take such steps as are reasonably necessary for its safe keeping until it is released or disposed of (reg. 3).
- On seizing a vehicle, the constable must give the driver a seizure notice unless it is impracticable to do so (reg. 4(1)).
- Where the driver is not the owner or registered keeper of the vehicle, the police officer or agent must take reasonably practicable steps to give a seizure notice to the keeper (and to the owner, if that is someone different) unless he/she is satisfied that this has already been done or the vehicle has been released in accordance with the regulations (reg. 4(2)).

The seizure notice must give specified details about the seizure and retention of the vehicle including:

- such information as can be (or could have been) ascertained from an inspection of the vehicle, or has been ascertained from any other source, relating to the registration mark and make of the vehicle;
- the place where the vehicle was seized and where it is being kept;
- a requirement that the owner (or keeper) claims it within a specified period of time not being less than seven working days from the day when the notice is given to the registered keeper or owner as the case may be;
- an indication that, unless the vehicle is claimed on or before that date, it may be disposed of; and
- an indication that a person must pay any relevant charges and must produce at a specified police station a valid licence and proof of insurance in respect of their use of the vehicle (or nominate a third person who can produce those documents in respect of that person's use of the vehicle to whom the vehicle can be released) (reg. 4(3)–(4)).

Regulation 5 deals with the procedure for releasing a vehicle. If, before a relevant motor vehicle is disposed of, someone:

- satisfies the authorised person that they are the registered keeper or the owner of that vehicle;
- pays to the authorised person such a charge in respect of its seizure and retention as provided for in reg. 6; and

- produces at a police station specified in the seizure notice a valid certificate of insurance covering their use of that vehicle *and* a valid licence authorising them to drive the vehicle,

the authorised person shall permit them to remove the vehicle.

Specific provision is made for cases where the person claiming the vehicle can demonstrate that he/she is the owner and pays the required fee but he/she nominates a third person who produces a valid certificate of insurance covering his/her use of that vehicle and a valid driving licence authorising him/her to drive that vehicle. In such circumstances, the authorised person must permit that person to remove the vehicle (reg. 5(2)).

Where a vehicle is not released, the conditions under which it can be disposed of are set out in reg. 7. In summary, the vehicle cannot be disposed of until at least 14 days after the date on which the vehicle was seized. If it is sold, the net proceeds are payable to the owner if claimed within a year.

The regulations also provide that the prescribed charges are not payable if the person claiming the vehicle was not driving it at the time of seizure, did not know it was being driven, had not consented to its being driven and could not reasonably have prevented its being driven (reg. 5(5)).

A key feature of the practical arrangements for enforcing the legislation in respect of uninsured drivers is the ability to get relevant information on vehicles and their insured status. This process is considered in **para. 3.6.2.10**.

3.6.2.10   Disclosure of Information about Insurance Status of Vehicles

Under s. 153 of the Serious Organised Crime and Police Act 2005 the Secretary of State may make provision for requiring the Motor Insurers' Information Centre (MIIC—a company limited by guarantee) to make available 'relevant vehicle insurance information' to the police with a view to making that information available for use by constables. The practical detail can be found in the Disclosure of Vehicle Insurance Information Regulations 2005 (SI 2005/2833). 'Relevant vehicle insurance information' means information (in any form) relating to vehicles that have previously been—but are no longer—insured under a policy of insurance (or security in respect of third party risks) complying with the relevant requirements of the Road Traffic Act 1988. This information will be set out in a 'periodic data list' taken from the motor insurance database. Effectively the legislation enables the police to have access to insurance industry data relating to vehicles whose use is no longer insured. The police are also able to link the processed data to Automated Number-Plate Reader (ANPR) units to assist them in detecting people driving without insurance.

Regulation 3 requires the MIIC to provide a list of vehicles, the use of which was covered by a policy of insurance on the reference date (a date before the periodic data list was produced) but is no longer covered under such a policy when the list is generated. The information which must be provided is the:

- registration mark
- make and model (where available to the MIIC) and
- date on which the vehicle ceased to have a record of insurance on the database.

Police officers may use the processed information to assist them in deciding whether to use their powers under s. 165 of the 1988 Act to require a person who is, or may have been, driving a vehicle to produce evidence that the vehicle is insured.

Any information provided to police officers should not be further disclosed by them except for the purposes of legal proceedings for contravening the 1988 Act or legislation made under it.

3.6.3 **Motor Insurers' Bureau**

All insurers in Great Britain are required to be members of the Motor Insurers' Bureau (MIB) (s. 145 of the Road Traffic Act 1988).

The purpose of the MIB is to provide compensation where someone is unable to pursue a valid claim against another following a road traffic accident because the other party is:

- not insured
- not known/traceable
- insured by a company now in liquidation.

The MIB has drawn up an agreement with the Secretary of State which sets out its terms of operation. Generally it will not pay compensation to those who are victims of deliberate criminal acts involving motor vehicles (including those who allow themselves to be carried in vehicles taken without the owner's consent), neither will it compensate those who 'use' vehicles without insurance ('use' here will be taken in the wide sense discussed in chapter 3.1 and will include some passengers (see e.g. *Stinton* v *Stinton* [1995] RTR 167 and *O'Mahoney* v *Joliffe and Motor Insurers' Bureau* [1999] RTR 245)). The Court of Appeal decided that a person injured by an uninsured or untraced driver cannot enforce a claim for compensation against the MIB by citing the 'direct effect' of EC Council Directive 84/5 which provides certain rights for citizens of EU Member States (*Mighell* v *Reading*; *Evans* v *Motor Insurers' Bureau*; *White* v *White* [1999] Lloyd's Rep IR 30).

The MIB scheme generates a considerable amount of civil litigation that, on the whole, is of little direct importance to police officers. However, there are key evidential areas that may arise during the course of an investigation into accidents and collisions. For instance, the MIB will generally deny liability for any damages or loss to passengers who knew, or ought to have known, that the driver was uninsured. Evidence of conversations between passengers and drivers before and during any journeys can therefore become highly relevant in subsequent litigation (see e.g. *Akers* v *Motor Insurers Bureau* [2003] EWCA Civ 18).

In order to help people seeking compensation generally for motor accidents across the European Economic Area, Member States have set up clearing houses where insurance information relating to vehicles within the relevant country are pooled. In the United Kingdom a company called the Motor Insurers' Information Centre (MIIC) has been set up for this purpose. Following an accident, a person in the relevant Member State will be entitled to specific information regarding the vehicle(s) and insurance policy details on application. Full details of the scheme, along with the entitlement to compensation and the role of the MIB within the scheme can be found in the Motor Vehicles (Compulsory Insurance) (Information Centre and Compensation Body) Regulations 2003 (SI 2003/37).

3.7 | Protection of Drivers and Passengers

3.7.1 Introduction

Safety considerations are uppermost in road policing and receive significant attention in the ACPO Road Policing Strategy.

This chapter deals with the main areas of legislation aimed at increasing—and enforcing—safety in the use of vehicles.

3.7.2 Seat Belts

Failure to wear seat belts has been identified by ACPO and the government as one of the four key behaviours contributing to avoidable deaths and injury.

The law governing the fitting of seat belts to vehicles comes under the Road Vehicles (Construction and Use) Regulations 1986 (SI 1986/1078) (**see chapter 3.9**); that which regulates the *wearing* of seat belts is provided by the Motor Vehicles (Wearing of Seat Belts) Regulations 1993 (SI 1993/176) and s. 14 of the Road Traffic Act 1988 for people over 14 years old, and by s. 15 of the Road Traffic Act 1988 for children under that age.

The regulations are made under s. 14 of the Road Traffic Act 1988.

> OFFENCE: **Contravention of Regulation Relating to Seat Belts—*Road Traffic Act 1988, s. 14(3)***
> * Triable summarily * Fine

It is an offence to:

* *drive* a **motor vehicle** or
* *ride* in a *front seat* of a **motor vehicle** or
* *ride* in the *rear seat* of a **motor car** or **passenger car**

in each case without wearing an adult seat belt.

Section 14(3) creates these offences by virtue of reg. 5 of the 1993 Regulations.

The above offences can only be committed by people aged 14 and over.

In these and the offences which follow, it is important to note the different definitions used (e.g. *drive, ride, motor vehicle, passenger car, rear seat* etc.).

The definitions can be found in the Road Traffic Act 1988, ss. 15(9) and 185; the Motor Vehicles (Wearing of Seat Belts) Regulations 1993 (as amended); the Motor Vehicles (Wearing of Seat Belts by Children in Front Seats) Regulations 1993 (SI 1993/31) (as amended) reg. 2, and the Road Vehicles (Construction and Use) Regulations 1986 (**see chapter 3.9**).

Section 14(3) goes on to say that, notwithstanding any enactment or rule of law, no person *other than the person actually committing the contravention* is guilty of an offence by reason of the contravention. This means that, irrespective of the general law relating to the aiding and abetting of offences, the driver of a vehicle will not be responsible for a passenger not wearing a seat belt.

This should be contrasted with the position under s. 15 of the 1988 Act in respect of children under 14 years of age who are not wearing seat belts (see below). In those cases the driver *is* responsible and, in theory at least, it would be possible for the child to be guilty of aiding and abetting the driver by not wearing a seat belt.

3.7.2.1 Exemptions

There are several general exemptions to the requirements of the regulations, many of them following common sense. Drivers of delivery vans, prisoner escorts, taxis and people reversing are all subject *to some degree* of exemption under reg. 6 of the Motor Vehicles (Wearing of Seat Belts) Regulations 1993, as are vehicles being used for police or fire brigade purposes. The general exemption relating to delivery drivers and their passengers is set out in s. 14(2)(b)(i) of the Road Traffic Act 1988. The section provides an exemption for the driver or a passenger in a motor vehicle constructed or adapted for carrying goods while on a journey which does not exceed the prescribed distance (50 metres—see reg. 6(1)(b) of the Motor Vehicles (Wearing of Seat Belts) Regulations 1993) *and* which is undertaken for the purpose of delivering or collecting any thing. An exemption may give a specific description, not only of the activity (e.g. taxis on hire business), but also of the *vehicle* to which it will apply (for instance, making deliveries in the family car would not attract the exemption because the vehicle used by delivery drivers must *be made or adapted* for making deliveries in order to be exempt).

In addition to these general exemptions, there are other occasions where the requirements will not apply. If there is no adult seat belt provided for the driver, or available for passengers aged 14 and over, the requirements will not apply (reg. 6).

Schedule 2 to the Regulations expands on a number of occasions where seat belts will be deemed not to be 'available'. These occasions include:

- where the seat is properly occupied by someone wearing the seat belt;
- where the seat is occupied by someone with a medical exemption.

If a person is unable to wear a seat belt owing to a disability, the seat belt will not be regarded for this purpose as being 'available'.

If a person holds a medical certificate signed by a doctor stating that the wearing of a seat belt by that person is inadvisable on medical grounds, that person will be exempt. Any such certificate must state the period over which it applies and carry the symbol prescribed in the regulations. If it is to be used in evidence in answer to a charge under s. 14(3) of the 1988 Act, such a certificate must be produced to a constable on request or to a police station within seven days (s. 14(4)).

3.7.2.2 Children under 14

The law in relation to the wearing of seat belts by children is contained in the Road Traffic Act 1988.

It is the *driver* who carries most responsibility in relation to the wearing of seat belts by children.

Section 15(1) of the Road Traffic Act 1988 states that, where a child under the age of 14 is in the front of a motor vehicle, a person must not without reasonable excuse drive the motor vehicle on a road unless the child is wearing a seat belt in conformity with the regulations.

The Road Traffic Act 1988, s. 15 states:

(1A) Where—
    (a) a child is in the front of a motor vehicle other than a bus,
    (b) the child is in a rear-facing child restraining device, and
    (c) the passenger seat where the child is placed is protected by a front air bag,
    a person must not without reasonable excuse drive the vehicle on a road unless the air bag is deactivated.
(3) Except as provided by regulations, where—
    (a) a child under the age of three years is in the rear of a motor vehicle, or
    (b) a child of or over that age but under the age of fourteen years is in the rear of a motor vehicle and any seat belt is fitted in the rear of that vehicle,
    a person must not without reasonable excuse drive the vehicle on a road unless the child is wearing a seat belt in conformity with regulations.
(3A) Except as provided by regulations, where—
    (a) a child who is under the age of 12 years and less than 150 centimetres in height is in the rear of a passenger car,
    (b) no seat belt is fitted in the rear of the passenger car, and
    (c) a seat in the front of the passenger car is provided with a seat belt but is not occupied by any person,
    a person must not without reasonable excuse drive the passenger car on a road.

OFFENCE: **Driving Motor Vehicle in Contravention of Requirement for Seat Belts for under 14s—*Road Traffic Act 1988, s. 15(2) and 15(4)***
    • Triable summarily • Fine

The Road Traffic Act 1988, s. 15 states:

(2) It is an offence for a person to drive a motor vehicle in contravention of subsection (1) or (1A) above.
  . . .
(4) It is an offence for a person to drive a motor vehicle in contravention of subsection (3) or (3A) above.

KEYNOTE

An air bag is regarded as 'deactivated' where it is designed or adapted in such a way that it cannot inflate enough to pose a risk of injury to a child travelling in a rear-facing child restraining device in the seat in question.

The suitability of seat belts, types of seat belt and the manner in which they must be worn by children are set out in the regulations, as are the further provisions which distinguish between smaller and larger children using them.

A 'small child' is defined as being under the age of 12 years and less than 135 cm in height.

A 'large child' is defined as being under the age of 14 years not being a 'small child'.

The consequences of this distinction are:

(a) a small child must wear a child restraint appropriate for his/her height and weight

(b) a large child must also wear a child restraint appropriate for his/her height and weight or may wear an adult belt

(c) a person aged 14 years or more must wear an adult belt.

If a person drives a motor vehicle in contravention of the regulations pertaining to children, he/she commits the offence under s. 15(2) or s. 15(4) above.

3.7.3   Motor Cycle Helmets

Under s. 16 of the Road Traffic Act 1988, the Secretary of State may make Regulations relating to the wearing of protective headgear by people riding motor cycles. The relevant regulations are the Motor Cycles (Protective Helmets) Regulations 1998 (SI 1998/1807) as amended.

The Regulations require every person driving or riding on a motor *bicycle* on a road to wear protective headgear (reg. 4).

OFFENCE: **Driving or Riding on Motor Cycle in Contravention of Regulations—**
Road Traffic Act 1988, s. 16(4)
  • Triable summarily • Fine

The Road Traffic Act 1988, s. 16 states:

(4)   A person who drives or rides on a motor cycle in contravention of regulations under this section is guilty of an offence. . .

KEYNOTE

The Regulations do not apply to all motor cycles; they only apply to motor bicycles.

Certain motor mowers are exempted by reg. 4(2) of the 1998 Regulations.

The helmet worn must either conform to one of the British Standards specified (in reg. 5) and be marked as such or it must give a similar (or greater) degree of protection as one which meets those Standards *and* be of a type manufactured for motor cyclists (reg. 4(3)(a)). If the helmet is unfastened or improperly fastened (e.g. with part of the chinstrap undone) the offence will be complete (reg. 4(3)(b) and (c)).

It is a summary offence under s. 17(2) to sell or let on hire a helmet for these purposes which does not meet the prescribed requirements. That offence will be committed even if the helmet is sold for off-road use (*Losexis Ltd* v *Clarke* [1984] RTR 174).

The wording of the Regulations suggests that no helmet is required by someone who is pushing a motor bicycle along but, if they straddled it and paddled it along with their feet, they would require one (see *Crank* v *Brooks* [1980] RTR 441 and **chapter 3.1**).

Section 16(2) creates an exemption for 'a follower of the Sikh religion while he is wearing a turban'.

The Motor Cycles (Eye Protectors) Regulations 1999 (SI 1999/535) as amended create an offence (under s. 18(3)) of using non-prescribed eye protectors when driving or riding on a motor cycle. These Regulations do not require the use of eye protectors; they impose standards on those appliances which motor cyclists choose to use. The definition of eye protector includes any appliance placed on the head intended for the protection of the eyes (which might include sunglasses). It is also an offence (s. 18(4)) to sell or let on hire eye protectors which do not meet the prescribed requirements.

3.7.3.1   Passengers

'Riding on' in the above offence means that pillion passengers must wear helmets but s. 16(1) of the 1988 Act exempts people in sidecars.

As with the seat belt provisions above, there is an exception to the general rule on aiding and abetting. Section 16(4) provides that only the person committing the offence of not wearing a helmet shall be liable *unless the person is under 16*. This means that, where a 16-year-old rider of a motor bicycle carries a 15-year-old pillion passenger who is not wearing a helmet, the 16-year-old will be responsible for the commission of the offence by the passenger as well as the passenger themselves. If the passenger were 16 years old, he/she alone would be responsible for his/her offence.

OFFENCE: **Passengers on Motor Cycles—*Road Traffic Act 1988, s. 23***
• Triable summarily • Fine • Discretionary disqualification

The Road Traffic Act 1988, s. 23 states:

(1) Not more than one person in addition to the driver may be carried on a motor bicycle.
(2) No person in addition to the driver may be carried on a motor bicycle otherwise than sitting astride the motor cycle and on a proper seat securely fixed to the motor cycle behind the driver's seat.
(3) If a person is carried on a motor cycle in contravention of this section, the driver of the motor cycle is guilty of an offence.

KEYNOTE

Under this section it is the *driver* who commits the offence (s. 23(3)), and the passenger can be convicted of aiding and abetting.

There is no specific requirement for the passenger to face the *front*—though this is presumably because it did not occur to the legislators that anyone would be daft enough to face the other way. Any person travelling as a passenger astride a motor cycle but facing the rear may commit an offence under the Road Vehicles (Construction and Use) Regulations 1986; he/she may also commit an offence of aiding and abetting the driver to drive dangerously.

Note that under the 1986 Regulations suitable supports for a passenger must be provided on a motor bicycle if it is to carry a passenger (reg. 102). There is no requirement that the supports be used by a passenger.

Note also the restrictions on learner drivers carrying passengers (**see chapter 3.10**).

3.7.4 Speeding and Speed Limits

Excessive and inappropriate speeding is—according to the ACPO Road Policing Strategy—one of the four key behaviours which contribute to avoidable deaths and injury by making collisions more likely, and by making the resultant injuries worse.

Speed limits may apply to particular roads (e.g. 'restricted' roads), particular vehicles (e.g. heavy commercial vehicles) or temporary conditions imposed in a given area. There are also further conditions regulating speed limits on motorways. As a general rule, the limit on motorways and dual carriageways for most cars will be 70 mph. However, there are many exceptions, and local regulations and orders should be consulted in cases of doubt.

Generally, the approval of the Secretary of State is required before speed limits of any great duration are imposed. However, that requirement has been removed in relation to speed limits of 20 mph by the Road Traffic Regulation Act 1984 (Amendment) Order 1999 (SI 1999/1608). As a result of this and other legislation (including the Traffic Signs Regulations and General Directions 2002 (SI 2002/3113)), local traffic authorities can create 20 mph zones under certain circumstances within their jurisdiction as part of a traffic calming scheme. Full guidance on the creation of such zones can be found in DETR Circular 05/99.

Under the Transport Act 2000, local authorities are empowered to designate roads as 'quiet lanes' or 'home zones', thereby placing greater restrictions on the use of them.

Although the imposition of a specific speed limit is a matter for legislation (either primary or in regulations and orders), the enforcement of those limits is an operational matter for the police force involved. While there is therefore a great deal of room for discretion in the enforcement of speed limits and there will always be exceptional cases, ACPO has produced guidelines setting out the *minimum* speeds at which it suggests enforcement action should be taken.

Note that since the Road Traffic Act 1991, increasing reliance has been placed on the use of automatic devices for detecting speeding offences and that the procedure of 'conditional offers' of fixed penalties are available for such offences.

The use of reflective or elaborately designed number plates to thwart speed cameras has been directly addressed in regulations.

The practice of drivers warning other motorists of the presence of a police speed detection operation can amount to an offence of obstructing a police constable in the execution of his/her duty. In such cases however it is critical that you can show that those warned were either exceeding the legal speed limit or were likely to do so at the location of the speed detection—*DPP* v *Glendinning* [2005] EWHC 2333 and *Betts* v *Stevens* [1910] 1 KB 1. In the absence of any such evidence, merely giving a warning to fellow drivers who were observing the speed limit at the time will not amount to this offence (see also *Bastable* v *Little* [1907] 1 KB 59).

3.7.4.1 Speed Limits on Restricted Roads

Section 81(1) of the Road Traffic Regulation Act 1984 provides that the speed limit on a 'restricted road' will be 30 mph. A restricted road is then defined under s. 82 as:

(1) Subject to the provisions of this section and of section 84(3) of this Act, a road is a restricted road for the purposes of section 81 of this Act if—
(a) in England and Wales, there is provided on it a system of street lighting furnished by means of lamps placed not more than 200 yards apart;
(b) (applies to Scotland only).
(2) The traffic authority for a road may direct—
(a) that the road which is a restricted road for the purposes of section 81 of this Act shall cease to be a restricted road for those purposes, or
(b) that the road which is not a restricted road for those purposes shall become a restricted road for those purposes.

KEYNOTE

By virtue of s. 85(5), where a road has such a system of street lamps the lack of any traffic signs specifically saying that the road is not a 'restricted' road will be evidence that it *is* a 'restricted' road.

If there are no such street lamps then there must be traffic signs stating what the speed limit is (s. 85(4)).

Although the two subsections above clearly overlap, the traffic authority can use the power under s. 82(2)(b) to impose 'restricted' status (and therefore a speed limit of 30 mph) on a road even though the road does not have a system of lighting as set out in s. 82(1)(a) (see *DPP* v *Evans* [2004] EWHC 2785).

3.7.4.2 Traffic Signs

The proper display of appropriate traffic signs is often critical to the enforcement of speed limits and successful prosecution for infringement.

Traffic signs generally must conform to the Traffic Signs Regulations and General Directions 2002. The specifications relating to signs marking the beginning and end of speed limits on roads are set out in part II of the Directions (particularly at paras 8–16) and make reference, *inter alia*, to the need for terminal signs to be properly illuminated during the hours of darkness. If the signs do not conform to the regulations there cannot be a conviction (*DPP v Butler* [2010] EWHC 669 (Admin)).

Section 81(1) of the 1984 Act states that it shall be unlawful for a person to drive a motor vehicle on a restricted road at a speed exceeding 30 mph.

However, failure by a local authority to erect signs does not amount to a breach of the general statutory duty to maintain highways nor the general duty to promote road safety (**see para. 3.8.2**). As the House of Lords has put it 'drivers [have] to take care for themselves and drive at a safe speed irrespective of whether or not there was a warning sign; they were not entitled to suppose that the need for care on their journeys would be highlighted so as to protect them from their own negligence' (*Gorringe v Calderdale MBC* [2004] UKHL 15).

Section 84 allows for speed limits to be imposed on roads other than restricted roads and motorways.

3.7.4.3 Temporary Speed Limits

Section 88 of the 1984 Act provides for both maximum and minimum temporary speed limits to be imposed on certain roads.

Traffic authorities may impose temporary speed *restrictions* in connection with road works or similar operations near to the road which present a danger to the public or serious damage to the highway (see ss. 14–16 of the Road Traffic Regulation Act 1984). These restrictions cannot generally exceed 18 months without approval from the Secretary of State.

As *restrictions* rather than speed limits, offences under this heading do not require notices of intended prosecution (*Platten v Gowing* [1983] Crim LR 184), neither do they require corroboration.

3.7.4.4 Speed Limits for Particular Classes of Vehicle

The Road Traffic Regulation Act 1984, s. 86 states:

(1) It shall not be lawful for a person to drive a motor vehicle of any class on a road at a speed greater than the speed specified in Schedule 6 to this Act as the maximum speed in relation to a vehicle of that class.
(2) Subject to subsections (4) and (5) below, the Secretary of State may by regulations vary, subject to such conditions as may be specified in the regulations, the provisions of that Schedule.
(3) Regulations under this section may make different provision as respects the same class of vehicles in different circumstances.
(4) . . .
(5) The Secretary of State shall not have power under this section to vary the speed limit imposed by section 81 of this Act.

KEYNOTE

Certain vehicles such as larger passenger carrying vehicles and goods vehicles are required to have 'speed limiters' under legislation emanating from European Directive 2002/85/EC. A speed limiter is basically a device designed to limit the maximum speed of a motor vehicle by controlling the power output from its engine (see reg. 36A(14) of the Road Vehicles (Construction and Use) Regulations 1986). The requirements in this area are complicated by the fact that, not only does the requirement for a vehicle to have a speed limiter fitted vary with the type of vehicle and the use to which it is being put, but also the dates by which they will have to comply vary from vehicle to vehicle. In each case the up-to-date regulations should be consulted. As a general rule, the Directive requires post-October 2001 diesel-engined goods vehicles over 3.5 tonnes and buses with more than eight passenger seats to be fitted with a speed limiter. There are many general exemptions to the need to have speed limiters fitted, one such being on qualifying vehicles that are being used for police, fire and rescue or ambulance purposes at the time (see the Road Vehicles (Construction and Use) Regulations 1986, reg. 36B(14)).

3.7.4.5 Exemption for Police, Fire and Ambulance Purposes

The Road Traffic Regulation Act 1984, s. 87 states:

(1) No statutory provisions imposing a speed limit on motor vehicles shall apply to any vehicle on an occasion when it is being used for fire brigade [or, in England, fire and rescue authority], ambulance or police purposes, if the observance of that provision would be likely to hinder the use of the vehicle for the purpose for which it is being used on that occasion.
(2) Subsection (1) above applies in relation to a vehicle being used—
    (a) for Serious Organised Crime Agency purposes, or
    (b) for training persons to drive vehicles for use for Serious Organised Crime Agency purposes,
    as it applies in relation to a vehicle being used for police purposes.

KEYNOTE

The above exemption is extended to cover employees of the Serious Organised Crime Agency (SOCA). Note however that s. 87(1) does not apply in relation to a vehicle being used for SOCA purposes unless it is being driven by a person who has been trained in driving vehicles at high speeds (except where it is being used for training the person by whom it is being driven)—s. 87(3).

It is the *purpose* to which the vehicle is being put which matters here. Consequently, a privately-owned vehicle used for police purposes may attract the exemption under s. 87 if it is driven in excess of the speed limit. However, a police vehicle being used for private purposes (i.e. doing some unauthorised 'shopping') would not attract the exemption. (Note that an ambulance here does not include organ transplant vehicles—unless it is an ambulance being used for that purpose at the time.)

Contrast this with the prohibition on the fitting and use of flashing lights where the focus of the exemption for emergency vehicles appears to be the construction and purpose of the vehicle itself.

Section 87 only applies to *speed*; it does not absolve drivers of emergency vehicles from any breaches of driving *standards*.

There is an ACPO Protocol in effect with regard to the reporting of speeding offences by roadside cameras in cases falling under the above provisions.

3.7.4.6 Proof of Speed

Section 89(2) of the 1984 Act requires that a person prosecuted for driving a motor vehicle at a speed exceeding the limit shall not be convicted solely on the evidence of one witness to the effect that, in his/her opinion, the defendant was exceeding the speed limit. Section 88(7) includes a similar provision for failing to attain a minimum speed limit.

The requirements for corroboration do not apply to general speeding offences on motorways (but they do for special classes of vehicle exceeding motorway speed limits).

Corroboration may be provided by the equipment in a police vehicle or by *Vascar* or similar speed measuring equipment (*Nicholas* v *Penny* [1950] 2 All ER 89). While it may be preferable, it is not *necessary* in such cases to prove the accuracy of the equipment being used (see e.g. *Darby* v *DPP* [1995] RTR 294).

Two police officers may provide sufficient evidence in a case of speeding but the court will decide how much weight to give to such evidence. It is important to show that both officers saw the vehicle at exactly the same time (*Brighty* v *Pearson* [1938] 4 All ER 127).

The signal emitted by a hand-held radar speed gun has been deemed *not* to amount to a 'communication' for the purposes of the Wireless Telegraphy Act 1949 and a person intercepting such signals cannot be prosecuted under that legislation (*R* v *Crown Court of Knightsbridge, ex parte Foot* [1999] RTR 21). See, however, the offences of encouraging or assisting an offence or obstruction.

The Road Traffic Offenders (Prescribed Devices) Order 1999 (SI 1999/162) makes provision for the use of speed cameras that calculate the average speed of a vehicle while passing between two points and allows these readings to be used as proof of the vehicle's speed under s. 20 of the Road Traffic Offenders Act 1988.

The Road Traffic Offenders Act 1988 (s. 20(1)) allows the prosecution to rely on documents such as those produced by prescribed speed detector devices. A condition of the use of such documents is that the document is served on the defendant not less than seven days before trial (see s. 20(8)). Where there has been a failure to provide the defendant with a copy of the document, however, the Road Traffic Offenders Act 1988 does not prevent the document being put before the court in the usual way (*DPP* v *Thornley* [2006] EWHC 312).

The heavy reliance on roadside cameras for enforcing speed limits has given rise to some inventive pleading. While it is possible to delay the whole prosecution process for many months—or even years—by demanding proof of technical and legal data about the cameras, arguing that the driver cannot be ascertained and so forth, such delay is usually simply postponing the inevitable. And for an example of the dim view that the courts will take if, having caused many years' delay, a defendant then seeks to rely on that delay as a reason to stay the prosecution against him/her see *R (On the Application of Johnson)* v *Stratford Magistrates' Court* [2003] EWHC 353.

3.7.4.7 Punishment of Speeding Offences

Speeding offences are punishable under the following Acts:

- Contravening speed limits generally (s. 89(1) of the Road Traffic Regulation Act 1984 and sch. 2 to the Road Traffic Offenders Act 1988).
- Contravening motorway speed limits (other than special classes of vehicle) (s. 17(4) of the Road Traffic Regulation Act 1984 and sch. 2 to the Road Traffic Offenders Act 1988).
- Contravening *minimum* speed limits made under s. 88(1)(b) of the Road Traffic Regulation Act 1984 (s. 88(7) of the Road Traffic Regulation Act 1984 and sch. 2 to the Road Traffic Offenders Act 1988).
- Contravening temporary speed *restrictions* made under s. 14 of the Road Traffic Regulation Act 1984 (s. 16(1) of the Road Traffic Regulation Act 1984 and sch. 2 to the Road Traffic Offenders Act 1988).

The Road Traffic Regulation Act 1984, s. 89(1) states:

(1) A person who drives a motor vehicle on a road at a speed exceeding a limit imposed by or under any enactment to which this section applies shall be guilty of an offence.

KEYNOTE

The enactments to which this section applies are the Road Traffic Regulation Act 1984 itself *except s. 17(2)* (ordinary classes of vehicles on motorways).

3.8 | Highways and Safety Measures

3.8.1 Introduction

In addition to the legislation regulating driver fitness and competence, there are many other provisions aimed at improving—and enforcing—safety. This chapter addresses some of the more common measures affecting safety, including the parking of vehicles.

3.8.2 Highways and Safety

OFFENCE: **Obstruction of the Highway**—*Highways Act 1980, s. 137*
- Triable summarily • Fine

The Highways Act 1980, s. 137 states:

(1) If a person, without lawful authority or excuse, in any way wilfully obstructs the free passage along a highway he is guilty of an offence . . .

> **KEYNOTE**
>
> If a person convicted of the above offence fails to remove an obstruction, a magistrates' court can make an order requiring him/her to do so. Failure to comply with that order is a further criminal offence triable summarily (see s. 137ZA). On many occasions this will be as much the fault of a company as an individual. Therefore, as a result of the Highways (Obstruction by Body Corporate) Act 2004, a director, manager or other officer of a company will also be guilty of the above offence (and of failure to comply with a magistrates' court order) if it can be proved that the offence was committed with the consent or connivance of the officer or that it was attributable to his/her neglect (see s. 314 of the Highways Act 1980).

OFFENCE: **Obstruction on a Road**—*Road Vehicles (Construction and Use) Regulations 1986, reg. 103*
- Triable summarily • Fine

The Road Vehicles (Construction and Use) Regulations 1986, reg. 103 states:

No person in charge of a motor vehicle or trailer shall cause or permit the vehicle to stand on a road so as to cause any unnecessary obstruction of the road.

OFFENCE: **Obstruction of Street**—*Town Police Clauses Act 1847, s. 28*
- Triable summarily • Fourteen days' imprisonment and/or a fine

The Town Police Clauses Act 1847, s. 28 states:

> Every person who in any street, to the obstruction, annoyance, or danger of the residents or passengers, . . . wilfully interrupts any public crossing, or wilfully causes any obstruction in any public footpath or other public thoroughfare . . .

KEYNOTE

The primary responsibility for maintaining highways rests with the highways authority for the relevant area. This includes a general statutory duty to maintain the highway itself (see Highways Act 1980, s. 41) and a duty—enforceable by individuals—serving statutory notice on the authority (e.g. under s. 130A of the 1980 Act). The general duty under s. 41 includes a duty, so far as reasonably practicable, to ensure that safe passage along the highway is not endangered by snow or ice (s. 41(1A)).

There is also a statutory duty on local authorities to promote road safety (see s. 39 of the Road Traffic Act 1988). Unlike the specific responsibilities with regard to highways above, the duty under s. 39 is 'a broad public duty to promote road safety and could not be converted into a common law duty' that individual road users can enforce (see *Gorringe* v *Calderdale MBC* [2004] UKHL 15).

One way in which local authorities can discharge this broad public duty is by consultation and participation in wider road policing strategies such as that set out within the Association of Chief Police Officers (ACPO) Road Policing Strategy.

What amounts to an obstruction is a question of fact for the magistrate(s) to decide in each case (*Wade* v *Grange* [1977] RTR 417; see also *DPP* v *Jones* [1999] 2 WLR 625). In arriving at that decision they will have regard to, amongst other things: 'the length of time the obstruction continued, the place where it occurred, the purpose for which it was done and whether it caused an actual as opposed to a potential obstruction' (Lord Parker CJ in *Nagy* v *Weston* [1965] 1 All ER 78).

Although primarily concerned with a trespassory assembly under the Public Order Act 1986, *DPP* v *Jones* (above) raised a number of significant points in relation to obstruction. In deciding that the public's rights in relation to the highway were not restricted to simply passing and re-passing, Lord Irvine said:

> . . . the public highway is a place which the public may enjoy for any reasonable purpose, provided the activity in question does not amount to a public or private nuisance and does not obstruct the highway by unreasonably impeding the primary right of the public to pass and re-pass: within these qualifications there is a public right of peaceful assembly on the highway.

His lordship gave examples of lawful use of the highway as including the handing out of leaflets (see *Hirst and Agu* v *Chief Constable of West Yorkshire* (1985) 85 Cr App R 143), making sketches and collecting for charity.

In addition, their lordships had been asked to consider the lawful use of the highway in the light of Article 11 of the European Convention on Human Rights, the article that protects a right of peaceful assembly generally. Lord Irvine stated that to view *any* assembly on the highway as being *prima facie* unlawful (as the Divisional Court had done) would not be compatible with Article 11.

Each of the above offences has different elements which are important in selecting the appropriate charge. The Highways Act 1980 offence can be committed by anyone using anything whereas the offence under reg. 103 refers to a person in charge of a motor vehicle or trailer. Similarly, the *place* being obstructed differs from a 'highway', 'road' or 'street' according to the enactment, while the *way* in which that place is obstructed may be either 'wilful' or 'unnecessary'.

Both of the offences, however, appear to require an unreasonable use of the road. Some examples of what might amount to obstruction have included:

- Parking a van in a lay-by to sell food and drink to passers by (*Waltham Forest LBC* v *Mills* [1980] RTR 201).

- Creating a queue of vehicles at a security gate at the entry to a factory (*Lewis* v *Dickson* [1976] RTR 431).
- Putting displays out on the footpath in front of a shop (*Hertfordshire County Council* v *Bolden* (1987) 151 JP 252).
- Street entertainers in a shopping street (*Waite* v *Taylor* (1985) 149 JP 551).

Where a person is convicted of an offence of obstruction under s. 137 of the 1980 Act above and the obstruction is not removed, the court can make an order requiring the person to remove the cause of the obstruction, provided that it is in that person's power to do so (s. 137ZA). Such an order can be made in addition to, or in place of any other punishment and will specify a reasonable period within which the cause of the obstruction must be removed. If the person fails without reasonable excuse to comply with such an order, he/she commits a summary offence punishable by a fine which will increase incrementally for every day that the obstruction remains.

A refusal to move a vehicle that is obstructing the highway when requested by a police officer can amount to an 'obstruction' of the officer under what is now s. 89(2) of the Police Act 1996 (*Gelberg* v *Miller* [1961] 1 WLR 153).

3.8.2.1 Stopping up Highways to Prevent Crime

The Highways Act 1980 has been amended to allow local highway authorities to stop up or divert highways where it is expedient to do so for the purposes of preventing or reducing crime which would otherwise disrupt the life of the community. The amendments (made by the Countryside and Rights of Way Act 2000) empower highway authorities to make a special order, either stopping up or diverting the relevant highway, where they are satisfied that premises adjoining or adjacent to the highway are affected by high levels of crime and that the existence of the highway is facilitating the persistent commission of criminal offences. If the relevant highway crosses school land an order can be made if it is expedient for the purposes of protecting the pupils or staff from violence or threats of violence, or from harassment, alarm or distress arising from unlawful activity. Neither a stopping up order (under s. 118B of the 1980 Act), nor a diversion order (under s. 119B) can be made until the highway authority has consulted the police authority for the area in which the highway lies. These orders must be submitted for confirmation by the Secretary of State. The majority of these powers came into effect in February 2003. For full details, see sch. 6 to the Countryside and Rights of Way Act 2000.

3.8.3 Causing Danger

OFFENCE: **Causing Danger to Other Road Users—*Road Traffic Act 1988, s. 22A***
- Triable either way • Seven years' imprisonment and/or a fine on indictment
- Six months' imprisonment and/or a fine summarily

The Road Traffic Act 1988, s. 22A states:

(1) A person is guilty of an offence if he intentionally and without lawful authority or reasonable cause—
  (a) causes anything to be on or over a road, or
  (b) interferes with a motor vehicle, trailer or cycle, or
  (c) interferes (directly or indirectly) with traffic equipment,
  in such circumstances that it would be obvious to a reasonable person that to do so would be dangerous.

(2) In subsection (1) above 'dangerous' refers to danger either of injury to any person while on or near a road, or of serious damage to property on or near a road; and in determining for the purposes of that subsection what would be obvious to a reasonable person in a particular case, regard shall be had not only to the circumstances of which he could be expected to be aware but also to any circumstances shown to have been within the knowledge of the accused.

(3) In subsection (1) above 'traffic equipment' means—

    (a) anything lawfully placed on or near a road by a highway authority;

    (b) a traffic sign lawfully placed on or near a road by a person other than a highway authority;

    (c) any fence, barrier or light lawfully placed on or near a road—

        (i) in pursuance of section 174 of the Highways Act 1980, or section 65 of the New Roads and Street Works Act 1991 (which provide for guarding, lighting and signing in streets where works are undertaken), or

        (ii) by a constable or a person acting under the instructions (whether general or specific) of a chief officer of police.

(4) For the purposes of subsection (3) above anything placed on or near a road shall unless the contrary is proved be deemed to have been lawfully placed there.

KEYNOTE

This offence requires a defendant to act both intentionally and without lawful authority. The intention in s. 22A only applies to the causing or interfering described. There is no need to show that the defendant *intended* to create danger—only that it would have been obvious to a reasonable person that to do so would be dangerous.

Like the requirements for dangerous driving under ss. 1 and 2 of the 1988 Act, the test here is primarily *objective* (the 'reasonable person' test) but it also has a *subjective* element in that regard will be had to any circumstances shown to be known to the defendant.

In assessing whether or not a person has committed the offence under s. 22A(1), the appropriate test is 'would a reasonable bystander (whether they are a motorist or not) consider that the act in question represented an obvious danger?' (*DPP* v *D* [2006] EWHC 314). This is a wider test than asking whether the danger would be obvious to a 'reasonable and prudent motorist driving at the correct speed', a test that the Divisional Court (in *DPP* v *D*) held to be too narrow. In the court's view a reasonable person would not expect all motorists to drive carefully and well and should realise that the placing of a traffic sign, for instance, could cause an accident—even if the primary factor of such an accident was excessive speed.

A 'road' for the purpose of this offence does not include a footpath (or bridleway) (s. 22A(5)).

3.8.3.1 Dangerous Activities on Highways

OFFENCE: **Dangerous Activity on Highways—*Highways Act 1980, ss. 161 to 162***

    • Triable summarily • Fine

The Highways Act 1980, ss. 161 to 162 state:

161.—(1) If a person, without lawful authority or excuse, deposits any thing whatsoever on a highway in consequence of which a user of the highway is injured or endangered, that person is guilty of an offence . . .

    (2) If a person, without lawful authority or excuse—

        (a) lights any fire on or over a highway which consists of or comprises a carriageway; or

        (b) discharges any firearm or firework within [15.24 metres] 50 feet of the centre of such a highway,

    and in consequence a user of the highway is injured, interrupted or endangered, that person is guilty of an offence . . .

    (3) If a person plays at football or any other game on a highway to the annoyance of a user of the highway he is guilty of an offence . . .

(4) If a person, without lawful authority or excuse, allows any filth, dirt, lime or other offensive matter or thing to run or flow on to a highway from any adjoining premises, he is guilty of an offence . . .

161A.—(1) If a person—

(a) lights a fire on any land not forming part of a highway which consists of or comprises a carriageway; or

(b) directs or permits a fire to be lit on any such land,

and in consequence a user of any highway which consists of or comprises a carriageway is injured, interrupted or endangered by, or by smoke from, that fire or any other fire caused by that fire, that person is guilty of an offence . . .

162.— A person who for any purpose places any rope, wire or other apparatus across a highway in such a manner as to be likely to cause danger to persons using the highway is, unless he proves that he had taken all necessary means to give adequate warning of the danger, guilty of an offence . . .

KEYNOTE

'Carriageway' means a way constituting or comprised in a highway, being a way (other than a cycle track) over which the public have a right of way for the passage of vehicles (s. 329 of the 1980 Act).

The offences at s. 161(1), (2) and (3) and s. 161A(1) are all offences of 'consequence', that is, you must show the relevant consequence (e.g. injury, annoyance, etc.).

Authorised fire-fighters and members of fire and rescue services have powers to stop and regulate traffic and to close highways.

3.8.4 Parking

A significant cause of traffic disruption, frustration and even danger is the parking of vehicles. While specific parking control in a location is more often than not a matter for the local authority, there are several key areas of general regulation that may be relevant; these are set out below.

3.8.4.1 Parking on Verges

OFFENCE: **Parking of Heavy Commercial Vehicles on Verges—*Road Traffic Act 1988, s. 19***
• Triable summarily • Fine

The Road Traffic Act 1988, s. 19 states:

(1) Subject to subsection (2) below, a person who parks a heavy commercial vehicle (as defined in section 20 of this Act) wholly or partly—

(a) on the verge of a road, or

(b) on any land situated between two carriageways and which is not a footway, or

(c) on a footway,

is guilty of an offence.

Defence

The Road Traffic Act 1988, s. 19 states:

(2) A person shall not be convicted of an offence under this section in respect of a vehicle if he proves to the satisfaction of the court—

(a) that it was parked in accordance with permission given by a constable in uniform, or

(b) that it was parked in contravention of this section for the purpose of saving life or extinguishing fire or meeting any other like emergency, or

(c) that it was parked in contravention of this section but the conditions specified in subsection (3) below were satisfied.

(3) The conditions mentioned in subsection (2)(c) above are—

(a) that the vehicle was parked on the verge of a road or on a footway for the purpose of loading or unloading, and

(b) that the loading or unloading of the vehicle could not have been satisfactorily performed if it had not been parked on the footway or verge, and

(c) that the vehicle was not left unattended at any time while it was so parked.

(4) In this section 'carriageway' and 'footway', in relation to England and Wales, have the same meanings as in the Highways Act 1980.

KEYNOTE

'Heavy commercial vehicle' means any goods vehicle which has an operating weight exceeding 7.5 tonnes (Road Traffic Act 1988, s. 20(1)).

The operating weight of a goods vehicle for the purposes of this section is:

- in the case of a motor vehicle not drawing a trailer or in the case of a trailer, its maximum laden weight,

- in the case of an articulated vehicle, its maximum laden weight (if it has one) and otherwise the aggregate maximum laden weight of all the individual vehicles forming part of that articulated vehicle, and

- in the case of a motor vehicle (other than an articulated vehicle) drawing one or more trailers, the aggregate maximum laden weight of the motor vehicle and the trailer or trailers attached to it.

For the purposes of this section: a 'carriageway' is a part of the highway (other than a cycle track) over which members of the public have a right of way for vehicles; a 'footway' is part of a highway that also comprises a carriageway, being a way over which the public has a right to pass on foot only (simply the pavement in most cases) (s. 329(1) of the Highways Act 1980).

3.8.4.2 Leaving Vehicles in Dangerous Positions

OFFENCE: **Leaving Vehicles in Dangerous Positions—*Road Traffic Act 1988, s. 22***
- Triable summarily • Fine • Discretionary disqualification

The Road Traffic Act 1988, s. 22 states:

If a person in charge of a vehicle causes or permits the vehicle or a trailer drawn by it to remain at rest on a road in such a position or in such condition or in such circumstances as to involve a danger of injury to other persons using the road, he is guilty of an offence.

KEYNOTE

This offence involves presenting a danger of injury to other road users by the *position, condition* or *circumstances* of the vehicle/trailer.

The danger presented by the condition or circumstances of the vehicle is not confined to occasions when it is stationary but will also apply to a vehicle/trailer which presents a danger by moving (such as where a driver fails to set the handbrake (*Maguire* v *Crouch* (1940) 104 JP 445)).

The risk must be to 'other persons using the road'.

3.8.4.3 Parking Regulations

Much of the responsibility for regulating the parking of vehicles on roads falls on local authorities. The Road Traffic Regulation Act 1984, ss. 45–56, makes provision for the parking of motor vehicles on highways and for the operation of parking meters. The designation of parking places by local authorities is provided for under s. 46 while s. 47 creates an offence of failing to comply with the conditions of such a designated parking place.

Special provision is made in relation to parking in London under part IV of the Greater London Authority Act 1999.

The Road Traffic Regulation Act 1984, ss. 1–8 allows for the creation of 'no waiting' orders. When creating these orders, local authorities must follow the procedure laid out in the relevant regulations.

It is worth noting that a council has a statutory duty (under s. 21 of the Housing Act 1985) to manage, regulate and control its houses. This has been held to empower a council to enforce regulations for the control of parking—for instance by clamping vehicles where appropriate (see *Akumah* v *Hackney London Borough Council* [2002] EWCA Civ 582). A council also has subsidiary powers to do anything that is conducive or incidental to the discharge of its functions (see s. 111 of the Local Government Act 1972). As a result, a council has the power to enforce measures for the proper regulation of parking without the need to make specific by-laws first.

OFFENCE: **Contravention of Traffic Regulation Order—*Road Traffic Regulation Act 1984, s. 5(1) (outside London); s. 8(1) (inside London)***
 • Triable summarily • Fine

The Road Traffic Regulation Act 1984, ss. 5 and 8 state:

5.—(1) A person who contravenes a traffic regulation order, or who uses a vehicle, or causes or permits a vehicle to be used in contravention of a traffic regulation order, shall be guilty of an offence.

8.—(1) Any person who acts in contravention of, or fails to comply with, an order under section 6 of this Act shall be guilty of an offence.

> **KEYNOTE**
>
> In order to be effective, signs showing 'no waiting' areas must be properly marked and displayed as required by the Road Traffic Regulation Act 1984, s. 64, along with the relevant regulations, traffic signs and general directions. If they are not, then no offence of contravention can be prosecuted (see *Hassan* v *DPP* [1992] RTR 209).

3.8.4.4 Badge Scheme: Disabled Drivers

Local authorities are empowered to issue 'badges' under the Chronically Sick and Disabled Persons Act 1970 (as amended) for motor vehicles driven by, or used for, the carriage of disabled persons.

Exemptions for disabled people driving or being carried in vehicles using a badge are covered by a number of regulations applicable to local authorities.

The regulation of the badge scheme *in England* falls under the Disabled Persons (Badges for Motor Vehicles) (England) Regulations 2000 (SI 2000/682). These Regulations came into force on 1 April 2000. In relation to Wales, the relevant law can be found in the Disabled Persons (Badges for Motor Vehicles) (Wales) Regulations 2000 (SI 2000/1786 (W. 123)) which came into force on 1 July 2000.

The 2000 Regulations were introduced to give effect to an EC Council Recommendation for a Community-model parking card for people with disabilities. These badges have a blue background.

In addition to continuing the individual badge scheme, the 2000 Regulations introduced an 'institutional' badge issued to a relevant institution for its motor vehicles when they are being used to carry people who are disabled within the meaning of the Regulations. The 2000 Regulations go on to make provision for the issuing, refusal, withdrawal and display of the individual and institutional badges.

Section 105 of the Road Traffic Regulation Act 1984 exempts vehicles displaying a current blue badge from being clamped (under s. 104) under some circumstances.

OFFENCE: **Wrongful Use of Disabled Person's Badge—*Road Traffic Regulation Act 1984, s. 117***

> • Triable summarily • Fine

The Road Traffic Regulation Act 1984, s. 117 states:

(1) A person who at any time acts in contravention of, or fails to comply with, any provision of an order under this Act relating to the parking of motor vehicles is also guilty of an offence under this subsection if at that time—

  (a) there was displayed on the motor vehicle in question a badge purporting to be of a form prescribed under section 21 of the Chronically Sick and Disabled Persons Act 1970, and

  (b) he was using the vehicle in circumstances where a disabled person's concession would be available to a disabled person's vehicle,

  but he shall not be guilty of an offence under this subsection if the badge was issued under that section and displayed in accordance with regulations made under it.

(1A) A person who at any time acts in contravention of, or fails to comply with, any provision of an order under this Act relating to the parking of motor vehicles is also guilty of an offence under this subsection if at that time—

  (a) there was displayed on the motor vehicle in question a badge purporting to be a recognised badge, and

  (b) he was using the vehicle in circumstances where a concession would, by virtue of section 21B of the Chronically Sick and Disabled Persons Act 1970, be available to a vehicle lawfully displaying a recognised badge,

  but he shall not be guilty of an offence under this subsection if the badge was a recognised badge and displayed in accordance with regulations made under section 21A of that Act.

  . . .

(3) In this section—

  'disabled person's concession' means—

  (a) an exemption from an order under this Act given by reference to disabled persons' vehicles; or

  (b) a provision made in any order under this Act for the use of a parking place by disabled persons' vehicles.

KEYNOTE

A local authority may require the return of a badge and may refuse to issue such a badge if the person concerned has held and subsequently misused it in a way which has led to at least three relevant convictions.

A driver who commits a parking offence and misuses a blue badge at the same time commits both the relevant parking offence *and* an offence under s. 117 above.

3.8.4.5 Removal and Immobilisation of Parked Vehicles

Sections 104–106 of the Road Traffic Regulation Act 1984 provide for the clamping of vehicles on roads using an 'approved' device (provided for under s. 104(9)). The Traffic Management Act 2004 also allows for further clamping legislation to be brought in by the relevant authority in England or Wales.

Wheel clamping on private land is a different matter. If an occupier of land decides to enforce a civil remedy of detaining the property of trespassers until compensation is paid (i.e. by clamping their vehicle), that is a civil matter. Where an occupier of private land displayed a clear notice that vehicles parking without authority would be clamped, the Divisional Court held that anyone who subsequently parked there without authority consented to their car being clamped. The vehicle owner could not be excused for causing criminal damage to the clamp by trying to remove it (*Lloyd* v *DPP* [1991] Crim LR 904).

The Private Security Industry Act 2001 created a Security Industry Authority whose remit includes the regulation of wheel clamping on private land and the introduction of a code of practice for clamping firms. The relevant activities that will be covered by this part of the Act are set out in sch. 2 (as amended). Generally this provides that immobilisation will only amount to regulated activity by a security operative where it is proposed to charge a fee for the release of the immobilised vehicle. Immobilisation in this way will include blocking in or other types of restriction of the vehicle's movement.

Note that under the Vehicle Excise Duty (Immobilisation, Removal and Disposal of Vehicles) Regulations 1997 (SI 1997/2439) vehicles may be clamped if they are not taxed.

Special provisions in relation to the disposal and immobilisation of vehicles in London are set out at s. 101 of the Road Traffic Regulation Act 1984. Responsibility for regulating traffic and parking in London has been transferred to 'Transport for London' by the Greater London Authority Act 1999.

3.8.5 Tampering with and Getting on to Vehicles

OFFENCE: **Tampering with Motor Vehicles—*Road Traffic Act 1988, s. 25***
- Triable summarily • Fine

The Road Traffic Act 1988, s. 25 states:

> If, while a motor vehicle is on a road or on a parking place provided by a local authority, a person—
> (a) gets on to the vehicle, or
> (b) tampers with the brake or other part of its mechanism,
> without lawful authority or reasonable cause he is guilty of an offence.

KEYNOTE

This offence, which only applies to 'motor vehicles' and not trailers, can only be committed where the vehicle is on a road or local authority parking place.

What constitutes a part of its mechanism—other than the brake—is open to interpretation but it would appear that anything falling within the ordinary meaning of 'mechanism' would suffice.

If a defendant has got on to or tampered with the vehicle in order to steal it or part of its load then the offence under s. 9 of the Criminal Attempts Act 1981 (interfering) may be appropriate.

This is a specified offence for the purposes of s. 3(4)(b) of the Vehicles (Crime) Act 2001.

If a defendant gets on to a *moving* vehicle—or trailer—he/she may commit the following offence.

OFFENCE: **Holding or Getting on to Vehicle in Motion—*Road Traffic Act 1988, s. 26***
- Triable summarily • Fine

The Road Traffic Act 1988, s. 26 states:

(1) If, for the purpose of being carried, a person without lawful authority or reasonable cause takes or retains hold of, or gets on to a motor vehicle or trailer while in motion on a road he is guilty of an offence.

(2) If, for the purpose of being drawn, a person takes or retains hold of a motor vehicle or trailer while in motion on a road he is guilty of an offence.

KEYNOTE

For this offence the vehicle or trailer must both be in motion and on a road.

3.8.6 Abandoning Vehicles

Those involved in road policing have a number of powers and obligations in this regard, the key ones being summarised in the rest of this paragraph.

In order to address this growing phenomenon, and to improve recycling efforts, the End-of-Life Vehicles (Producer Responsibility) Regulations 2005 (SI 2005/263) have been enacted. The regulations impose a series of requirements on vehicle manufacturers and importers in respect of certain vehicles that have effectively become waste—basically, those that have reached the end of their useful life (the specific definition of 'waste' is set out in Council Directive 75/442/EC). The regulations require 'producers' (the vehicle manufacturer or the professional importer of a vehicle into the United Kingdom) to register with the Secretary of State and declare responsibility for those vehicles that they have placed on the market (reg. 7). Producers are obliged to make provision for vehicles for which they have declared responsibility under reg. 7 or for which responsibility has been ascribed to them by the Secretary of State (see reg. 8) or where their business is transferred to another person as set out in reg. 9. In practice there will be a rolling programme under which producers must establish collection networks to receive their own brands of certain vehicles that have become waste. The programme—which contains several either way offences—will be overseen and enforced by the Secretary of State with the assistance of the Environment Agency.

OFFENCE: **Abandoning Motor Vehicle—*Refuse Disposal (Amenity) Act 1978, s. 2(1)***

• Triable summarily • Fine

The Refuse Disposal (Amenity) Act 1978, s. 2 states:

(1) Any person who, without lawful authority,—
    (a) abandons on any land in the open air, or on any other land forming part of a highway, a motor vehicle or anything which formed part of a motor vehicle and was removed from it in the course of dismantling the vehicle on the land; or
    (b) abandons on any such land any thing other than a motor vehicle, being a thing which he has brought to the land for the purpose of abandoning it there,
    shall be guilty of an offence.

3.8.6.1 Duty of Local Authority to Remove Abandoned Vehicles

The Refuse Disposal (Amenity) Act 1978, s. 3 states:

(1) Where it appears to a local authority that a motor vehicle in their area is abandoned without lawful authority on any land in the open air or on any other land forming part of a highway, it shall be the duty of the authority, subject to the following provisions of this section, to remove the vehicle.

'Motor vehicle' is defined under s. 11 of the Act as:

> . . . a mechanically propelled vehicle intended or adapted for use on roads, whether or not it is in a fit state for such use, and includes any trailer intended or adapted for use as an attachment to such a vehicle, any chassis or body, with or without wheels, appearing to have formed part of such a vehicle or trailer, and anything attached to such a vehicle or trailer.

KEYNOTE

Before it can remove a vehicle under this section, a local authority must follow the requirements of the Act and of the Removal and Disposal of Vehicles Regulations (SI 1986/183) in relation to affixing of notices advising the owner (of both the vehicle, and the land if occupied) of its intention. In order to combat the growing problem of abandoned cars, the notice period required to be given by a local authority in relation to a vehicle which appears to have been abandoned and ought to be destroyed has been reduced from seven days to 24 hours (see reg. 10).

Where an authority has removed a vehicle which is not in such a condition that it ought to be destroyed, and the authority has located the owner, the period during which the owner must remove the vehicle after service of the relevant notice is now seven days (see reg. 14).

3.8.6.2 Police Power to Remove Vehicles from Roads

In certain circumstances police officers can require a vehicle to be removed from a particular road or place.

The Removal and Disposal of Vehicles Regulations 1986, reg. 3 states:

> (2) A constable may require the owner, driver or other person in control or in charge of any vehicle to which this Regulation applies to move or cause to be moved the vehicle and any such requirement may include a requirement that the vehicle shall be moved from that road to a place which is not on that or any other road, or that the vehicle shall not be moved to any such road or to any such position on a road as may be specified.

KEYNOTE

These regulations are made under s. 99 of the Road Traffic Regulation Act 1984.

The vehicles to which this regulation applies are vehicles which:

- have broken down, or been permitted to remain at rest, on a road in such a position or in such condition or in such circumstances as to cause obstruction to persons using the road or as to be likely to cause danger to such persons, or
- have been permitted to remain at rest or have broken down and remained at rest on a road in contravention of a prohibition or restriction contained in, or having effect under, any of the enactments mentioned in sch. 1 to these Regulations.

Note that this regulation is not restricted to 'motor' vehicles and it applies to any vehicle, whatever its condition, including chassis or bodies, with or without wheels, appearing to have formed part of a vehicle (Road Traffic Regulation Act 1984, s. 99(5)).

'Obstruction' for these purposes is not to be construed in the same way as an obstruction under the Highways Act 1980 or reg. 103 of the Road Vehicles (Construction and Use) Regulations 1986. There, an obstruction requires an unreasonable use of the road or highway. Under reg. 3 above the requirement to move the vehicle can be made, not only where the vehicle is *actually* obstructing other traffic, but also where it is *potentially* obstructing other road users that may be expected at some time in the future (*Carey* v *Chief Constable of Avon and Somerset* [1995] RTR 405). This power can be used if the offending vehicle is

---

considered (by the officer) to be 'obstructing the passage of road users along the highway; hindering them or preventing them from getting past' (per Hutchinson LJ in *Carey* above).

Regulation 4A provides traffic wardens with a power to remove or arrange for the removal of vehicles to which reg. 3 applies under certain circumstances. The powers in regulations made under s. 99 of the Road Traffic Regulation Act 1984 are among those that can be conferred on a Community Support Officer designated under sch. 4 to the Police Reform Act 2002 and a person accredited under sch. 5 to that Act.

Schedule 1 lists most offences relating to unlawful parking (e.g. 'no waiting' areas, pedestrian crossing areas, etc.).

These provisions extend to vehicles parked in contravention of an order made under s. 48 of the Terrorism Act 2000.

The Removal and Disposal of Vehicles Regulations 1986, reg. 4 states:

> Where a vehicle—
> (a) is a vehicle to which Regulation 3 of these Regulations applies, or
> (b) having broken down on a road or on any land in the open air, appears to a constable to have been abandoned without lawful authority, or
> (c) has been permitted to remain at rest on a road or on any land in the open air in such a position or in such condition or in such circumstances as to appear to a constable to have been abandoned without lawful authority,
>
> then, subject to the provisions of sections 99 and 100 of the Road Traffic Regulation Act 1984, a constable may remove or arrange for the removal of the vehicle, and, in the case of a vehicle which is on a road he may remove it or arrange for its removal from that road to a place which is not on that or any other road, or may move it or arrange for its removal to another position on that or another road.

KEYNOTE

Section 99 of the Road Traffic Regulation Act 1984 provides for the removal of vehicles illegally parked or abandoned, while s. 100 deals with the interim disposal of such vehicles.

This power might be used where an officer wishes to move a vehicle and either cannot find the driver or the driver refuses to move it.

Regulation 4 also empowers a police officer to remove vehicles that have broken down on land in the open air.

Regulation 4 confers two powers on the police officer: a personal power to remove the vehicle and a power to arrange for the vehicle's removal by another (*Rivers* v *Cutting* [1983] RTR 105). If the officer arranges for a reputable contractor to remove the vehicle under this power and chooses that contractor with reasonable care, the officer is not liable for any damage caused by the contractor.

In a case involving the theft of a car which had been abandoned by thieves, the Court of Appeal reviewed the use of these powers by police officers. The court held that the correct approach under s. 99 of the Act and reg. 4 of the Regulations was not whether a vehicle had been abandoned, but whether, in the wording of reg. 4, the vehicle had been *left in a position so as to appear to the police officer* that it had been abandoned (*Clarke* v *Chief Constable of the West Midlands Police* [2001] EWCA Civ 1169).

The powers conferred by regulations made under s. 99 of the Road Traffic Regulation Act 1984 are among those that can be conferred on a designated person under sch. 4 to the Police Reform Act 2002.

3.8.7 **Off-road Driving**

OFFENCE: **Driving Motor Vehicle on Land other than a Road—*Road Traffic Act 1988, s. 34(1)***

- Triable summarily • Fine

The Road Traffic Act 1988, s. 34 states:

(1) Subject to the provisions of this section, if without lawful authority a person drives a mechanically propelled vehicle—

    (a) on to or upon any common land, moorland or land of any other description, not being land forming part of a road, or

    (b) on any road being a footpath, bridleway or restricted byway,

    he is guilty of an offence.

KEYNOTE

Note that this offence applies to mechanically propelled vehicles. A 'restricted byway' means a highway over which the public have rights of way on foot, on horseback, or using vehicles other than mechanically propelled vehicles.

Where a constable in uniform has reasonable grounds for believing that a mechanically propelled vehicle is being used or has been used on any occasion in a manner which contravenes s. 34, and is causing (or is likely to cause), alarm, distress or annoyance to members of the public, he/she has the powers set out in s. 59 of the Police Reform Act 2002.

3.8.7.1 **Exception**

The Road Traffic Act 1988, s. 34 states:

(3) It is not an offence under this section to drive a mechanically propelled vehicle on any land within fifteen yards of a road, being a road on which a motor vehicle may lawfully be driven, for the purpose only of parking the vehicle on that land.

KEYNOTE

This exception only applies if the driver's purpose in driving on the land is to park on it. Although s. 34(3) could be interpreted as limiting such driving to 15 yards the point is unclear. If, however, the driver's purpose is to do something other than park on the land (e.g. to turn round) the offence will be made out. The section includes any land 'of any other description' which is not part of a road.

There is a further, general defence under s. 34 which states:

(4) A person shall not be convicted of an offence under this section with respect to a vehicle if he proves to the satisfaction of the court that it was driven in contravention of this section for the purpose of saving life or extinguishing fire or meeting any other like emergency.

KEYNOTE

Note that it is still a summary offence under s. 72 of the Highway Act 1835 wilfully to ride or drive on the footway and the offence is not limited to 'motor vehicles'. 'Wilfully' means doing so on purpose and any accidental or inadvertent driving onto the footway would not come under this offence (*Fearnley* v *Ormsby* (1879) 43 JP 384).

3.8.8 Skips

OFFENCE: **Depositing Builders' Skip on the Highway—*Highways Act 1980, s. 139***
  • Triable summarily • Fine

The Highways Act 1980, s. 139 states:

(1) A builder's skip shall not be deposited on a highway without the permission of the highway authority for the highway.

(2) A permission under this section shall be a permission for a person to whom it is granted to deposit, or cause to be deposited, a skip on the highway specified in the permission, and a highway authority may grant such permission either unconditionally or subject to such conditions as may be specified in the permission including, in particular, conditions relating to—

(a) the siting of the skip;

(b) its dimensions;

(c) the manner in which it is to be coated with paint and other material for the purpose of making it immediately visible to oncoming traffic;

(d) the care and disposal of its contents;

(e) the manner in which it is to be lighted or guarded;

(f) its removal at the end of the period of permission.

(3) . . .

(4) Where a builder's skip has been deposited on a highway in accordance with a permission granted under this section, the owner of the skip shall secure—

(a) that the skip is properly lighted during the hours of darkness and, where regulations made by the Secretary of State under this section require it to be marked in accordance with the regulations (whether with reflecting or fluorescent material or otherwise), that it is so marked;

(b) that the skip is clearly and indelibly marked with the owner's name and with his telephone number or address;

(c) that the skip is removed as soon as practicable after it has been filled;

(d) that each of the conditions subject to which that permission was granted is complied with; and, if he fails to do so, he is, subject to subsection (6) below, guilty of an offence. . .

KEYNOTE

Any permission has to be given in writing and it is an offence to fail to comply with any condition imposed upon that permission. 'Blanket' permissions are not permitted (*York District Council* v *Poller* [1976] RTR 37) and the offence will be complete if the owner fails to remove the skip after the permission has expired (*Craddock* v *Green* [1983] RTR 479). It is important to note from a practical perspective that the responsibility for lighting etc. of the skip is with the owner rather than the hirer.

In addition, the 1980 Act goes on to allow for regulations to be made requiring notification of specific details with regard to the placing of builders' skips and also allowing the highway authority to levy a charge for the depositing of such skips on highways. Breach of these regulations may amount to a criminal offence triable summarily.

Under s. 139(11) skips for this purpose are containers:

. . . designed to be carried on a road vehicle and to be placed on a highway or other land for the storage of builders' materials, or for the removal and disposal of builders' rubble, waste, household and other rubbish or earth . . .

KEYNOTE

They must also comply with the Builders' Skips (Markings) Regulations 1984 (SI 1984/1933).

The owner of a skip that is the subject of a hiring or hire purchase agreement is defined under s. 139(11) as the person in possession of it, provided that the agreement is for a period of *not less than* one month.

3.8.8.1 Defence

The Highways Act 1980, s. 139 states:

> (6) In any proceedings for an offence under this section it is a defence, subject to subsection (7) below, for the person charged to prove that the commission of the offence was due to the act or default of another person and that he took all reasonable precautions and exercised all due diligence to avoid the commission of such an offence by himself or any person under his control.

3.8.8.2 Police Powers

Under s. 140 of the 1980 Act a constable in uniform may require the removal of a skip from the highway. Failure to do so is an offence under s. 140(3) but the requirement must be made *in person*. If the requirement to remove the skip is made by the officer telephoning the owner, the offence will not be made out (*R v Worthing Justices, ex parte Waste Management Ltd* [1988] Crim LR 458).

3.8.9 Pedestrian Crossings

The regulations governing this area are fairly detailed and what follows is a summary of the main provisions.

Section 25 of the Road Traffic Regulation Act 1984 allows the Secretary of State to make regulations with respect to pedestrian crossings.

The current regulations are the Zebra, Pelican and Puffin Pedestrian Crossings Regulations and General Directions 1997 (SI 1997/2400) and these regulations are the ones referred to throughout the following section. Combined pedestrian and cyclist crossings (Toucan crossings) come under reg. 49 of the Traffic Signs Regulations and General Directions 2002 (SI 2002/3113).

OFFENCE: **Contravening Regulations made under s. 25 of the Road Traffic Regulation Act 1984—*Road Traffic Regulation Act 1984, s. 25(5)***
  • Triable summarily • Fine • Discretionary disqualification

The Road Traffic Regulation Act 1984, s. 25 states:

> (5) A person who contravenes any regulations made under this section shall be guilty of an offence.

KEYNOTE

Offences committed against the following crossings regulations will generally be prosecuted under the Road Traffic Regulation Act 1984, s. 25. However, some behaviour will involve a breach of a regulation made under s. 64 of the Road Traffic Regulation Act 1984 (e.g. ignoring a crossing light). In such cases the offence will be triable summarily, attracting a fine but no endorsement or liability to be disqualified unless the relevant regulation applies (s. 36 of the Road Traffic Act 1988).

3.8.9.1 The Regulations

The Puffin crossing gets its name from the Pedestrian User-friendly Intelligent crossing! Puffin crossings differ from their less intelligent counterparts by incorporating a pedestrian sensor that delays traffic as long as is necessary while people are on the crossing but not once the crossing is clear.

The Zebra, Pelican and Puffin Pedestrian Crossings Regulations and General Directions 1997 (SI 1997/2400) set out the relevant requirements for each type of crossing, together with the obligations on drivers when at a crossing.

Regulation 3 provides the many definitions found within the 1997 Regulations. The various dimensions of each type of crossing and their respective markings are laid out in regs 5–7 and in schs 1–4.

Under regs 8 and 9, provision is made for traffic authorities to add further apparatus or equipment at crossings (e.g. equipment to help people with disabilities).

Although the prescribed dimensions and markings must be adopted by traffic authorities when erecting such crossings, minor irregularities which do not materially affect the appearance or proper operation of a crossing will not prevent it from being treated as 'a crossing' for the purposes of offences and traffic regulation (reg. 10).

3.8.9.2 Lights at Crossings

Lights placed at crossings are 'traffic signs' for the purposes of the Road Traffic Regulation Act 1984 (reg. 11).

Regulations 12 and 13 set out the significance of the lights and signals at pelican and puffin crossings respectively. These regulations state what meanings each signal shall have and what action may or may not be taken by drivers on seeing those signals.

Special provision is made within regs 12 and 13 in relation to vehicles being used for the purposes of:

- police;
- fire (and rescue);
- ambulance; or
- national blood service.

If a vehicle is being used for one of those purposes *and* if the observance of the steady amber or red signal (or the red-with-amber at a puffin crossing) would be likely to hinder the use of the vehicle for that purpose, the driver of the vehicle may proceed beyond the 'stop' line under certain conditions (regs 12(1)(e) and 13(1)(f)).

Those conditions are that the driver:

- accords precedence to any pedestrian who is on the carriageway within the limits of the crossing; and
- does not proceed in a manner or at a time likely to endanger any person/vehicle approaching or waiting at the crossing; or
- does not proceed in a manner or at a time likely to cause the driver of any such vehicle to change its speed or course in order to avoid an accident.

For a discussion of the standards of police driving in general, **see para. 3.2.12**.

3.8.9.3 Give-way Lines at Zebra Crossings

Regulation 14 of the 1997 Regulations states:

A give-way line included in the markings placed pursuant to regulation 5(1)(b) and Part II of Schedule 1 shall convey to vehicular traffic proceeding towards a Zebra crossing the position at or before which a vehicle should be stopped for the purpose of complying with regulation 25 (precedence of pedestrians over vehicles at Zebra crossings).

3.8.9.4 Pedestrian Light Signals

Regulation 15 of the 1997 Regulations states:

(1) The significance of the red and steady green pedestrian light signals whilst they are illuminated at a Pelican crossing and of the red and green figures on a pedestrian demand unit whilst they are illuminated at a Puffin crossing shall be as follows—

(a) the red pedestrian light signal and the red figure shall both convey to a pedestrian the warning that, in the interests of safety, he should not cross the carriageway; and

(b) the steady green pedestrian light signal and the steady green figure shall both indicate to a pedestrian that he may cross the carriageway and that drivers may not cause vehicles to enter the crossing.

(2) The flashing green pedestrian light signal at a Pelican crossing shall convey—

(a) to a pedestrian who is already on the crossing when the flashing green signal is first shown the information that he may continue to use the crossing and that, if he is on the carriageway or a central reservation within the limits of that crossing (but not if he is on a central reservation which lies between two crossings which form part of a system of staggered crossings) before any part of a vehicle has entered those limits, he has precedence over that vehicle within those limits; and

(b) to a pedestrian who is not already on the crossing when the flashing green light is first shown the warning that he should not, in the interests of safety, start to cross the carriageway.

(3) Any audible signal emitted by any device for emitting audible signals provided in conjunction with the steady green pedestrian light signal or the green figure, and any tactile signal given by any device for making tactile signals similarly provided, shall convey to a pedestrian the same indication as the steady green pedestrian light signal or as the green figure as the case may be.

3.8.9.5 Movement of Traffic at Crossings

Section IV of the 1997 Regulations contains the relevant regulations which restrict the movement of vehicles at crossings. Regulations 18 to 26 state:

18. The driver of a vehicle shall not cause the vehicle or any part of it to stop within the limits of a crossing unless he is prevented from proceeding by circumstances beyond his control or it is necessary for him to stop to avoid injury or damage to persons or property.

19. No pedestrian shall remain on the carriageway within the limits of a crossing longer than is necessary for that pedestrian to pass over the crossing with reasonable despatch.

20.—(1) For the purposes of this regulation and regulations 21 and 22 the word 'vehicle' shall not include a pedal bicycle not having a sidecar attached to it, whether or not additional means of propulsion by mechanical power are attached to the bicycle.

(2) Except as provided in regulations 21 and 22 the driver of a vehicle shall not cause it or any part of it to stop in a controlled area.

21. Regulation 20 does not prohibit the driver of a vehicle from stopping it in a controlled area—

(a) if the driver has stopped it for the purpose of complying with regulation 25 or 26;

(b) if the driver is prevented from proceeding by circumstances beyond his control or it is necessary for him to stop to avoid injury or damage to persons or property; or

(c) when the vehicle is being used for police, fire brigade or, in England, fire and rescue authority or ambulance purposes.

22.—(1) Regulation 20 does not prohibit the driver of a vehicle from stopping it in a controlled area—

(a) for so long as may be necessary to enable the vehicle to be used for the purposes of—

(i) any building operation, demolition or excavation;

(ii) the removal of any obstruction to traffic;

(iii) the maintenance, improvement or reconstruction of a road; or

(iv) the laying, erection, alteration, repair or cleaning in or near the crossing of any sewer or of any main, pipe or apparatus for the supply of gas, water or electricity, or of any electronic communications apparatus kept installed for the purposes of an electronic communications code network or of any other electronic communications apparatus lawfully kept installed in any position,

but only if the vehicle cannot be used for one of those purposes without stopping in the controlled area; or

(b) if the vehicle is a public service vehicle being used—
  (i) in the provision of a local service; or
  (ii) to carry passengers for hire or reward at separate fares,

and the vehicle, having proceeded past the crossing to which the controlled area relates, is waiting in that area in order to take up or set down passengers; or

(c) if he stops the vehicle for the purpose of making a left or right turn.

(2) In paragraph (1) 'local service' has the meaning given in section 2 of the Transport Act 1985 but does not include an excursion or tour as defined by section 137(1) of that Act.

23. When vehicular light signals at a Pelican or Puffin crossing are displaying the red light signal the driver of a vehicle shall not cause it to contravene the prohibition given by that signal by virtue of regulation 12 or 13.

24.—(1) Whilst any motor vehicle (in this regulation called 'the approaching vehicle') or any part of it is within the limits of a controlled area and is proceeding towards the crossing, the driver of the vehicle shall not cause it or any part of it—

(a) to pass ahead of the foremost part of any other motor vehicle proceeding in the same direction; or

(b) to pass ahead of the foremost part of a vehicle which is stationary for the purpose of complying with regulation 23, 25 or 26.

(2) In paragraph (1)—

(a) the reference to a motor vehicle in sub-paragraph (a) is, in a case where more than one motor vehicle is proceeding in the same direction as the approaching vehicle in a controlled area, a reference to the motor vehicle nearest to the crossing; and

(b) the reference to a stationary vehicle is, in a case where more than one vehicle is stationary in a controlled area for the purpose of complying with regulation 23, 25 or 26, a reference to the stationary vehicle nearest the crossing.

25.—(1) Every pedestrian, if he is on the carriageway within the limits of a Zebra crossing, which is not for the time being controlled by a constable in uniform or traffic warden, before any part of a vehicle has entered those limits, shall have precedence within those limits, over that vehicle and the driver of the vehicle shall accord such precedence to any such pedestrian.

(2) Where there is a refuge for pedestrians or central reservation on a Zebra crossing, the parts of the crossing situated on each side of the refuge for pedestrians or central reservation shall, for the purposes of this regulation, be treated as separate crossings.

26. When the vehicular light signals at a Pelican crossing are showing the flashing amber signal, every pedestrian, if he is on the carriageway or a central reservation within the limits of the crossing (but not if he is on a central reservation which forms part of a system of staggered crossings) before any part of a vehicle has entered those limits, shall have precedence within those limits over that vehicle and the driver of the vehicle shall accord such precedence to any such pedestrian.

KEYNOTE

The expression 'pedestrian' replaced the former one of 'foot passengers' which had given rise to many debates about people pushing bicycles and skateboarders, rollerbladers, etc. It remains to be seen how the expression will be interpreted in relation to crossings.

Failing to observe the 1997 Regulations will amount to an offence under s. 25 of the 1984 Act above.

If a police officer, traffic warden or other authorised person is directing traffic at a crossing, it will for the time being cease to be 'uncontrolled' and their directions must be followed, even if they contravene the regulations. Failure to follow such directions may amount to an offence.

Part I of sch. 1 to the 1997 Regulations requires Zebra crossings to be marked with yellow globes mounted at or near each end of the crossing. The globes must show a flashing or—where so authorised—a constant light (para. 1). If the globes have been disfigured, discoloured or have failed to light, the crossing will still be deemed to be properly marked for the purposes of enforcement (para. 4).

The globes may be fitted with boards to increase their visibility or prevent their light from reaching adjoining properties (para. 3).

The 'limits' of a Zebra crossing will be defined by the line of studs on each side of the black and white stripes. Anything or anyone who is outside those lines of studs is consequently outside the limits of the crossing (*Moulder* v *Neville* [1974] RTR 53).

Although the failure of a driver to stop at a crossing in contravention of the Regulations is *absolute* (that is, you need not show any particular state of mind), if control of the vehicle is temporarily and unavoidably taken from the driver—say, by being shunted from behind by another vehicle—the driver will not commit an offence (*Burns* v *Bidder* [1966] 3 All ER 29).

Failure to observe crossing regulations is not of itself conclusive proof of driving without due care or consideration (*Gibbons* v *Kahl* [1956] 1 QB 59).

3.8.9.6   School Crossings

The Road Traffic Regulation Act 1984 makes provision for the patrolling of school crossings (ss. 26–29). Section 28 states:

(1) When a vehicle is approaching a place in a road where a person is crossing or seeking to cross the road, a school crossing patrol wearing a uniform approved by the Secretary of State shall have power, by exhibiting a prescribed sign, to require the person driving or propelling the vehicle to stop it.

(2) When a person has been required under subsection (1) above to stop a vehicle—

   (a) he shall cause the vehicle to stop before reaching the place where a person is crossing or seeking to cross and so as not to stop or impede his crossing, and

   (b) the vehicle shall not be put in motion again so as to reach the place in question so long as the sign continues to be exhibited.

OFFENCE: **Failing to Comply—*Road Traffic Regulation Act 1984, s. 28(3)***
   • Triable summarily • Fine • Discretionary disqualification

The Road Traffic Regulation Act 1984, s. 28 states:

(3) A person who fails to comply with paragraph (a) of subsection (2) above, or who causes a vehicle to be put in motion in contravention of paragraph (b) of that subsection, shall be guilty of an offence.

KEYNOTE

School crossing patrols are no longer restricted to stopping traffic when children are crossing and can operate at any time.

Section 28 enables patrols to stop traffic in order to allow anyone to cross safely. This section creates two separate offences:

• s. 28(2)(a)—failing to stop in a way which does not impede the people crossing; and

• s. 28(2)(b)—having stopped, putting the vehicle in motion again while the sign continues to be exhibited.

The Road Traffic Regulation Act 1984, s. 28 goes on to state:

(4) In this section—
    (a) 'prescribed sign' means a sign of a size, colour and type prescribed by regulations made by the Secretary of State or, if authorisation is given by the Secretary of State for the use of signs of a description not so prescribed, a sign of that description;
    (b) 'school crossing patrol' means a person authorised to patrol in accordance with arrangements under section 26 of this Act;

and regulations under paragraph (a) above may provide for the attachment of reflectors to signs or for the illumination of signs.

(5) For the purposes of this section—
    (a) where it is proved that a sign was exhibited by a school crossing patrol, it shall be presumed, unless the contrary is proved, to be of a size, colour and type prescribed, or of a description authorised, under subsection (4)(b) above, and, if it was exhibited in circumstances in which it was required by the regulations to be illuminated, to have been illuminated in the prescribed manner; and
    (b) where it is proved that a school crossing patrol was wearing a uniform, the uniform shall be presumed, unless the contrary is proved, to be a uniform approved by the Secretary of State.

KEYNOTE

The dimensions and details of the crossing sign exhibited by crossing patrol staff are set out in the School Crossing Patrol Sign (England and Wales) Regulations 2006 (SI 2006/2215). School crossings may also be marked with warning lights and these are provided for under the Traffic Signs Regulations and General Directions 2002.

Traffic wardens may act as school crossing patrols under the Functions of Traffic Wardens Order 1970 (SI 1970/1958) and when they do there is no need for them to wear the prescribed uniform (although they must display the approved sign).

3.8.10 Fire and Rescue Services

The role of the fire and rescue services has several areas of significance for the policing of roads and highways. The key aspects of the relevant legislation are set out below. When considering the legislation applicable to fire authorities it is important to bear in mind that the precise constitution of what are loosely referred to as 'fire brigades' is complex and historical, with many local variations. In addition, many responsibilities have, in the case of Wales, been devolved to the National Assembly and some further local variations may apply. In England there has been a significant reorganisation of fire brigades which, among other things, have become fire and rescue authorities. The London Fire and Civil Defence Authority became the London Fire and Emergency Planning Authority under the Greater London Authority Act 1999.

The main relevance of the legislative provisions so far as road policing is concerned lies in the statutory powers given to some fire authority personnel. The majority of the Fire and Rescue Services Act 2004 applies to England and Wales, with most of the powers given to the Secretary of State being read as though they were also given to the Welsh National Assembly.

3.8.10.1 Powers of Fire-fighters in an Emergency

The Fire and Rescue Services Act 2004, s. 44 states:

(1) An employee of a fire and rescue authority who is authorised in writing by the authority for the purposes of this section may do anything he reasonably believes to be necessary—

(a) if he reasonably believes a fire to have broken out or to be about to break out, for the purpose of extinguishing or preventing the fire or protecting life or property;

(b) if he reasonably believes a road traffic accident to have occurred, for the purpose of rescuing people or protecting them from serious harm;

(c) if he reasonably believes an emergency of another kind to have occurred, for the purpose of discharging any function conferred on the fire and rescue authority in relation to the emergency;

(d) for the purpose of preventing or limiting damage to property resulting from action taken as mentioned in paragraph (a), (b) or (c).

KEYNOTE

The above powers are very widely drafted and clearly allow fire and rescue personnel with the appropriate *written authority* to exercise significant practical powers in connection with accidents and emergencies. Emergencies of 'another kind' would include terrorist activities and threats.

The Act goes on to make specific provision for such authorised employees to move or break into a vehicle without the consent of its owner (see s. 44(2)(b)). As such this power would provide a defence to offences such as taking a vehicle without the owner's consent.

In addition, s. 44(2) empowers an authorised employee to close a highway or to stop and regulate traffic in the circumstances set out at s. 44(1).

Obstructing an employee of a fire and rescue authority without reasonable excuse when that employee is taking authorised action under this section is a summary offence (s. 1(1) of the Emergency Workers (Obstruction) Act 2006).

3.8.10.2 Fire Hydrants

The Fire and Rescue Services Act 2004 requires a water undertaker to cause the location of every fire hydrant provided by it to be clearly indicated by a notice or distinguishing mark and that, in so doing, the water undertaker may place such a notice or mark on a wall or fence adjoining a highway or public place (see s. 42). It is a summary offence for a person to use, damage or obstruct a fire hydrant, otherwise than in consequence of use for the purposes of fire-fighting or for any other purposes of a fire and rescue authority (or purpose authorised by the water undertaker/owner)—see s. 42(6) and (7).

3.8.11 Street Works

The New Roads and Street Works Act 1991 contains a number of specific provisions to ensure safety on roads and streets where there is work taking place. These have been extended (by the Traffic Management Act 2004) and now require the appropriate undertaker to ensure that their works are properly signed, guarded and lit—particularly with regard to the needs of people having a disability. Taking down, altering or removing any fence, barrier, traffic sign or light (or extinguishing a light) at such a site without lawful authority or excuse is a summary offence (see s. 65(6)).

3.8.12 Playgrounds

Section 29 of the Road Traffic Regulation Act 1984 makes provision for local traffic authorities to create orders prohibiting or restricting vehicular access to certain roads so that the roads may be used as 'street playgrounds'.

OFFENCE: **Contravention of Street Playground Order—*Road Traffic Regulation Act 1984, s. 29(3)***

• Triable summarily • Fine • Discretionary disqualification

The Road Traffic Regulation Act 1984, s. 29 states:

(3) A person who uses a vehicle, or causes or permits a vehicle to be used, in contravention of an order in force under this section shall be guilty of an offence.

KEYNOTE

This offence does not apply to vehicles or drivers in the public service of the Crown.

3.9 | Construction and Use

3.9.1 Introduction

The use of vehicles in a poor or dangerous condition is not only likely to amount to a specific offence or offences, but it can often be an indication of wider criminal behaviour. As such, matters affecting the construction and use of vehicles fall within the ACPO Road Policing Strategy.

The law governing the construction and use of road vehicles is mainly to be found— as the name suggests—in the Road Vehicles (Construction and Use) Regulations 1986 (SI 1986/1078). The Regulations deal with everything from motor cycle sidestands (reg. 38) to the placing of mascots (reg. 53). These Regulations are frequently amended and continue to be amended as the law develops. (For full details of the current Regulations, see *The Encyclopedia of Road Traffic Law & Practice* (Sweet & Maxwell).)

Although 'vehicles' for many purposes, pedal cycles have their own construction and use regulations.

3.9.2 Vehicle Defect Rectification Scheme

The Vehicle Defect Rectification Scheme (VDRS) was introduced to streamline the process for dealing with vehicles having minor defects and to ensure that those defects were in fact rectified rather than simply punished. The scheme is voluntary and a motorist does not have to participate. The VDRS, which represents the next non-prosecution stage after a verbal warning, involves the person responsible being issued with a form by a police officer setting out the relevant defect in his/her vehicle. Once the defect has been pointed out and the person has accepted the form, he/she must have the defect remedied and then submit the vehicle for examination at a Department of Transport approved testing station. The testing station will certify that the defect has been rectified and the form, so endorsed, must be returned to the central police ticket office by the responsible person within 14 days. Failure to return the form within that time will result in the matter being considered for prosecution in the normal manner. A copy of the form is returned to the originating officer after 21 days.

3.9.3 Type Approval

Part I of the Regulations, which govern the way in which vehicles are built and equipped, are gradually being replaced by the 'type approval' system.

The type approval system has come about as a result of the United Kingdom's membership of the European Union whose common transport policy has had a significant impact on this area of law (see the Road Vehicles (Approval) Regulations 2009 (SI 2009/717)).

The eventual aim of the policy is standardisation of the construction of all vehicles and their component parts.

When dealing with any potential breach of the legislation in this area, it is important to make sure whether a type approval system applies. In doing so you should refer to reg. 6 which contains guidance on compliance with Community Directives and EC Regulations.

Whether or not a particular type approval scheme applies to a vehicle or a part used in one will largely be determined by the date of its first use or of its manufacture. It is important to distinguish which of these applies in any particular case.

The law which currently regulates this area is to be found in ss. 54–65A of the Road Traffic Act 1988 which makes it an offence to use, cause or permit to be used a vehicle subject to the type approval requirements on a road without a certificate of conformity (s. 63(1)).

Additionally, under s. 80 of the 1988 Act the Secretary of State may designate the marking of motor vehicle parts to indicate conformity with a type approved by any country. Examples of such 'type approval marks' can be found under the Motor Vehicles (Designation of Approval Marks) Regulations 1979 (SI 1979/1088), as amended, which relate to braking systems and seat belt anchorage systems. Applying a 'mark' in a way that is likely to deceive is an offence under s. 1 of the Trade Descriptions Act 1968.

3.9.4 The Road Vehicles (Construction and Use) Regulations 1986

Many of the principal rules relating to the use of vehicles on roads are to be found in the Road Vehicles (Construction and Use) Regulations 1986. These have been amended many, many times and the most up-to-date copy should be referred to. Some of the offences are aimed at the driving or control of the vehicle but most are concerned with the condition of the vehicle, its equipment and specifications.

Regulation 3 sets out the relevant definitions; where there is no specific definition, those used under the Road Traffic Act 1988 will usually apply.

In bringing a prosecution for an offence under these Regulations it is important to establish whether the correct offence is 'using', 'causing' or 'permitting'. It is also important to establish whether a particular regulation applies to vehicles *first used* on or after a certain date; *first registered* on or after a certain date; or *manufactured* on or after a certain date (see e.g. *Mackinnon* v *Peate* [1936] 2 All ER 240). In addition to the general condition and use of the relevant vehicle, the regulations can require the fitting of specific equipment to vehicles and this can be of considerable practical significance. For example, certain vehicles such as those with eight or more passenger seats are (or will be) required to have 'speed limiters'. As the many and various requirements under the regulations are often complicated by fine detail (including the 'first used' or 'first manufactured' issues referred to above), it is important to consult an up-to-date copy of the regulations in each case.

Certain vehicles are exempted from the Regulations (see reg. 4) and again it is important to check that a vehicle in a particular case does fall within those categories.

3.9.4.1 Brakes

Regulations 15–19 set out the requirements as to braking systems on vehicles, together with those for their maintenance. It is not absolutely *necessary* for the person testing the braking system of a vehicle to be a 'qualified examiner' (see *Stoneley* v *Richardson* [1973] RTR 229 where a constable testified to being able to push the defendant's car along with the hand-brake applied).

The offence of breaching the requirement in relation to brakes is prosecuted under s. 41A of the Road Traffic Act 1988.

See also s. 75 of the Road Traffic Act 1988 for the offence of selling unroadworthy vehicles.

3.9.4.2 Tyres

Section 41A of the 1988 Act also applies where the requirements in relation to tyres have been breached.

Regulation 24 sets out the requirements as to what tyres must be fitted to which vehicles, while reg. 25 restricts the speed limits and loads for such vehicles. Regulation 27 sets out a number of specific defects that will make tyres unlawful. It also contains exemptions for certain vehicles. The defects, in reg. 27, are where:

(1) . . .

    (a) the tyre is unsuitable having regard to the use to which the motor vehicle or trailer is being put or to the types of tyres fitted to its other wheels;

    (b) the tyre is not so inflated as to make it fit for the use to which the motor vehicle or trailer is being put;

    (c) the tyre has a cut in excess of 25mm or 10% of the section width of the tyre, whichever is the greater, measured in any direction on the outside of the tyre and deep enough to reach the ply or cord;

    (d) the tyre has any lump, bulge or tear caused by separation or partial failure of its structure;

    (e) the tyre has any of the ply or cord exposed;

    (f) the base of any groove which showed in the original tread pattern of the tyre is not clearly visible;

    (g) either—

        (i) the grooves of the tread pattern of the tyre do not have a depth of at least 1 mm throughout a continuous band measuring at least three-quarters of the breadth of the tread and round the entire outer circumference of the tyre; or

        (ii) if the grooves of the original tread pattern of the tyre did not extend beyond three-quarters of the breadth of the tread, any groove which showed in the original tread pattern does not have a depth of at least 1mm; or

    (h) the tyre is not maintained in such condition as to be fit for the use to which the vehicle or trailer is being put or has a defect which might in any way cause damage to the surface of the road or damage to persons on or in the vehicle or to other persons using the road.

Regulation 27 also places restrictions on 'recut' tyres (reg. 27(5)) and provides for many exemptions from the above conditions.

KEYNOTE

The entire outer circumference of a tyre does not usually include the outer walls or shoulder as they are not in contact with road (see *Coote* v *Parkin* [1977] RTR 61).

In the case of:

• 'passenger vehicles other than motor cycles constructed or adapted to carry no more than 8 seated passengers in addition to the driver'

• 'goods vehicles with a maximum gross weight which does not exceed 3500 kg'

• 'light trailers'

(first used on or after 3 January 1933 in each case) the depth of tread requirement is increased to 1.6 mm throughout a continuous band across the central 3/4 section of the tyre and around the entire circumference. For these three types of vehicle paras 27(1)(f) and 27(1)(g) shall not apply.

To avoid the defect at reg. 27(1)(b) the tyre must be inflated so as to make it fit for the use to which the vehicle is being put at the material time; it does not have to be so inflated as to make it fit for some *future* use, however probable that use might be (*Connor* v *Graham* [1981] RTR 291).

Evidence as to the defective condition of a tyre may be given by anyone who saw it and it is no defence to argue that the tyre was not examined by an authorised vehicle examiner (*Phillips* v *Thomas* [1974] RTR 28).

Regulation 26 generally prohibits the mixing of different types of tyre (e.g. diagonal ply, bias-belted or radial ply) on both the same axle or different axles (although some combination is permissible). The use on roads of some 'knobbly' tyres or others which are designed for off-road use (on vehicles such as quad-bikes) may be prosecuted under reg. 27(1)(a) if it can be shown that the tyres were 'unsuitable having regard to the use to which the vehicle was put'.

'Tread pattern' includes plain surfaces as well as cut grooves but it does *not* cover tie-bars and tread wear indicators as used on the tyres of many goods and heavy vehicles.

In relation to the selling of unsafe tyres, see the Motor Vehicles Tyres (Safety) Regulations 1994 (SI 1994/3117) and the Consumer Protection Act 1987, s. 12(5).

Exemptions

Regulation 27(4) sets out a number of exemptions to the provisions at (a)–(g) above, the main ones being:

- agricultural motor vehicles driven at not more than 20 mph
- agricultural trailers
- broken down vehicles or vehicles proceeding to a place to be broken up, being drawn in either case, by a motor vehicle at not more than 20 mph.

The onus appears to be on the defendant to show that his/her vehicle falls into an exempted category and that burden is not discharged simply by showing that the vehicle's excise licence describes it as being in one such category (*Wakeman* v *Catlow* [1977] RTR 174).

3.9.4.3 Mirrors

Regulation 33 sets out the requirements for mirrors on vehicles, including exemptions for certain types of vehicle. At reg. 33(1) there is a table showing the various types of mirror(s) required by different vehicles. Regulation 33(4) sets out the requirement for the stability and visibility of a vehicle's mirrors, together with the ability of the driver to adjust them.

3.9.4.4 Exhaust Systems and Audible Warning Instruments

Regulations 54 and 57 regulate the fitting and use of silencers. The regulations provide that every vehicle propelled by an internal combustion engine shall be fitted with an exhaust system including a silencer and the exhaust gases from the engine shall not escape into the atmosphere without passing through the silencer and exhaust system. The silencer shall be maintained in good and efficient working order and shall not be altered so as to increase the noise made by the escape of exhaust gases.

Regulations 37 and 99 regulate the fitting and use of audible warning instruments. Every motor vehicle which has a maximum speed of more than 20 mph shall be fitted with a horn, not being a reversing alarm or a two-tone horn. This does not apply to an agricultural motor vehicle, unless it is being driven at more than 20 mph. The sound emitted by any horn, other than a reversing alarm, boarding aid alarm or a two-tone horn, fitted to a wheeled vehicle first used on or after 1 August 1973, shall be continuous, uniform and not strident. A general prohibition on the use of an audible warning instrument while the vehicle is stationary on a road (except to warn of danger) is made by reg. 99, which also prohibits the use of such instruments between 11.30 pm and 7 am on a restricted road.

Generally, no motor vehicle shall be fitted with a bell, gong, siren or two-tone horn but a bell, gong, or siren may be fitted to prevent theft or attempted theft of the motor vehicle or its contents and also to a bus to summon help for the driver, conductor or an inspector. If the device is fitted to prevent theft and the vehicle was first used on or after 1 October 1982, another device must be fitted so as to stop the bell, gong or siren after it has sounded continuously for more than five minutes. Every such device shall be maintained in good working order.

As an exception to the general rule, a bell, gong, siren or two-tone horn may be fitted to a vehicle, examples of which include:

- if used for fire brigade, ambulance or police purposes;
- if used by a body formed primarily for the purposes of fire salvage and used for those or similar purposes;
- if used by the Forestry Commission or local authority for fighting fires;
- if used for bomb disposal;
- if used by the blood transfusion service;
- if used as a Coastguard vehicle;
- if used for mine rescue;
- if used by the RAF mountain rescue service;
- if used by the Royal National Lifeboat Institute for the purpose of launching lifeboats;
- if used for mountain rescue purposes.

3.9.4.5 Quitting

Regulation 107 prohibits the leaving of a motor vehicle unattended on a road unless the engine has been stopped *and* the brake set; both must be done (*Butterworth* v *Shorthouse* [1956] Crim LR 341). Any person left 'attending' the vehicle must be someone who is licensed to drive it and in a position to intervene otherwise reg. 107 is breached. This sort of behaviour is very common (particularly outside cashpoints etc.) and, owing to the danger it presents, can often be dealt with under s. 22 of the Road Traffic Act 1988 (**see chapter 3.8**).

There are some exceptions to this prohibition when the vehicle is being used for certain purposes (e.g. for police, ambulance or fire and rescue services).

3.9.4.6 Stopping of Engine

Regulation 98 provides that the driver of a vehicle when it is stationary shall stop the action of any machinery attached to or forming part of the vehicle so far as may be necessary for the prevention of noise *or exhaust emissions*. The italicised addition was inserted by the Road Vehicles (Construction and Use) (Amendment) Regulations 1998 (SI 1998/1) and has significant implications for vehicles such as taxis waiting at ranks. The exceptions to reg. 98 are:

- when the vehicle is stationary owing to the necessities of traffic;
- where it is necessary to examine machinery following its failure or derangement, or where it is required to be worked for a purpose other than driving the vehicle; or
- where a vehicle is propelled by gas produced in plant carried on the vehicle, the exception applies to that plant itself.

3.9.4.7 Dangerous Use or Condition

Regulation 100 contains a catch-all provision to prevent the use of vehicles in a way which presents a danger to others. There are many ways in which that danger can be brought about (e.g. insecure loading, using the vehicle in a way which causes a nuisance, having the vehicle in a poor general condition). This regulation, which would apply to vehicles carrying too many people or vehicles being used for an unsuitable purpose, overlaps to a large extent with the offences under ss. 22A and 40A of the Road Traffic Act 1988.

Regulation 104 makes provision to ensure that drivers maintain proper control of their vehicles and maintain a full view of the traffic ahead together with restrictions on the distances which drivers can reverse.

This regulation would cover the improper use of equipment such as mobile phones and stereos if, in using them, the driver failed to maintain proper control of the vehicle and a full view of the traffic ahead.

3.9.4.8 Reversing

Regulation 106 prohibits the reversing of a motor vehicle on a road further than may be requisite for the safety or reasonable convenience of the occupants or of other traffic (unless the vehicle is a road roller engaged in the construction, maintenance or repair of the road).

3.9.4.9 Special Types of Vehicle

The Road Vehicles (Authorisation of Special Types) (General) Order 2003 (SI 2003/1998) exempts a diverse collection of vehicles from the provisions of the 1986 Regulations.

The list of exemptions includes some track-laying, hedge-trimming, grass-cutting, life-saving, rotavating and excavating vehicles, together with some military and pedestrian-controlled vehicles. In the case of any vehicle which falls outside the conventional classes of cars, motor cycle, lorries and buses in terms of its size, construction or use, it is worth checking these exemptions.

3.9.4.10 Motor Cycles

A number of the construction and use regulations relate specifically to motor cycles.

Regulations 57 and 57A set out the construction requirements in relation to noise limits and exhaust systems on motor cycles.

Regulation 84 imposes restrictions on the drawing of trailers by motor cycles on a road, while regs 92 and 93 make provision for the attachment and use of sidecars.

3.9.4.11 Offences

OFFENCE: **Using a Vehicle in Dangerous Condition etc.—*Road Traffic Act 1988, s. 40A***
- Triable summarily • Fine • Obligatory disqualification if committed within three years of a previous conviction of the offender under s. 40A. Discretionary disqualification in any other case

The Road Traffic Act 1988, s. 40A states:

> A person is guilty of an offence if he uses, or causes or permits another to use, a motor vehicle or trailer on a road when—
> (a) the condition of the motor vehicle or trailer, or of its accessories or equipment, or
> (b) the purpose for which it is used, or

(c) the number of passengers carried by it, or the manner in which they are carried, or

(d) the weight, position or distribution of its load, or the manner in which it is secured,

is such that the use of the motor vehicle or trailer involves a danger of injury to any person.

KEYNOTE

Section 40A creates an offence of:

- using, causing or permitting another to use
- on a road
- a motor vehicle or trailer
- which, for whatever reason, involves a danger of injury
- to any person.

The existence of any danger is a question of fact, although s. 40A has to be read in conjunction with reg. 100(1) of the Road Vehicles (Construction and Use) Regulations 1986 (*DPP* v *Potts* [2000] RTR 1).

Given the broad wording of the offence, it would seem to invite an objective test of the use of the motor vehicle or trailer and whether or not that did in fact create a potential danger to anyone including the driver. However, the offence applies to *motor* vehicles and trailers only and not to any other type of vehicle.

The test in relation to the potential for injury is an objective one and will consider the anticipated eventualities of the ordinary course of driving including the need for sudden braking, swerving, etc. (*Akelis* v *Normand* 1997 SLT 136). For example, in *Gray* v *DPP* [1999] RTR 339, a seven-year-old boy was seen to be travelling in the open back of an uncovered jeep without any fitted restraints. The boy was steadying himself by holding on to the vehicle's roll-bars. The court held that, even though he had travelled in that way without incident many times in the past and that his father, the driver, was generally a responsible parent, the objective test as to the potential for injury meant that the offence (under s. 40A(c) above) had been committed.

OFFENCE: **Breach of Requirement: Brakes, Steering Gear or Tyres—*Road Traffic Act 1988, s. 41A***

- Triable summarily • Fine • Discretionary disqualification under specified conditions

The Road Traffic Act 1988, s. 41A states:

A person who—

(a) contravenes or fails to comply with a construction and use requirement as to brakes, steering-gear or tyres, or

(b) uses on a road a motor vehicle or trailer which does not comply with such a requirement, or causes or permits a motor vehicle or trailer to be so used,

is guilty of an offence.

OFFENCE: **Breach of Weight Requirements—Goods and Passenger Vehicles—*Road Traffic Act 1988, s. 41B***

- Triable summarily • Fine

The Road Traffic Act 1988, s. 41B states:

(1) A person who—

(a) contravenes or fails to comply with a construction and use requirement as to any description of weight applicable to—

(i) a goods vehicle, or

(ii) a motor vehicle or trailer adapted to carry more than eight passengers, or

(b) uses on a road a vehicle which does not comply with such a requirement, or causes or permits a vehicle to be so used,

is guilty of an offence.

Defence

The Road Traffic Act 1988, s. 41B states:

(2) In any proceedings for an offence under this section in which there is alleged a contravention of or failure to comply with a construction and use requirement as to any description of weight applicable to a goods vehicle, it shall be a defence to prove either—

(a) that at the time when the vehicle was being used on the road—

(i) it was proceeding to a weighbridge which was the nearest available one to the place where the loading of the vehicle was completed for the purpose of being weighed, or

(ii) it was proceeding from a weighbridge after being weighed to the nearest point at which it was reasonably practicable to reduce the weight to the relevant limit, without causing an obstruction on any road, or

(b) in a case where the limit of that weight was not exceeded by more than 5 per cent—

(i) that that limit was not exceeded at the time when the loading of the vehicle was originally completed, and

(ii) that since that time no person has made any addition to the load.

Weights

The weight of a vehicle will often determine its classification and the use to which it may be put, together with the licensing conditions of those who drive it.

Reference will usually be made to the laden weight or the gross weight of a vehicle in offences involving its construction and use, while offences concerning the speed and excise duty of larger vehicles will usually be concerned with laden and unladen weight.

Calculation of a vehicle's unladen weight for most purposes is contained under s. 190 of the Road Traffic Act 1988.

Most locomotives, motor tractors and heavy motor cars are required to show their unladen weight, either on their nearside or on the relevant plating certificate(s) (see Road Vehicles (Construction and Use) Regulations 1986, regs 66 and 71).

For construction and use purposes, the gross weight under reg. 3(2) of the 1986 Regulations will be:

- For motor vehicles—the sum of the weights transmitted to the road surface by all its wheels.
- For trailers—the sum of the weights transmitted to the road surface by all its wheels *and* of any weight of the trailer which is imposed on the drawing vehicle.

Axle weights are, generally, the sum of the weights transmitted to the road surface by all the wheels of that axle.

OFFENCE: **Breach of Requirements as to Control of Vehicle, Mobile Telephones etc.—*Road Traffic Act 1988, s. 41D***

    • Triable summarily • Fine • Discretionary disqualification • Obligatory endorsement—Three points

The Road Traffic Act 1988, s. 41D states:

A person who contravenes or fails to comply with a construction and use requirement—

(a) as to not driving a motor vehicle in a position which does not give proper control or a full view of the road and traffic ahead, or not causing or permitting the driving of a motor vehicle by another person in such a position, or

(b) as to not driving or supervising the driving of a motor vehicle while using a hand-held mobile telephone or other hand-held interactive communication device, or not causing or permitting the driving of a motor vehicle by another person using such a telephone or other device,

is guilty of an offence.

OFFENCE: **Breach of Other Construction and Use Requirements—*Road Traffic Act 1988, s. 42***

• Triable summarily • Fine

The Road Traffic Act 1988, s. 42 states:

A person who—
(a) contravenes or fails to comply with any construction or use requirement other than one within section 41A(a) or 41B(1)(a) or 41D of this Act, or
(b) uses on a road a motor vehicle or trailer which does not comply with such a requirement, or causes or permits a motor vehicle or trailer to be so used,
is guilty of an offence.

KEYNOTE

Under s. 44 of the Act the Secretary of State may make regulations allowing road use by vehicles that would otherwise contravene the above sections. Such vehicles are usually of extraordinary dimensions such as construction equipment or vehicles for moving abnormal indivisible loads.

3.9.5 Lights

The law which governs the fitting and use of lights on vehicles is to be found in the Road Vehicles Lighting Regulations 1989 (SI 1989/1796). In common with most of the key sets of regulations affecting road policing, these Regulations are regularly amended and the latest version should be referred to. They are made under s. 41 of the Road Traffic Act 1988, for all vehicles except cycles (which are made under s. 81).

The main lights are themselves divided into:

• headlamps (main beam and dipped)
• front and rear position lamps (side lights)
• front and rear fog lamps
• stop lamps
• reversing lamps
• optional lamps
• rear registration plate lamps.

Among other things, the Regulations restrict the use of blue lights (as used by the emergency services) and other non-emergency use of flashing lights such as amber lights used when escorting abnormal loads.

Also included in the 1989 Regulations are reflectors and markers.

3.9.5.1 Offences

Offences contravening the lighting regulations are charged under s. 41 of the Road Traffic Act 1988 in the same ways as the other construction and use offences above.

Note the wording of a prohibition under the relevant regulation may be aimed at the fitting of a light and not necessarily its use.

3.9.5.2 Definitions

Regulation 3 sets out the definitions for the purposes of the 1989 Regulations. Again, where none is specified, the corresponding definition under the Road Traffic Act 1988 will usually apply.

The Regulations separate a 24-hour period into:

- the period between sunset and sunrise
- the period between sunrise and sunset.

Where the old distinction of 'daytime hours' and 'hours of darkness' apply, reg. 3 defines them as 'the time between half an hour before sunrise and half an hour after sunset' and 'the time between half an hour after sunset and half an hour before sunrise' respectively.

3.9.5.3 Exemptions

Regulations 4–9A list the exemptions which include:

4. ...
    (3) Nothing in these Regulations shall require any lamp or reflector to be fitted between sunrise and sunset to—
        (a) a vehicle not fitted with any front or rear position lamp,
        (b) an incomplete vehicle proceeding to a works for completion,
        (c) a pedal cycle,
        (d) a pedestrian-controlled vehicle,
        (e) a horse-drawn vehicle,
        (f) a vehicle drawn or propelled by hand, or
        (g) a combat vehicle.
5. Temporarily imported vehicles and vehicles proceeding to a port for export
6. Vehicles towing or being towed
7. Military vehicles
8. Invalid carriages
9. Vehicles drawn or propelled by hand
9A. Tram cars.

Other exemptions will apply to some parked vehicles (see e.g. reg. 24).

An important class of exempt vehicles is 'emergency vehicles'. These are defined in reg. 3 and include the usual emergency services vehicles (police, ambulance, fire) and also in some cases (e.g. use of blue lights) vehicles used by other agencies such as HM Revenue & Customs and the Ministry of Defence.

3.9.5.4 Fitting of Lights

Regulations 11–22 cover the fitting of lights, reflectors and rear markings. The vehicles shown in sch. 1 must be fitted with the corresponding lights etc. and it is an offence to use, or to cause or permit to be used such a vehicle which does not comply with those regulations.

Regulation 11 deals with the colours of lights and reflectors which must or must not be fitted, while regs 13 and 16 address the fitting of flashing lights and warning beacons. This includes the use of coloured flashing lights on any emergency vehicles (such as police and ambulance vehicles). The definition of emergency vehicles is no longer restricted to *motor* vehicles and any form of emergency vehicle may use the appropriate flashing lights permitted by these regulations. Note that emergency services personnel using their own private vehicle which is not constructed or adapted for relevant 'emergency' purposes will not generally be allowed to use flashing lights even if they are using the vehicle in the course of their work (see *Ashton* v *DPP* (2005) EWHC 2729).

Regulations 21 and 22 deal with the fitting of additional lights to long vehicles and trailers.

3.9.5.5 Rear Registration Lamps

Although rear registration lamps are addressed under the 1989 Regulations, there is also an offence under the Vehicle Excise and Registration Act 1994.

3.9.5.6 Headlamps

Schedules 4 and 5 contain the specifications for headlamps.

Regulation 25 makes it an offence to use or cause or permit to be used, a vehicle with obligatory headlamps on a road unless they are kept lit during the hours of darkness and in seriously reduced visibility. (There is an exception to this requirement which applies to vehicles on 'restricted' roads per s. 81 of the Road Traffic Regulation Act 1984 where the street lights are on.)

3.9.5.7 Position Lamps

Schedules 2 and 10 set out the specification for front and rear position lamps respectively. Regulation 24 makes it an offence to use, or to cause or permit to be used, a vehicle on a road between sunset and sunrise or in motion in seriously reduced visibility, unless every position lamp, rear registration lamp and side-marker lamp required by it are lit.

3.9.5.8 Maintenance and Use

Regulations 23–27 govern the maintenance of lights and reflectors, together with their use. Regulation 23 makes it an offence to use, or to cause or permit to be used, a vehicle on a road unless the relevant lamps and reflectors (including some optional ones) are clean and in good working order.

The general exception to reg. 23 is if the vehicle is being used during daytime hours and the defect only happened during the journey or if arrangements have been made to rectify it with all reasonable expedition (reg. 23(3)).

Regulation 27 sets out a table showing the ways in which certain lights may/may not be used. Regulation 27 states that no person shall use (or cause or permit to be used) on a road, any vehicle on which any lamp, hazard warning signal/device or beacon of a type specified in column 2 of the table in a manner specified in column 3.

3.9.6 Testing

Section 47 of the Road Traffic Act 1988 requires all motor vehicles which were first registered more than three years before the time when they are being used on a road to pass a test. That requirement includes vehicles manufactured abroad (s. 47(2)(b)).

Some vehicles need to be tested after one year, notably:

- motor vehicles having more than eight seats (excluding the driver's seat) which are used to carry passengers
- taxis
- ambulances.

The procedure for testing of vehicles is set out in the Motor Vehicles (Tests) Regulations 1981 (SI 1981/1694), as amended. These and their many amending Regulations lay down both the instructions for carrying out a test and also specify those items which will be tested.

Tests can only be carried out by 'authorised examiners' and others listed in s. 45(3) and vehicle examiners appointed under s. 66A (as amended by the Road Traffic (Vehicle Testing)

Act 1999). Many garages are so authorised. Roadside tests may also be carried out in some circumstances.

Where a garage returned a car to its owner on the understanding that it had been repaired and had passed its MOT when in fact it was unroadworthy, the garage was held to have committed the offence of 'supplying' an unroadworthy vehicle contrary to s. 75 of the Road Traffic Act 1988 (*Devon County Council* v *DB Cars* [2001] EWHC Admin 521). In that case the High Court held that the word 'supply' involved no more than a transfer of physical control of an item from one person to another in order to provide the other person with something that he/she wanted. As the garage owner transferred physical control of the car to the owner he had, on that definition, 'supplied' it. (See also *Formula One Autocentres Ltd* v *Birmingham City Council* [1999] RTR 195.)

For the scope of Regulations that may be made in relation to the testing of vehicles, see s. 46 of the Road Traffic Act 1988. The Road Traffic (Vehicle Testing) Act 1999 made a number of significant changes to the statutory framework for the testing of vehicles. It introduced a system to operate a national computerised database of vehicles and their respective issue/need for MOTs. The 1999 Act allows for changes to be made in respect of a number of aspects including:

- the supervision of MOT testing centres
- the training of staff
- access to information held on the database
- the admissibility/use of records as an alternative to production of the test certificate itself.

The items tested on a vehicle include:

- brakes
- tyres
- seat belts
- steering
- certain lights/reflectors
- stop lights
- exhausts
- wipers and washers
- direction indicators
- suspension
- bodywork
- horn.

Satisfactory completion of the test results in the issuing of a certificate under s. 45(2)(b).

In order to further the overall objective of ensuring that vehicles used on the roads are safe and fit for purpose, several legislative provisions have been made to assist the Vehicle and Operator Services Agency (VOSA) in their regulatory role. An example relevant to road policing is the Road Vehicles (Construction and Use) (Amendment) (No. 4) Regulations 2005 (SI 2005/3165) and the Road Vehicles Lighting (Amendment) (No. 2) Regulations 2005 (SI 2005/3169) which provide exemptions for vehicles used by VOSA examiners from having to comply with certain requirements of the Road Vehicles (Construction and Use) Regulations 1986 and the Road Vehicles Lighting Regulations 1989. The exemptions allow VOSA examiners, posing as members of the public, to drive a vehicle with specific, recorded defects, to and from an MOT testing station in order to see whether the MOT tester not only applies the correct testing standards when conducting the MOT test but is also able to identify the relevant defective components.

Clearly if the examiner exceeds the permitted parameters of the scheme, or uses the vehicle for some purpose other than that envisaged by the legislation, he or she will not be able to rely on these exemptions and will be liable for any offences revealed. In order to come within the exemptions the examiner must:

- be authorised in writing by the Secretary of State to drive the defective vehicle and
- reasonably believe that the defects will not cause a danger of injury to anyone while being so used.

This means that the vehicles will not have major braking, steering or tyre defects for example. The defects that will be imposed on these vehicles will generally be minor such as horns and washers not working, rear seat belts missing or defective, and defects with boot locks, bonnet fastenings etc.

OFFENCE: **Using, Causing or Permitting Use of Vehicle without Test Certificate—**
Road Traffic Act 1988, s. 47(1)
- Triable summarily • Fine

The Road Traffic Act 1988, s. 47 states:

(1) A person who uses on a road at any time, or causes or permits to be so used, a motor vehicle to which this section applies, and as respects which no test certificate has been issued within the appropriate period before that time, is guilty of an offence.
In this section and section 48 of this Act, the 'appropriate period' means a period of twelve months or such shorter period as may be prescribed.

KEYNOTE

Where someone applies for a vehicle excise licence (under the Vehicle Excise and Registration Act 1994):

- the person applying must provide an effective test certificate for the vehicle, or
- show from records maintained under s. 45(6B) of the 1988 Act evidence that such a test certificate has been granted, or
- make a declaration in the specified form.

Alternatively, in the case of an exempt vehicle (see below) the owner of the vehicle can declare in writing the year in which the vehicle was manufactured, and the period of three years from the date of manufacture has not expired. (see the Motor Vehicles (Evidence of Test Certificates) Regulations 2004 (SI 2004/1896)).

As ever, there are numerous exemptions to the requirements of s. 47, most of which relate to larger vehicles, track-laying vehicles and some pedestrian-controlled vehicles (see reg. 6 of the 1981 Regulations).

Some military vehicles, some electrically-powered goods vehicles and vehicles temporarily in Great Britain are also exempt.

Vehicles *provided* (as opposed to 'used') for police purposes are exempt if they are maintained in an approved police workshop (reg. 6(1)(xiv)). Other exemptions exist in relation to vehicles seized or detained by the police or customs and excise officers.

Special provision is made (under s. 48) for the issue of temporary exemption certificates in the case of certain public service vehicles.

An exemption exists where the person using the vehicle is taking it to or from a testing centre. This exemption is only applicable where the test has been previously arranged with the garage. A further exemption exists where a test certificate has been refused and the vehicle is:

- being delivered by prior arrangement, or brought from the place where the relevant work is to be/has been carried out; or
- being towed to a place where it is to be broken up.

Provision is made in reg. 6 for the use of a vehicle by an authorised examiner or inspector during the test.

The provisions of s. 165 of the Road Traffic Act 1988 apply to test certificates.

This means that an officer may issue a form HORT/1 in respect of such a certificate.

Note that the offences under s. 173 (forging documents) and s. 175 (issuing false documents) of the Road Traffic Act 1988 apply to test certificates.

3.9.6.1 Goods Vehicles

The testing of goods vehicles is governed by ss. 49–53 of the Road Traffic Act 1988 and the Goods Vehicles (Plating and Testing) Regulations 1988 (SI 1988/1478), as amended.

They are tested and 'plated' at government testing stations under the ambit of the Secretary of State and these tests must be carried out annually.

Schedule 2 to the Regulations lists the many vehicles which are exempt, a list which includes snow ploughs, hearses, fire fighting vehicles and road rollers.

Where an application is made under the Vehicle Excise and Registration Act 1994 for a compulsory goods vehicle licence, the person applying must:

- provide evidence that an effective goods vehicle test certificate is in force for the vehicle;
- make a declaration in the specified form; or
- produce a certificate of temporary exemption (issued under s. 53(5)(b) of the Road Traffic Act 1988), for a period which includes the date on which the licence is to come into force

(see the Goods Vehicles (Evidence of Test Certificates) Regulations 2004 (SI 2004/2577)).

OFFENCE: **Using, Causing or Permitting Use of Goods Vehicle without Test Certificate—*Road Traffic Act 1988, s. 53(2)***
- Triable summarily • Fine

The Road Traffic Act 1988, s. 53 states:

(2) If any person at any time on or after the relevant date—
  (a) uses on a road a goods vehicle of a class required by regulations under section 49 of this Act to have been submitted for a goods vehicle test, or
  (b) causes or permits to be used on a road a goods vehicle of such a class,
  and at that time there is no goods vehicle test certificate in force for the vehicle, he is guilty of an offence.
  In this subsection 'relevant date', in relation to any goods vehicle, means the date by which it is required by the regulations to be submitted for its first goods vehicle test.

Section 53(1) creates a similar offence in relation to Plating Certificates.

3.9.6.2 Roadside Tests

Section 67 of the Road Traffic Act 1988 allows 'authorised examiners' to carry out roadside tests on motor vehicles, in relation to the brakes, steering, tyres, lights and noise and fume emission. Authorised examiners include police constables so authorised by their chief officer of police. Other examiners may be appointed (e.g. by the Secretary of State or a police authority) but they must produce their authority to act as such if required to do so (s. 67(5)). Obstructing such an examiner is a summary offence under s. 67(9). The Road Vehicles (Powers to Stop) Regulations 2011 (SI 2011/996) enables the appointment of uniformed stopping officers with powers to stop vehicles on roads for a number of purposes.

Section 67(6) allows for drivers to ask for the examination to be deferred (in accordance with the time limits set out at sch. 2 to the 1988 Act). However, s. 67 goes on to state:

(7) Where it appears to–
   (a) a constable, or
   (b) in the case of a vehicle to which subsection (3B) applies, a stopping officer, that, by reason of an accident having occurred owing to the presence of the vehicle on a road, it is requisite that a test should be carried out forthwith, the constable or stopping officer may require it to be so carried out and, if the constable or stopping officer is not to carry it out himself, may require that the vehicle shall not be taken away until the test has been carried out.
(8) Where in the opinion of–
   (a) a constable, or
   (b) in the case of a vehicle to which subsection (3B) applies, a stopping officer, the vehicle is apparently so defective that it ought not to be allowed to proceed without a test being carried out, the constable or stopping officer may require the test to be carried out forthwith.
(9) If a person obstructs an authorised examiner acting under this section, or fails to comply with a requirement of this section or Schedule 2 to this Act, he is guilty of an offence.
(10) In this section and in Schedule 2 to this Act—
   (a) 'test' includes 'inspect' or 'inspection', as the case may require, and
   (b) references to a vehicle include references to a trailer drawn by it.

KEYNOTE

Section 68 provides a power for vehicle examiners to inspect goods vehicles, PSVs and some larger passenger carrying vehicles. It also provides a power for a police officer in uniform to direct such a vehicle to a suitable place of inspection when found on a road, provided that that place of inspection is not more than five miles from the place where the requirement is made. Refusal or neglect to comply is a summary offence. The power is only available in relation to vehicles that are 'stationary' on a road. Presumably if the vehicle is moving, the officer need only stop it (using the general power under s. 163) before directing it to be driven to a place of inspection.

3.9.6.3 Testing and Inspection

Regulation 74 of the Road Vehicles (Construction and Use) Regulations 1986 provides a power to test and inspect the:

- brakes
- silencers
- steering gear
- tyres

of any vehicle on any premises where that vehicle is located.

The power applies to police officers in uniform and other authorised vehicle examiners (see reg. 74(1)(a)–(f)). Regulation 74 provides no power of entry and stipulates that the person empowered shall produce his/her authorisation if required to do so. It also provides that no such test or inspection shall be carried out unless:

- the owner of the vehicle consents;
- notice has been given to that owner (either personally or left at his/her address not less than 48 hours before the time of the proposed test/inspection, or sent to him/her by recorded delivery at least 72 hours before the proposed test/inspection); or
- the test or inspection is made within 48 hours of a reportable accident in which the vehicle was involved.

3.10 Driver Licensing and Forgery of Documents

This chapter is only tested in the Sergeants' examination—Inspectors' examination candidates should not study this material.

3.10.1 Introduction

The law regulating driver licensing is governed primarily by the Motor Vehicles (Driving Licences) Regulations 1999 (SI 1999/2864). As with most statutory instruments in the area of road traffic, these principal Regulations have themselves been amended many times and it is important to refer to the most up-to-date list of such amendments when dealing with licensing matters. In cases of any doubt, the DVLA are generally the best source of information.

Most of the relevant legislation governing the licensing of drivers to drive motor vehicles can be found in the 1999 Regulations, together with:

- part III of the Road Traffic Act 1988
- the Road Traffic (Driver Licensing and Information Systems) Act 1989
- the Road Traffic (New Drivers) Act 1995.

The 1999 Regulations, which have consolidated many of their predecessors, should be consulted when considering offences or entitlements to drive. Infringement is generally charged under the Road Traffic Offenders Act 1988, s. 91.

3.10.2 Driving Otherwise than in Accordance with Licence

Since the implementation of the EC directive on driving licences (Council Directive 91/439/EEC) the categories of vehicles for the purposes of driving licences have been altered. The current categories are to be found in sch. 2 to the 1999 Regulations.

OFFENCE: **Driving Otherwise than in Accordance with Licence—*Road Traffic Act 1988, s. 87***

- Triable summarily • Fine • Discretionary disqualification for s. 87(1) under specified circumstances

The Road Traffic Act 1988, s. 87 states:

(1) It is an offence for a person to drive on a road a motor vehicle of any class otherwise than in accordance with a licence authorising him to drive a motor vehicle of that class.

(2) It is an offence for a person to cause or permit another person to drive on a road a motor vehicle of any class otherwise than in accordance with a licence authorising that other person to drive a motor vehicle of that class.

KEYNOTE

Where a defendant is charged with driving otherwise than in accordance with a licence and driving without insurance, once the prosecution have proved that the defendant has driven on a public highway, it is for him or her to show that he/she had a driver's licence and insurance as those matters were within the defendant's knowledge. In addition, there is no obligation on the police to serve any request for production of the relevant documentation (e.g. a HORT/1)—*DPP* v *Hay* [2005] EWHC 1395.

This offence will apply where a person has a particular licence and has failed to abide by any conditions attached to it, or where a person does not hold a licence at all. In proving such an offence, you must show that the defendant drove a motor vehicle on a road; it is then for the defendant to show that he/she had a licence to do so (see *John* v *Humphreys* [1955] 1 All ER 793).

Section 88 provides a long list of exceptions to the general prohibition imposed by s. 87. Those exemptions include:

- Drivers who have had their licence revoked on disqualification and who have re-applied for another.

- Drivers who have a 'qualifying application' lodged with the Secretary of State.

- Drivers from overseas becoming resident in Great Britain.

Section 88 sets out a number of exemptions to the requirements of s. 87.

3.10.3 The Licence

A driving licence must be issued in the form prescribed by the Secretary of State under s. 98 of the Road Traffic Act 1988. The photocard driving licence was introduced in 1998 as part of the harmonisation process between our domestic road traffic legislation and that of the rest of the European Union (see the Driving Licences (Community Driving Licence) Regulations 1998 (SI 1998/1420)). In addition to the photocard licence, there is a paper counterpart containing much of the same detail as the plastic card but not the holder's photograph.

Photocard licences are *pink* for full licence holders and *green* for provisional licence holders. Licences held by drivers in Wales are printed in both Welsh and English.

Photocard licences are the same size as a credit card and contain the holder's:

- name
- address
- date of birth
- driver number
- driving entitlement
- photograph
- electronically copied signature
- information codes showing any restrictions that apply to the holder.

They can be of particular practical importance and will indicate, for instance, whether the driver is supposed to be wearing spectacles or some other form of visual correction.

A licence holder must surrender his/her licence to the Secretary of State on changing name or address and failure to do so is a summary offence under s. 99(5) of the Road Traffic Act 1988. The Secretary of State may also revoke driving licences under certain conditions (see e.g. s. 93 of the 1988 Act).

The European Commission has recently published a draft directive on standardising driving licences across Member States.

3.10.3.1 Expiry of Licences

The photocard licence is renewable every 10 years, and a reminder, with the appropriate form, is generally sent by DVLA to the address on their records.

Licences will *generally* last until the holder's 70th birthday or for three years, whichever is the longer (see s. 99 of the Road Traffic Act 1988). On reaching 70, a driver may renew his/her licence every three years. This applies to full driving licences and most provisional licences.

Large goods vehicles and passenger carrying vehicles licences last until the driver's 45th birthday or five years, whichever is the longer. If the driver is between 45 and 65 they last for five years or until the holder's 66th birthday, whichever is the *shorter*. After the driver has reached 65 the licence must be renewed annually.

Provisional licences for motor cycles remain generally valid until the holder's 70th birthday (reg. 15 as amended by the Motor Vehicles (Driving Licences) (Amendment) Regulations 2001 (SI 2001/53)).

3.10.3.2 Use of Full Licence as Provisional Licence For Other Vehicles

Full licences can act as provisional licences in many cases (except e.g. motor cycles over 125cc) and you should refer to the licence itself, together with the 1999 Regulations and the provisions of s. 97 in establishing whether a particular licence does entitle the holder to drive other vehicles as a provisional licence holder.

3.10.4 Police Powers

The police now have access to the DVLA database which allows them to check some aspects of driver records. However, the power to demand that a person, in certain circumstances, produces a licence is still valid. Certainly under the present fixed penalty system the need to be able to demand the production of a driving licence is essential.

3.10.4.1 Power to Demand Production of Driving Licence

The Road Traffic Act 1988, s. 164 states:

(1) Any of the following persons—
  (a) a person driving a motor vehicle on a road,
  (b) a person whom a constable or vehicle examiner has reasonable cause to believe to have been the driver of a motor vehicle at a time when an accident occurred owing to its presence on a road,
  (c) a person whom a constable or vehicle examiner has reasonable cause to believe to have committed an offence in relation to the use of a motor vehicle on a road, or
  (d) a person—
    (i) who supervises the holder of a provisional licence while the holder is driving a motor vehicle on a road, or
    (ii) whom a constable or vehicle examiner has reasonable cause to believe was supervising the holder of a provisional licence while driving, at a time when an accident occurred owing to the presence of the vehicle on a road or at a time when an offence is suspected of having been committed by the holder of the provisional licence in relation to the use of the vehicle on a road,

must, on being so required by a constable or vehicle examiner, produce his licence and its counterpart for examination, so as to enable the constable or vehicle examiner to ascertain the name and address of the holder of the licence, the date of issue, and the authority by which they were issued.

KEYNOTE

In order to have met with the requirement to 'produce' a licence—or other documentation—the person must allow the constable (or vehicle examiner) a reasonable time to check the name and address of the holder, the date of issue and the authority under which the licence was issued (*Tremelling* v *Martin* [1971] RTR 196). Therefore simply flashing the licence at a police officer or waving it under his/her nose would not discharge the requirements of s. 164.

The requirement under s. 164(1)(a) is worded in the present tense. Therefore the power to require a licence under this subsection ceases when the driver ceases 'driving' (as to which, **see chapter 3.1**) (*Boyce* v *Absalom* [1974] RTR 248). Unfortunately the legislators did not use the same wording when drafting s. 164(1)(d)(i) in relation to supervisors of learner drivers. It is submitted, however, that the same restrictions would apply and that the power under this section would only apply if the relevant person were still supervising a learner at the time of the demand.

Clearly if a driver is reasonably believed to *have been* driving under the circumstances described in s. 164(1)(b), (c) and (d)(i) then the power to demand the relevant licence would not be restricted to the present tense.

Note that the requirement is to produce both the driving licence *and* its counterpart. It also applies to Community licences (s. 164(11)).

A vehicle examiner is an examiner appointed under s. 66A of the 1988 Act (s. 164(11)).

Unlike a certificate of insurance (**see chapter 3.6**) driving licences must be produced in person.

3.10.4.2 Power to Demand Date of Birth

The Road Traffic Act 1988, s. 164 states:

> (2) A person required by a constable under subsection (1) above to produce his licence must in prescribed circumstances, on being so required by the constable, state his date of birth.

KEYNOTE

The 'prescribed circumstances' are set out under reg. 83 of the Motor Vehicles (Driving Licences) Regulations 1999 and are:

- where the person *fails* to produce the licence *forthwith* (although the regulation says nothing about the *counterpart*); or

- where the person *produces* a licence which the police officer has reason to suspect
  - was not granted to that person
  - was granted to that person in error
  - contains an alteration to the particulars on the licence *other than the driver number*, made with intent to deceive; or
  - in which the driver number has been altered, removed or defaced; *or*

- where the person is/was a supervisor of a learner driver as specified under s. 164(1)(d) *and* the police officer has reason to suspect that he/she is under 21 years of age.

Failing to state one's date of birth when lawfully required is a summary offence under s. 164(6).

Where a person does state his/her date of birth as required, the Secretary of State may serve a written notice on that person requiring him/her to provide evidence verifying that date of birth. If the person's name differs from his/her name at birth, the Secretary of State may also serve a similar notice requiring a statement from the person as to his/her name when born (s. 164(9)). Knowingly failing to do so is a summary offence (s. 164(9)).

3.10.4.3 | Other Powers

Where a police officer has reasonable cause to believe that the holder of a driving licence has knowingly made a false statement to obtain it, the officer may require the production of that licence and its counterpart (s. 164(4)). Failure to do so is a summary offence under s. 164(6).

Where the rider of a motor bicycle produces a provisional driving licence to a police officer and that officer has reasonable cause to believe that the holder was not driving the motor bicycle as part of training on an approved course, he/she may require the production of a prescribed certificate in relation to the completion of, or exemption from, such a course (s. 164(4A)). Failure to produce such a certificate when lawfully required is a summary offence under s. 164(6).

3.10.4.4 | Failure to Produce or Deliver Licence

Failing to produce a licence and its counterpart when lawfully required is a summary offence under s. 164(6) of the 1988 Act.

Where a person has had his/her licence revoked in relation to a disability or because it has expired and he/she fails to deliver the licence to the DVLA, a police officer or vehicle examiner may require the licence to be produced and may then seize it (s. 164(3)). Similar powers apply where the licence holder has been ordered to produce his/her licence to a court (s. 164(5)). Failure to do so is a summary offence under s. 164(6).

Licences Surrendered under Fixed Penalty Procedure

If a person has surrendered his/her licence and its counterpart to a police officer in connection with a fixed penalty offence (**see chapter 3.11**) he/she cannot produce it if required under s. 164. Therefore s. 164(7) provides that, if such a person produces:

- a *current* receipt (under s. 56 of the Road Traffic Offenders Act 1988) to that effect (either then and there or within seven days) and
- *if required to do so*, produces the licence and counterpart on his/her return to a police station

he/she does not commit an offence under s. 164(6).

Defence

The Road Traffic Act 1988, s. 164 states:

(8) In proceedings against any person for the offence of failing to produce a licence and its counterpart it shall be a defence for him to show that—
  (a) within seven days after the production of his licence and its counterpart was required he produced them in person at a police station that was specified by him at the time their production was required, or
  (b) he produced them in person there as soon as was reasonably practicable, or
  (c) it was not reasonably practicable for him to produce them there before the day on which the proceedings were commenced,
  and for the purposes of this subsection the laying of the information . . . shall be treated as the commencement of the proceedings.

KEYNOTE

This general defence allows for the issuing of an HORT/1 in respect of driving licences and counterparts; it also applies to the certificate showing that a licence holder has completed his/her compulsory training in relation to motor bicycles or that he/she is exempt from having to complete such a course (s. 164(8A)). Section 164(8) and (8A) also allow for occasions where the production of the relevant documents is not possible at the time.

3.10.4.5 Failure to Provide Signature or Sign Licence on Receipt

It is a summary offence—under reg. 20 of the Motor Vehicles (Driving Licences) Regulations 1999 and s. 91 of the Road Traffic Offenders Act 1988—to fail to sign a driving licence in ink as soon as it is received by the holder. Holders of the photocard licence (**see para. 3.10.3**) are required to provide a signature on the relevant form in order that the DVLA can reproduce his/her signature electronically on that photocard and both failures are provided for under the wording of reg. 20.

3.10.5 Classes and Categories of Vehicle Licensed

Section 87 of the Road Traffic Act 1988 requires that any person driving a motor vehicle on a road does so in accordance with a licence authorising him/her to drive a motor vehicle *of that class* (**see para. 3.10.2**).

The classification of vehicles is created by virtue of reg. 4 of the Motor Vehicles (Driving Licences) Regulations 1999 and sch. 2 to those Regulations. In relation to licences granted before 1 January 1997, provisions for the change from the 'old' categories to the new ones are to be found in reg. 76.

Regulation 7 of the 1999 Regulations sets out the categories of vehicle that a driver will be deemed as competent to drive by virtue of holding a licence. This regulation restricts drivers who passed tests in relation to certain restricted classes of vehicle (e.g. those with an automatic transmission) to vehicles falling within that category or sub-category. Similar provisions apply under reg. 7 to drivers having adaptations in relation to a disability. The categories of vehicle that a licence holder is entitled to drive will be clearly marked on his/her licence and its counterpart and any relevant restrictions will appear in the information codes in section 12.

3.10.6 Minimum Ages

The ages at which a person may drive the relevant category are generally to be found in the Road Traffic Act 1988, s. 101—although some of the restrictions on additional categories under reg. 7 above also include references to minimum ages.

That table is amended in certain cases by the provisions of reg. 9 of the 1999 Regulations. Those amendments are principally in the areas of:

- Large motor bicycles where, under certain circumstances, the age is raised to 21 years (unless the person has passed a relevant test or the vehicle is owned by the Secretary of State for Defence/is being used for military purposes by a member of the armed forces).
- Some small agricultural and forestry tractors without trailers or with smaller trailers, where the limit is lowered to 16 years.

- Small vehicles without trailers driven by someone in receipt of certain disability allowances where the limit is lowered to 16 years.
- Medium-sized goods vehicles drawing a trailer where the maximum authorised mass of the combination exceeds 7.5 tonnes where the limit is raised to 21 years.
- Large goods and large passenger carrying vehicles driven under certain circumstances in relation to NHS and Primary Care Trust ambulances, training scheme employees and holders of provisional or full PSV licences operating under a PSV operators' licence. In the specified circumstances, the limit is lowered to 18 years.
- Some vehicles owned or operated by the armed forces and some road rollers.

These amendments are very detailed and are frequently updated. Therefore reference should be made to the Regulations themselves wherever possible and again the DVLA are probably the best source of up-to-date information in this respect.

KEYNOTE

If a person takes and passes a test on a motor cycle between 120 cc and 125 cc and capable of more than 100 kph, he/she will be entitled to a full standard group A licence. The person is then restricted to motor cycles of up to 25 KW for two years. After the two-year period has elapsed, that person can ride any size of motor cycle.

However, to enable older riders access to ride larger machines there is a direct or accelerated access method. This allows riders over 21 years of age, or those who reach 21 before the end of the two-year restricted period, to ride larger motor cycles. To obtain a licence to ride such motor cycles the rider must successfully complete a compulsory basic training course, pass a theory test if required and pass a practical test on a machine with a power output of at least 35 KW. When training and practising, riders can use larger motor cycles with 'L' plates on public roads, but must be accompanied by an approved instructor using another motor cycle and who is in radio contact.

3.10.7 Driving Tests

Sections 89 and 89A of the Road Traffic Act 1988 impose the need to pass a prescribed driving test before being granted a licence, while part III of the Motor Vehicles (Driving Licences) Regulations 1999 (as amended) makes provisions for those driving tests—along with the various exemptions from any part of the test that may apply. The content of the test itself includes a two-part theory test, with the second part covering hazard perception.

The 1999 Regulations set out the requirements for the testing of drivers for specific categories of vehicle.

A person conducting a driving test must be satisfied as to the applicant's identity. The only document that is acceptable as proof of identity in this regard is a valid passport (except in relation to tests run by the armed forces)—reg. 38. Purporting to be someone else when taking a test will involve offences of fraudulently creating or using documents. Under regs 23 and 24, chief officers of police may conduct driving tests for their personnel under certain conditions.

Section 99ZA was inserted into the Road Traffic Act 1988 from 1 May 2002. This effectively allows the Secretary of State to make regulations requiring people to complete driving training courses before taking certain driving tests or before driving certain vehicles on a provisional licence.

3.10.8 | Disqualified Drivers

Most disqualifications are imposed by the courts under part II of the Road Traffic Offenders Act 1988. Some special provisions exist in relation to the disqualification of holders of large goods or passenger-carrying vehicles licences (see the Road Traffic Act 1988 s. 115 and the Driving Licences (Community Driving Licence) Regulations 1998 (SI 1998/1420)). Many drivers also find themselves disqualified by reason of the 'totting up' procedure whereby, once you have accumulated 12 penalty points within three years of the commission of the first offence, you are subject to a mandatory minimum period of six months' disqualification. There is a separate, more stringent, system in place for new drivers. In addition, s. 146 of the Powers of Criminal Courts (Sentencing) Act 2000 makes provision for courts to disqualify defendants convicted of any offence, instead of or as well as any other punishment. Section 147 allows the Crown Court to impose disqualification where the person has been convicted of an offence punishable on indictment with two years or more imprisonment, or any offence involving assault provided the court is satisfied that a motor vehicle was used for the purpose of committing, or facilitating the commission of, the offence in question.

The Powers of Criminal Courts (Sentencing) Act 2000 gives courts the power to disqualify any defendant from holding or obtaining a driving licence when convicting that person of any criminal offence (see s. 146). Other than in very serious cases, this disqualification may be made instead of, as well as in addition to any other penalty and the disqualification can be for any period.

Similarly, where a court convicts a person of common assault or of any other offence involving an assault (including an offence of aiding, abetting, counselling or procuring, or inciting), that person can be disqualified if the assault was committed by driving a motor vehicle. In the case of the Crown Court, if it is satisfied that a motor vehicle was used *by the person convicted or by anyone else* for the purpose of committing, or facilitating the commission of, the offence in question, the court may order the person convicted to be disqualified (see s. 147). Facilitating the commission of an offence includes the taking of any steps after the offence has been committed for the purpose of disposing of any property to which it relates or of avoiding apprehension or detection (s. 147(6)).

OFFENCE: **Driving while Disqualified—*Road Traffic Act 1988, s. 103(1)(b)***
• Triable summarily • Six months' imprisonment and/or a fine • Discretionary disqualification

The Road Traffic Act 1988, s. 103 states:

(1) A person is guilty of an offence if, while disqualified for holding or obtaining a licence, he—
(a) . . .
(b) drives a motor vehicle on a road.

OFFENCE: **Obtaining Licence while Disqualified—*Road Traffic Act 1988, s. 103(1)(a)***
• Triable summarily • Fine

The Road Traffic Act 1988, s. 103 states:

(1) A person is guilty of an offence if, while disqualified for holding or obtaining a licence, he—
(a) obtains a licence . . .

KEYNOTE

A licence obtained by a person who is disqualified is of no effect (s. 103(2)).

The Court of Appeal has taken the opportunity to set out the key issues to be considered when looking at an offence of driving while disqualified. In that case (*Shackleton* v *Chief Constable of Lancashire Police* [2001] EWCA Civ 1975), the defendant was known to be a disqualified driver and was seen by a police officer to be 'jogging' away from a parked Ford Escort. The officer followed and arrested him under the former statutory power. In hearing the defendant's appeal against the lawfulness of his arrest, the court said that the primary issue was whether the defendant had driven the car or whether the police officer had the reasonable belief that he had driven it. Guidance on this issue was to be found in *Pinner* v *Everett* [1969] 1 WLR 1266 where the House of Lords concluded that each case had to be considered on its merits. Their lordships had also held that there was no requirement for the vehicle to be in motion and that the key considerations in assessing each case on its merits were whether the defendant:

- had actually stopped driving or intended to carry on driving (e.g. at a set of traffic lights)

- was still driving

- had arrived at his/her destination or intended to continue to a further location

- had been prevented or persuaded from driving by someone else.

If the person is disqualified *by reason of age* (under s. 101), neither this offence *nor the power of arrest* will apply; the relevant offence would be under s. 87(1) (see para. 3.10.2).

The offence of driving while disqualified is one of strict liability and there is no need to show that the driver knew of the disqualification (*Taylor* v *Kenyon* [1952] 2 All ER 726).

You must *prove* that the person who was driving the motor vehicle was in fact disqualified. This may sound pretty obvious but it has occasionally been overlooked causing problems at trial (*R* v *Derwentside Magistrates' Court, ex parte Heaviside* [1996] RTR 384). Although one—and perhaps the best—way of proving that a defendant was disqualified at the time of driving is by a certificate under s. 73(4) of the Police and Criminal Evidence Act 1984, this is by no means the *only* way of so proving. The courts have accepted the evidence of someone who was present in court at the time the person was disqualified (*Derwentside* above); they have also accepted the defendant's own admission that he/she was disqualified, both in interview under caution and in evidence before the court (see *Moran* v *CPS* (2000) 164 JP 562 and *DPP* v *Mooney* [1997] RTR 434).

A person may still commit the offence(s) above even if the disqualification is later quashed on appeal; the offence is complete as long as he/she was disqualified at the relevant time (*R* v *Lynn* [1971] RTR 369).

As the offence of driving while disqualified is a summary offence, it cannot be 'attempted'.

If a passenger genuinely believes that the driver is entitled to drive the vehicle in which they are both found, that belief will prevent him/her being charged with 'aiding and abetting' the offence under s. 103(1)(b) (*Bateman* v *Evans* (1964) 108 SJ 522). In the case of someone supervising a 'learner driver' who turns out to be disqualified, it seems reasonable to expect a supervisor to establish that the driver under his/her supervision has a current and valid licence before venturing out onto the road.

3.10.8.1 Disqualification Until Test is Passed

The Road Traffic Offenders Act 1988, s. 36 states:

(1) Where this subsection applies to a person the court must order him to be disqualified until he passes the appropriate driving test.

(2) Subsection (1) above applies to a person who is disqualified under section 34 of this Act on conviction of—

    (a) manslaughter, or in Scotland culpable homicide, by the driver of a motor vehicle, or

    (b) an offence under section 1 (causing death by dangerous driving) or section 2 (dangerous driving) of the Road Traffic Act 1988.

(3) Subsection (1) above also applies—

    (a) to a person who is disqualified under section 34 or 35 of this Act in such circumstances or for such period as the Secretary of State may by order prescribe, or

    (b) to such other persons convicted of such offences involving obligatory endorsement as may be so prescribed.

(4) Where a person to whom subsection (1) above does not apply is convicted of an offence involving obligatory endorsement, the court may order him to be disqualified until he passes the appropriate driving test (whether or not he has previously passed any test).

(5) In this section—

'appropriate driving test' means—

    (a) an extended driving test, where a person is convicted of an offence involving obligatory disqualification or is disqualified under section 35 of this Act,

    (b) a test of competence to drive, other than an extended driving test, in any other case,

'extended driving test' means a test of competence to drive prescribed for the purposes of this section, and 'test of competence to drive' means a test prescribed by virtue of section 89(3) of the Road Traffic Act 1988.

KEYNOTE

Section 36 gives the court the power to disqualify a person from holding or obtaining a licence (s. 98(1)) until the person passes an 'appropriate' test. If the person is disqualified under the provisions for 'totting up' penalty points (see s. 35) or is found guilty of an offence involving obligatory disqualification (see s. 34), the 'appropriate' test is an *extended* test as defined at s. 36(5)(b). In other cases the 'appropriate' test will be a regular driving test under s. 89(3) of the Road Traffic Act 1988.

The relevant offences are set out at s. 36(2)(a) and (b), namely manslaughter, causing death by dangerous driving and dangerous driving itself.

Section 36(3)(b) enables the Secretary of State to add further offences to the list. This has been done in relation to an offence under s. 3A of the Road Traffic Act 1988—causing death by careless driving when under the influence of drink or drugs (see the Driving Licences (Disqualification until Test Passed) (Prescribed Offence) Order 2001 (SI 2001/4051)). In the case of an offence under s. 3A the relevant test is an extended driving test.

Where a person is convicted of an offence involving obligatory disqualification that is not covered by s. 36(1) and (2) (e.g. an offence under s. 4(1) of the Road Traffic Act 1988; **see para. 3.5.2**), the court *may* order disqualification until that person passes an appropriate driving test (s. 36(4)). Here the appropriate test will generally be the regular driving test (unless the disqualification involves 'totting up'). In determining whether or not to disqualify a person in such a case, the court must have regard to the safety of road users (s. 36(6)).

Section 36(7) to (13) makes provisions for the extent and effect of a disqualification until a test is passed and also provides for tests of competence in certain other European countries to be treated as meeting the requirements of s. 36.

A person disqualified from holding a licence until he or she has passed another driving test is a disqualified person for the purposes of s. 103. Such persons are forbidden to drive unless they can bring themselves within the provisions of the Act with regard to provisional licences. In effect, they are given a limited right to drive, as an exception, notwithstanding the fact that they have been disqualified (see *Scott* v *Jelf* [1974] RTR 256). One effect of this is that where a person so disqualified obtains a provisional licence and then drives without supervision or 'L' plates, he/she commits an offence of driving while disqualified under s. 103 (*Scott* v *Jelf*). In addition, this also means that the burden of proving that the exception applies rests with the driver (partly as a result of s. 101 of the Magistrates' Courts Act 1980). The practical effect of this is that it will fall to the driver to show that, not only did he/she have a provisional licence at the time, but that he/she was driving in accordance with the conditions of that licence. The absence of any such evidence means that, once it is proved that a defendant was the driver of a vehicle at a particular time, the court should have convicted him/her of the offence of driving while disqualified (*DPP* v *Barker* [2004] EWHC 2502).

A person who has been disqualified until he/she has passed a test can apply for a provisional licence and can drive in accordance with the conditions of such a licence (s. 37(3)). After all, it is the purpose of such a disqualification that the offender be required to prove his/her competence to drive, rather than simply removing him/her from the road.

The courts have a power to impose an interim disqualification under certain conditions. Where a defendant has been convicted of a relevant offence under ss. 34–36 and the magistrates' court commits him/her to the Crown Court *for sentence*, the court may order an interim disqualification (see s. 26(1) of the Road Traffic Offenders Act 1988 and s. 6 of the Powers of Criminal Court (Sentencing) Act 2000). The magistrates' court may also impose an interim disqualification when:

- remitting the person to another magistrates' court (under s. 10 of the Powers of Criminal Court (Sentencing) Act 2000);
- deferring passing a sentence on the person; or
- adjourning after convicting the person but before dealing with him/her for the offence.

A magistrates' court cannot impose an interim disqualification when committing a defendant *for trial*.

3.10.8.2 After Disqualification has Expired

- Once a period of disqualification ends, the person may apply for another licence.
- On application for another licence the person falls within the category of someone who 'has held and is entitled to obtain' a licence under s. 88 of the Road Traffic Act 1988.
- Section 88 provides an exemption to the offence of driving otherwise than in accordance with a licence (s. 87).
- The person can begin to drive again as soon as a proper application has been received by the Driver and Vehicle Licensing Agency.

If a person drives before applying for a new licence he/she commits the offence under s. 87.

A person disqualified until he/she passes a driving test may (or, if they are ever going to drive again, *must*) apply for a provisional licence. On application he/she may begin to drive in accordance with the conditions below.

A person who receives a disqualification period of less than 56 days (called a Short Period Disqualification) will have his/her counterpart licence stamped by the court with details of the disqualification and the licence will be handed back to him/her. The licence will become valid again the day after the expiry of the disqualification and he/she can then drive again without the need to apply to the DVLA for return of the licence (see s. 37(1A) of the Road Traffic Offenders Act 1988).

3.10.8.3 Driving Whilst Disqualified in Another Country

Disqualification from holding or obtaining a licence in one country does not generally prevent the person from driving in another country. And even within the United Kingdom there have been loopholes whereby disqualification by the courts has not prevented the offender from driving elsewhere. However a number of initiatives have been put in place to deal with these anomalies. A person who is disqualified by a court in Northern Ireland from holding or obtaining a Northern Ireland licence will also be disqualified from holding or obtaining a driving licence issued by the DVLA (see s. 102A of the Road Traffic Act 1988).

3.10.9 | Learner Drivers

Learner drivers are generally required to hold provisional licences (**see para. 3.10.3**). The granting of provisional licences is governed by s. 97(3) of the Road Traffic Act 1988 which states:

(3) A provisional licence—
- (a) shall be granted subject to prescribed conditions,
- (b) shall, in any cases prescribed for the purposes of this paragraph, be restricted so as to authorise only the driving of vehicles of the classes so prescribed,
- (c) may, in the case of a person appearing to the Secretary of State to be suffering from a relevant disability or a prospective disability, be restricted so as to authorise only the driving of vehicles of a particular construction, or design specified in the licence, and . . .

KEYNOTE

Drivers—or potential drivers—may apply for provisional licences specifically to drive certain categories of vehicles or they may be able to use a licence that they already hold. The type of provisional entitlement that each category of vehicle requires is governed by s. 97 of the Road Traffic Act 1988 and reg. 11 of the Motor Vehicles (Driving Licences) Regulations 1999.

Some sub-categories of vehicle can only be driven by certain learner drivers who hold a full licence in another, specified category. These categories are set out in the table found under reg. 11. Regulation 11 makes exemptions in relation to full-time members of the armed forces.

Further provision is made (by s. 98(2) of the Road Traffic Act 1988) to allow full licences in some categories to count as provisional licences for others. These categories are set out in the table found under reg. 19.

3.10.9.1 | Motor Bicycles and Mopeds

The Road Traffic Act 1988, s. 97 goes on to state that a provisional licence:

(3) . . .
- (d) shall not authorise a person under the age of 21 years, before he has passed a test of competence to drive a motor bicycle,—
  - (i) to drive a motor bicycle without a side-car unless it is a learner motor bicycle (as defined in subsection (5) below) or its first use (as defined in regulations) occurred before January 1, 1982 and the cylinder capacity of its engine does not exceed 125 cubic centimetres, or
  - (ii) to drive a motor bicycle with a side-car unless its power to weight ratio is less than or equal to 0.16 kilowatts per kilogram.
- (e) except as provided under subsection (3B) below, shall not authorise a person, before he has passed a test of competence to drive, to drive on a road a motor bicycle or moped except where he has successfully completed an approved training course for motor cyclists or is undergoing training on such a course and is driving the motor bicycle or moped on the road as part of the training.

(3A) Regulations may make provision as respects the training in the driving of motor bicycles and mopeds of persons wishing to obtain licences authorising the driving of such motor bicycles and mopeds by means of courses of training provided in accordance with the regulations; and the regulations may in particular make provision with respect to—
- (a) the nature of the courses of training;
- (b) the approval by the Secretary of State of the persons providing the courses and the withdrawal of his approval;
- (c) the maximum amount of any charges payable by persons undergoing the training;
- (d) certificates evidencing the successful completion by persons of a course of training and the supply by the Secretary of State of the forms which are to be used for such certificates; and

(e) the making, in connection with the supply of forms of certificates, of reasonable charges for the discharge of the functions of the Secretary of State under the regulations;

and different provision may be made for training in different classes of motor bicycles and mopeds.

KEYNOTE

The restrictions at s. 97(3)(d)(i) and (ii) apply to motor bicycles—which includes a sidecar combination. Therefore learner riders are generally restricted to using 'learner motor bicycles', motor *cycles* (i.e. mainly those having more than two wheels) and older motor bicycles first used before 1 January 1982 whose engine capacity does not exceed 125 cc. For the respective definitions, **see chapter 3.1**.

Unless a driver is exempted by the Regulations, he/she may not drive a motor bicycle or moped on a road before passing an approved training course or while on such a course as part of that training (s. 97(3)(e)). The regulation of approved training courses (also known as compulsory basic training—'CBT') for riders of motor bicycles is governed by part V of the 1999 Regulations. Among the other qualifications that such a person must have, an approved CBT instructor must show the Secretary of State that he/she is a 'fit and proper person'.

On completion of a CBT course a person will be issued with a certificate. After 1 February 2001 this certificate will be valid for two years (reg. **68** as amended by the Motor Vehicles (Driving Licences) (Amendment) Regulations 2001 (SI 2001/53)).

As with other provisional licence holders, learner riders will be subject to the conditions set out in reg. 16 (see below). The requirement to have a qualified driver supervising him/her on the vehicle does not apply when the licence holder is riding a moped, or motor bicycle with or without a sidecar (reg. 16(3)(b)).

Regulation 16(6) provides that the holder of a provisional licence authorising the driving of a moped, or motor bicycle with or without a sidecar, shall not drive such a vehicle while carrying another person. This creates an absolute ban on passengers, qualified or otherwise, on such vehicles being driven by provisional licence holders.

The government's Advisory Group on Motorcycling has recently reported back on a number of areas with regard to motorcycle safety, training and other practical matters affecting the relevant law. Although not enacted at the time of writing, their recommendations may become the subject of legislation in the near future.

A person learning to ride a 'large motor bicycle' must:

- hold a provisional licence authorising the driving of motor bicycles other than learner motor bicycles (category A1)
- be at least 21 years old (see below) and must abide by the requirements of reg. 16(7).

Regulation 16(7) requires such learners to:

- be in the presence and under the supervision of a certified direct access instructor
- be able to communicate with the instructor by means of a non hand-held radio system
- be wearing apparel (together with the instructor) which is fluorescent or, if during the hours of darkness, is either fluorescent or luminous.

An exception to the requirement for the learner to be in radio contact with the instructor has been inserted to cover the situation where the learner has a hearing impairment (reg. 16(11)). In such cases, it will suffice that the learner and the instructor employ a 'satisfactory means of communication' which they agree upon before the start of the journey.

The requirements that must be met by a 'direct access instructor' are set out under reg. 65. Note that, while conducting the above training, the maximum number of 'trainees' that a direct access instructor can supervise is two (reg. 67).

As a further result of the Motor Vehicles (Driving Licences) (Amendment) Regulations 2001 above, additional requirements have been imposed on holders of provisional licences to drive learner motor bicycles or mopeds. These regulations add reg. 16(7A) to the 1999 Regulations. In essence, reg. 16(7A) says that the holder of a provisional licence for a learner motor bicycle or moped must not drive such a vehicle on a road when undergoing training (other than as part of an approved motor cyclists' training course) by a paid instructor unless the instructor is at all times present with him/her on the road and is supervising no more than three other such provisional licence holders.

3.10.9.2 Full Licences used as Provisional

As mentioned above, s. 98(2) of the Road Traffic Act 1988 provides that a person holding a full licence for certain classes of vehicle may drive motor vehicles of other classes as if authorised by a provisional licence for those other classes. However, reg. 19(5) of the 1999 Regulations modifies the effect of s. 98(2) in relation to motor bicycles. In the case of a licence that authorises the driving only of learner or standard motor bicycles, s. 98(2) will not apply so as to authorise the driving of a large motor bicycle by a person under the age of 21. Therefore a person who holds a licence for a learner or standard motor bicycle but who is under the age of 21 cannot use that licence as a provisional licence for a large motor bicycle. Further restrictions are imposed on holders of full licences for 'standard' motor bicycles who wish to use the licence as a provisional licence to drive large motor bicycles.

3.10.9.3 General Requirements for Provisional Licence Holders

A holder of a provisional licence must not drive or ride a motor vehicle of a class authorised by the licence unless he/she is under the supervision of a 'qualified driver' (see below) (reg. 16(2)(a) of the 1999 Regulations). He/she must also display the 'distinguishing mark' (L plate) in the form set out at part 1 to sch. 4 in such a manner that it is clearly visible to other persons using the road from within a reasonable distance from the front and back of the vehicle (reg. 16(2)(b)). Provisional licence holders driving a motor vehicle on a road in Wales may display the alternative distinguishing mark (a 'D' plate, signifying *dysgwr* or 'learner' (reg. 16(4)).

The requirement to have a qualified driver supervising him/her on the vehicle does not apply to invalid carriages or vehicles in certain categories that are constructed or adapted to carry only one person (reg. 16(3)), neither does it apply to motor bicycles or mopeds (see above).

Provisional licence holders are generally prohibited from drawing trailers although certain classes of vehicles are exempt from this provision (reg. 16(2)(c)).

If a person is disqualified until he/she passes another test and then fails to abide by the provisions of the new provisional licence, he/she commits the offence of driving while disqualified (under s. 103 of the Road Traffic Act 1988).

If a driver holding a provisional licence receives penalty points, those points will count towards the total number of points taken into account under the provisions of the Road Traffic (New Drivers) Act 1995.

If a person is a 'new driver' and has his/her licence revoked after accumulating six penalty points under s. 3 of the Road Traffic (New Drivers) Act 1995, he/she will not be counted as 'disqualified' but will revert to the position of a learner driver.

If a provisional licence holder fails to observe these conditions, he/she commits an offence under s. 91 of the Road Traffic Offenders Act 1988 (i.e. breaching the Regulations); if the person does *not have* a provisional licence he/she commits the offence under s. 87 of driving otherwise than in accordance with a licence.

3.10.9.4 | **Between Driving Test and Issue of Licence**

Regulation 16(10) of the 1999 Regulations makes provision for the situation where a provisional licence holder has been issued the relevant certificate stating that he/she has passed a driving test but has not yet received his/her full licence. In such cases, the requirements to display 'L' (or 'D') plates and to be supervised, together with the restrictions on the carrying of passengers are removed.

3.10.9.5 | **Supervision of Learner Drivers**

There is only one acceptable minimum standard of driving and all drivers, including learners, must observe it; if not, they commit the offence of careless driving (*McCrone* v *Riding* [1938] 1 All ER 157).

A supervisor of a learner driver is required not to provide tuition to the learner, but to 'supervise'. That means doing whatever might reasonably be expected to prevent the learner driver from acting carelessly or endangering others (see *Rubie* v *Faulkner* [1940] 1 All ER 285). The duty includes being in a position to take control of the vehicle in an emergency. If the supervisor is not able to do this, either because of his/her physical state (e.g. drunk) or their being out of the vehicle (e.g. giving directions), the condition will not have been fulfilled.

In fact in the context of drink driving offences, the role of the supervisor is particularly relevant—both to the offence and any available *defences*. The situation was considered by the Divisional Court in *DPP* v *Janman* [2004] EWHC 101. There it was held that, in any ordinary case, the person supervising a learner driver was in control of the vehicle and this was the obvious and normal consequence of their role. This factual state of affairs did not require proof that the supervisor was a 'qualified driver' under the regulations (see below). Therefore, if the supervisor's blood/alcohol level exceeded the prescribed limit, he/she would commit the offence under s. 5(1)(b) of the Road Traffic Act 1988 simply by supervising a learner driver on a road or in a public place. Additionally, the contingent role of the supervisor, whereby he/she has to be ready to take actual control of the vehicle at any point, means that it is almost impossible for him/her to argue the defence under s. 5(2) of the Act—because that defence requires the defendant to show that there was no likelihood of his/her driving while still over the limit. The whole purpose of supervising a learner is to intervene as and when it becomes necessary and therefore there is every likelihood of the supervisor having to drive during the journey.

Whether or not a supervisor fulfilled his/her duty will be a question of fact for a court to determine in each case. If it can be shown that the qualified person was not actually 'supervising' the driver then the requirement under reg. 16 above will not have been observed and the offence (under s. 91 of the Road Traffic Offenders Act 1988) will be committed. That offence will be aided and abetted by the so-called supervisor.

A 'supervisor' can also be convicted of aiding and abetting where the learner driver is over the prescribed limit or unfit through drink or drugs (*Crampton* v *Fish* (1969) 113 SJ 1003).

The duties of a supervisor extend to ensuring compliance with other legislative requirements made of drivers such as remaining at the scene of an accident (*Bentley* v *Mullen* [1986] RTR 7).

Supervisors of learner drivers must generally not use hand-held mobile telephones or other specified devices while supervising the provisional licence holder. This is because of their active responsibilities in being ready to take charge of the vehicle as discussed above, responsibilities that are reflected in the relevant legislation regarding mobile phones (the Road Vehicles (Construction and Use) Regulations 1986 (SI 1986/1078)).

The supervisor must be a 'qualified driver' under reg. 17 of the 1999 Regulations which now states:

(1) Subject to paragraphs (2) and (2A), a person is a qualified driver for the purposes of regulation 16 if he—
   (a) is 21 years of age or over,
   (b) holds a relevant licence,
   (c) has the relevant driving experience, and
   (d) in the case of a disabled driver, he is supervising a provisional licence holder who is driving a vehicle of a class included in Categories B, C, D, C + E, or D + E and would in an emergency be able to take control of the steering and braking functions of the vehicle. . .

(2A) For the purposes of supervising the holder of a provisional licence driving a vehicle of a class included in sub-category C1, C1+E, D1 or D1+E ('the learner vehicle') which the holder is authorised to drive by that licence, a person is not a qualified driver unless that person has, in addition to meeting the requirements specified in paragraph (1), passed a test in which the vehicle used in the practical test fell within the same sub-category as that of the learner vehicle.

KEYNOTE

A 'relevant licence' means a full licence (including a Northern Ireland or Community licence) authorising the driving of vehicles of the same class as the vehicle being driven by the provisional licence holder (reg. 17(3)(c)). In the case of disabled drivers it means a full licence authorising the driving of a class of vehicles in category B other than invalid carriages. The reference to paragraph (2) is to people who are members of the armed forces acting in the course of their duties. 'Relevant driving experience' is defined at reg. 17(3)(e). *Generally* a person will have relevant driving experience if they have held the relevant full licence for a continuous or aggregate period of not less than three years including any period when they have held a provisional licence and a valid test pass certificate entitling them to a full licence for the driving of vehicles of the same class. Other conditions setting out 'relevant driving experience' are imposed by reg. 17(3) in relation to the supervision of people driving vehicles in categories C, D, C + E and D + E.

Specific provision is made for the supervision of learner drivers by drivers who are disabled.

OFFENCE: **Supervisor of Learner Driver Failing to Give Details—*Road Traffic Act 1988, s. 165(5)***
   • Triable summarily • Fine

The Road Traffic Act 1988, s. 165 states:

(5) A person—
   (a) who supervises the holder of a provisional licence granted under Part III of this Act while the holder is driving on a road a motor vehicle (other than an invalid carriage), or
   (b) whom a constable or vehicle examiner has reasonable cause to believe was supervising the holder of such a licence while driving, at a time when an accident occurred owing to the presence of the vehicle on a road or at a time when an offence is suspected of having been committed by the holder of the provisional licence in relation to the use of the vehicle on a road,
   must, on being so required by a constable or vehicle examiner, give his name and address and the name and address of the owner of the vehicle.

KEYNOTE

Regulation 80 makes provision for holders of foreign licences to be treated as holders of relevant driving licences under part III of the Road Traffic Act 1988 for certain purposes. These requirements only apply in relation to the requirements of s. 87(1) (driving otherwise than in accordance with a licence) and therefore do not entitle such licence holders to supervise learner drivers. Holders of such licences may, if they take out a provisional licence in the United Kingdom, not have to comply with the general requirements imposed on learner drivers (see above) (reg. 18).

3.10.10 Instruction of Learner Drivers

Anyone is able to give driving lessons provided they do not charge money or money's worth in return. If a person wants to give driving instruction for payment, he/she must be registered in accordance with the provisions of part V of the Road Traffic Act 1988 (see s. 123). The purpose of the regulation of driving instructors was examined in *Mahmood* v *Vehicle Inspectorate* (1998) 18 WRTLB 1. There it was held by the Divisional Court that notions of contractual payment under civil law were not particularly helpful or relevant. What mattered was whether or not the defendant (instructor) had some sort of arrangement with the learner driver and that the arrangement had a 'commercial flavour'.

Police driving instructors are exempt from this requirement (s. 124) (this includes the proper giving of instruction in accordance with arrangements by the Serious Organised Crime Agency).

Free driving lessons offered by someone in the business of buying and selling cars will be deemed to be given for payment if they are given in connection with the supply of a vehicle (s. 123(3)).

These restrictions only apply to 'motor cars' as specifically designed for this purpose, therefore it would not prevent someone charging for driving lessons on motor cycles or other vehicles falling outside the definition.

The relevant conditions for driving instructors and instruction are set out in the Motor Cars (Driving Instruction) Regulations 2005 (SI 2005/1902) (as amended). These regulations consolidate the previous statutory instruments governing driving tests and the general level of competence required, broadening the requirements in some aspects (e.g. carrying out of safety checks by the test applicant) and the fitness of the registered instructor to conduct driving instruction.

The Road Traffic (Driving Instruction by Disabled Persons) Act 1993 introduced provisions for driving lessons to be provided by disabled people and those provisions can be found in ss. 125A and 125B and ss. 133A–133D of the Road Traffic Act 1988.

3.10.11 New Drivers

Once a learner driver has passed the prescribed test, there are further specific considerations with regard to their standard of driving in the first two years. The Road Traffic (New Drivers) Act 1995 places additional requirements on recently qualified drivers by setting out a probationary period during which time the accumulation of a reduced number of penalty points will result in their licence being revoked.

The Road Traffic (New Drivers) Act 1995 states:

> 1.—(1) For the purposes of this Act, a person's probationary period is, subject to section 7, the period of two years beginning with the day on which he becomes a qualified driver.
>
> (2) For the purposes of this Act, a person becomes a qualified driver on the first occasion on which he passes—

(a) any test of competence to drive mentioned in paragraph (a) or (c) of section 89(1) of the Road Traffic Act 1988;

(b) any test of competence to drive conducted under the law of

(i) another EEA State,

(ii) the Isle of Man,

(iii) any of the Channel Islands, or

(iv) Gibraltar.

2.—(1) Subsection (2) applies where—

(a) a person is the holder of a licence;

(b) he is convicted of an offence involving obligatory endorsement;

(c) the penalty points to be taken into account under section 29 of the Road Traffic Offenders Act 1988 on that occasion number six or more;

(d) the court makes an order falling within section 44(1)(b) of that Act in respect of the offence;

(e) the person's licence shows the date on which he became a qualified driver, or that date has been shown by other evidence in the proceedings; and

(f) it appears to the court, in the light of the order and the date so shown, that the offence was committed during the person's probationary period.

(2) Where this subsection applies, the court must send to the Secretary of State—

(a) a notice containing the particulars required to be endorsed on the counterpart of the person's licence in accordance with the order referred to in subsection (1)(d); and

(b) on their production to the court, the person's licence and its counterpart.

KEYNOTE

The above legislation sets out a probationary period of two years beginning when the driver passed a test of competence to drive either in the United Kingdom or in another European Economic Area country. If, during that time, the driver receives six or more penalty points on his or her licence, the full entitlement to drive will be lost and the driver will have to pass another test of competence in the category of vehicle which he or she was entitled to drive (s. 4). The Divisional Court has confirmed that, if a driver attracts penalty points as a result of an offence committed while he or she held a *provisional* licence and then receives further points in the first two years of holding a full licence taking him or her to six or more points in all, the Secretary of State has no alternative but to revoke the licence under the provisions of s. 3—*R (On the Application of Adebowale) v Bradford Crown Court* [2004] EWHC 1741.

3.10.12 Drivers from Other Countries

The entitlement of drivers living outside the United Kingdom to drive here under the authority of their overseas permits is governed by the Motor Vehicles (International Circulation) Order 1975 (SI 1975/1208). If such drivers hold a domestic or Convention driving permit issued abroad or a British Forces driving licence, they may drive the vehicles covered by those authorities in Great Britain for one year (Article 2). Regulation 80 of the Motor Vehicles (Driving Licences) Regulations 1999 makes similar provisions in relation to people who become resident in the United Kingdom. That permit allows the holder to take a driving test in that 12 month period. If they do not do so successfully then they will need a GB provisional licence. The permit alone does not allow them to supervise learner drivers.

Visitors and new residents holding a valid driving licence may also use that licence during the first 12 months and, if they apply for a GB provisional licence during that period, they will be exempt from the conditions imposed on provisional licence holders (reg. 18).

Members of visiting forces and their dependants are covered by the Motor Vehicles (International Circulation) Order 1975, as amended (Article 3).

The former requirement for drivers from EU Member States to exchange their licences within one year of becoming a resident in Great Britain has been removed. The law governing such drivers can now be found in the Driving Licences (Community Driving Licence) Regulations 1996 (SI 1996/1974).

Drivers from EU Member States must meet the fitness requirements of British drivers and, provided they are not disqualified, drivers meeting those physical requirements may exchange their licence for a part III licence if they have become normally resident in Great Britain (s. 89 of the Road Traffic Act 1988).

The 1988 Act also makes provision for the exchange of other licences from some non-EU countries.

3.10.13 Physical Fitness and Disability

The Road Traffic Act 1988, s. 92 states:

(1) An application for the grant of a licence must include a declaration by the applicant, in such form as the Secretary of State may require, stating whether he is suffering or has at any time (or, if a period is prescribed for the purposes of this subsection, has during that period) suffered from any relevant disability or any prospective disability.

(2) In this Part of this Act—
'disability' includes disease and the persistent misuse of drugs or alcohol, whether or not such misuse amounts to dependency,
'relevant disability' in relation to any person means—
(a) any prescribed disability, and
(b) any other disability likely to cause the driving of a vehicle by him in pursuance of a licence to be a source of danger to the public, and
'prospective disability' in relation to any person means any other disability which—
(a) at the time of the application for the grant of a licence or, as the case may be, the material time for the purposes of the provision in which the expression is used, is not of such a kind that it is a relevant disability, but
(b) by virtue of the intermittent or progressive nature of the disability or otherwise, may become a relevant disability in course of time.

(3) If it appears from the applicant's declaration, or if on inquiry the Secretary of State is satisfied from other information, that the applicant is suffering from a relevant disability, the Secretary of State must, subject to the following provisions of this section, refuse to grant the licence.

KEYNOTE

Part VI of the Motor Vehicle (Driving Licences) Regulations 1999 sets out the specific requirements as to the physical fitness of drivers and includes the standard of eyesight demanded of drivers of different vehicle groups; it also makes specific provisions for drivers with controlled epilepsy.

3.10.13.1 Driving with Uncorrected Defective Eyesight

OFFENCE: **Driving with Uncorrected Defective Eyesight—*Road Traffic Act 1988, s. 96(1)***
• Triable summarily • Fine

The Road Traffic Act 1988, s. 96 states:

(1) If a person drives a motor vehicle on a road while his eyesight is such (whether through a defect which cannot be or one which is not for the time being sufficiently corrected) that he cannot

comply with any requirement as to eyesight prescribed under this Part of this Act for the purposes of tests of competence to drive, he is guilty of an offence.

KEYNOTE

Under s. 96(2) a constable having reason to suspect that a person driving a motor vehicle may be guilty of this offence may require him/her to submit to an eyesight test. Refusing to do so is a further offence under s. 96(3).

The specific requirements as to eyesight are set out at regs 72–73 and sch. 8 to the Motor Vehicles (Driving Licences) Regulations 1999. These regulations have been amended several times. They *generally* require a potential driver, existing licence holder and participant in compulsory basic training courses for motor cycles to be able to read:

- characters 79 mm high and 57 mm wide

- on a registration mark

- fixed to a motor vehicle

- at 20.5 metres

- in good light (with the aid of corrective lenses if worn at the time).

However, one amendment to the regulations takes into account the changes to the dimensions of vehicle registration plate characters and, if the narrower characters (50 mm wide) are used, the relevant distance for the above test is generally 20 metres (this is a lesser requirement than that imposed on applicants taking driving tests, where the relevant distance is generally 27 metres—see the Motor Cars (Driving Instruction) Regulations 2005 (SI 2005/1902) (as amended). For this reason it would seem that an eyesight test under s. 96(2) ought to be carried out under the same conditions, though there is no direct authority on the point.

One source of a police officer's 'reasonable suspicion' under s. 96(2) might be the information code on the driver's photocard licence which will state whether the holder has any eyesight correction.

Inability to read the characters as set out in the regulations will amount to a prescribed disability for the purposes of s. 92(2) (see above).

The 1999 Regulations also set out the conditions under which the Secretary of State may require (under s. 94) an applicant for a licence to undergo a medical examination if he/she has convictions for drink/driving offences.

If a driving licence has been refused or revoked on medical grounds (including eyesight), the Secretary of State may serve a notice (under s. 94(5)(c) of the Road Traffic Act 1988) requiring the applicant to take a specific driving test in order to assess his/her fitness—a 'disability assessment test'. In such cases the person may be granted a disability assessment licence which is an authority to drive only *for the purposes of taking such a test*.

The 1999 Regulations make special provision for drivers who suffer from epilepsy who may obtain a Group 1 licence as long as they have been free from an attack over the preceding 12 months or have only suffered from those attacks while asleep.

A person refused a licence may appeal against that decision under s. 100.

A court has a duty to notify the Secretary of State if it appears that a person has a relevant disease or disability (s. 22 of the Road Traffic Offenders Act 1988).

The Secretary of State may attach conditions to a licence in light of any disability of the holder. If the holder does not observe those conditions, he/she commits the offence under s. 87(1).

Section 94 imposes a requirement for a licence holder to notify the Secretary of State *in writing*, of any relevant disability which has either not been disclosed in the past or which has become more acute since the licence was granted.

3.10.13.2 | Notification of Disability

OFFENCE: **Failing to Give Notification of Relevant Disability—*Road Traffic Act 1988, s. 94(3)***
* Triable summarily • Fine

The Road Traffic Act 1988, s. 94 states:

(3) A person who fails without reasonable excuse to notify the Secretary of State as required by sub-section (1) above is guilty of an offence.

OFFENCE: **Driving Motor Vehicle before Giving Notification of Disability—*Road Traffic Act 1988, s. 94(3A)***
* Triable summarily • Fine • Discretionary disqualification

The Road Traffic Act 1988, s. 94 states:

(3A) A person who holds a licence authorising him to drive a motor vehicle of any class and who drives a motor vehicle of that class on a road is guilty of an offence if at any earlier time while the licence was in force he was required by subsection (1) above to notify the Secretary of State but has failed without reasonable excuse to do so.

3.10.13.3 | Driving after Refusal or Revocation of Licence

OFFENCE: **Driving Motor Vehicle after Refusal or Revocation—*Road Traffic Act 1988, s. 94A***
* Triable summarily • Six months' imprisonment and/or a fine • Discretionary disqualification

The Road Traffic Act 1988, s. 94A states:

(1) A person who drives a motor vehicle of any class on a road otherwise than in accordance with a licence authorising him to drive a motor vehicle of that class is guilty of an offence if—
  (a) at any earlier time the Secretary of State—
    (i) has in accordance with section 92(3) of this Act refused to grant such a licence,
    (ii) has under section 93 of this Act revoked such a licence, or
    (iii) has served notice on that person in pursuance of section 99C(1) or (2) or 109B of this Act requiring him to deliver to the Secretary of State a Community licence or Northern Ireland licence authorising him to drive a motor vehicle of that or a corresponding class, and
  (b) since that earlier time he has not been granted—
    (i) a licence under this Part of this Act, or
    (ii) a Community licence or Northern Ireland licence,
  authorising him to drive a motor vehicle of that or a corresponding class.

3.10.14 | The Road Traffic (Driver Licensing and Information Systems) Act 1989

The purpose of this Act is to provide a unified information system about and for drivers, under the authority of the Secretary of State.

Part I of the 1989 Act introduces a unified licensing system, abolishing the former special licences for heavy goods vehicles (HGV) and public service vehicles (PSV).

The Act provides for the licensing of drivers of such vehicles and sets out the requirements of those drivers, including their suitability to hold the relevant licence.

The Act provides the Secretary of State with powers to refuse driving licences to some applicants or to revoke existing licences on grounds of physical unfitness.

Part II of the Act provides for the introduction of driver information systems which will collect, store, process and transmit data on 'driver information'. Such systems are intended to help drivers in relation to traffic routes, congestion, etc. The systems are to be provided by operators licensed to do so by the Secretary of State. Operating an unlicensed system is an offence (s. 9).

3.10.14.1 Access to Driver Licensing Records

Under s. 71(2) of the Criminal Justice and Court Services Act 2000, the Secretary of State may make available any information held by him/her (e.g. by the DVLA) under part III of the Road Traffic Act 1988 to the police and the Serious Organised Crime Agency. When making this information available, the Secretary of State may determine the *purposes* for which constables may be given that information and also the *circumstances* under which constables may further disclose the information they have been given.

In the Motor Vehicles (Access to Driver Licensing Records) Regulations 2001 (SI 2001/3343), the Secretary of State has set out both the purposes for which the information may be given to police officers and the circumstances under which officers can further disclose it.

Under reg. 2 of the 2001 Regulations, the purposes are the prevention, investigation or prosecution of a contravention of any provision under the following:

- the Road Traffic Act 1988
- the Road Traffic Offenders Act 1988

and also for ascertaining whether a person has had an order made in relation to them under the various statutes that allow for their disqualification from driving (namely the Child Support Act 1991, s. 40B and the Criminal Justice Act 2003, s. 301(2)).

Under reg. 3, the circumstances under which officers may further disclose the information that they have been given are:

- where the information is passed to an employee of a police authority
- for any purpose ancillary to, or connected with, the use of the information by the officers.

A new system of endorsing driving licences enables the Secretary of State to make arrangements for the access to information held on a person's 'driving record' as held at the DVLA, irrespective of whether or not that person holds a driving licence. The driving record will contain particulars of any endorsements. This is particularly relevant when dealing with an offence under the fixed penalty procedure when it is important to be able to ascertain if the person has existing penalty points which, when added to the penalty points available for the offence under consideration, would make them liable to disqualification under the 'totting up procedure' (**see para. 3.11.4.1**). The Road Traffic Offenders Act 1988 provides:

97A Meaning of 'driving record'
(1) In this Act 'driving record', in relation to a person, means a record in relation to the person maintained by the Secretary of State and designed to be endorsed with particulars relating to offences committed by the person under the Traffic Acts.
(2) The Secretary of State may make arrangements for the following persons to have access, by such means as the Secretary of State may determine, to information held on a person's driving record—
(a) courts,
(b) constables,

> (c) fixed penalty clerks,
> (d) the person in respect of whom the record is maintained and persons authorised by him, and
> (e) other persons prescribed in regulations made by the Secretary of State.
>
> (3) The power to make regulations under subsection (2)(e) above shall be exercisable by statutory instrument.
> (4) No regulations shall be made under subsection (2)(e) above unless a draft of the instrument containing them has been laid before, and approved by a resolution of, each House of Parliament.

3.10.15 Forgery and Falsification of Documents

Much of the law regulating road traffic depends on the production and examination of documents. The following deals with occasions where a defendant has, or uses, false documentation. When dealing with such occasions, it is important to consider the overlapping legislation which deals with deception, forgery and fraud generally.

3.10.15.1 The Offences

Road traffic law is heavily reliant on forms and documents. Therefore it is important that any documents are genuine and reliable. Many further road traffic offences involve the fraudulent creation and use of documents, some of which are summarised below.

3.10.15.2 Forgery of Documents

OFFENCE: **Forgery of Documents—*Road Traffic Act 1988, s. 173***
  • Triable either way • Two years' imprisonment and/or a fine on indictment
  • Fine summarily

The Road Traffic Act 1988, s. 173 states:

> (1) A person who, with intent to deceive—
>   (a) forges, alters or uses a document or other thing to which this section applies, or
>   (b) lends to, or allows to be used by, any other person a document or other thing to which this section applies, or
>   (c) makes or has in his possession any document or other thing so closely resembling a document or other thing to which this section applies as to be calculated to deceive,
>   is guilty of an offence.

KEYNOTE

'Forges' for this purpose means making a false document or other thing in order that it may be used as genuine (s. 173(3)).

In each of the circumstances set out in s. 173(1)(a) to (c) you must show an intention to deceive, making this a crime of 'specific intent'.

The documents to which these offences apply are set out in s. 173(2) and include:

• licences

• test certificates

• certificates of insurance

- certificates exempting the wearing of seat belts

- international road haulage permits

- any document evidencing the successful completion of a driver training course provided in accordance with regulations under s. 99ZA of the Act

- goods vehicle plates.

'Calculated to deceive' (s. 173(1)(c)) means likely to deceive. Where a defendant produces a certificate of insurance issued under a policy which has since been cancelled, this offence may be made out (see *R* v *Cleghorn* [1938] 3 All ER 398).

3.10.15.3   False Statements or Withholding Information

OFFENCE: **False Statements and Withholding Information—*Road Traffic Act 1988, s. 174***

> - Triable either way • Two years' imprisonment on indictment • Six months' imprisonment and/or fine summarily

The Road Traffic Act 1988, s. 174 states:

(1) A person who knowingly makes a false statement for the purpose—
  (a) of obtaining the grant of a licence under any Part of this Act to himself or any other person, or
  (b) of preventing the grant of any such licence, or
  (c) of procuring the imposition of a condition or limitation in relation to any such licence, or
  (ca) of obtaining a document evidencing the successful completion of a driver training course provided in accordance with regulations under section 99ZA of this Act, or
  (d) of securing the entry or retention of the name of any person in the register of approved instructors maintained under Part V of this Act, or
  (dd) of obtaining the grant to any person of a certificate under section 133A of this Act, or
  (e) of obtaining the grant of an international road haulage permit to himself or any other person,
  is guilty of an offence.

(2) A person who, in supplying information or producing documents for the purposes either of sections 53 to 60 and 63 of this Act or of regulations made under sections 49 to 51, 61, 62 and 66(3) of this Act—
  (a) makes a statement which he knows to be false in a material particular or recklessly makes a statement which is false in a material particular, or
  (b) produces, provides, sends or otherwise makes use of a document which he knows to be false in a material particular or recklessly produces, provides, sends or otherwise makes use of a document which is false in a material particular,
  is guilty of an offence.

(3) A person who—
  (a) knowingly produces false evidence for the purposes of regulations under section 66(1) of this Act, or
  (b) knowingly makes a false statement in a declaration required to be made by the regulations,
  is guilty of an offence.

(4) A person who—
  (a) wilfully makes a false entry in any record required to be made or kept by regulations under section 74 of this Act, or
  (b) with intent to deceive, makes use of any such entry which he knows to be false,
  is guilty of an offence.

(5) A person who makes a false statement or withholds any material information for the purpose of obtaining the issue—

(a) of a certificate of insurance or certificate of security under Part VI of this Act, or

(b) of any document issued under regulations made by the Secretary of State in pursuance of his power under section 165(2)(a) of this Act to prescribe evidence which may be produced in lieu of a certificate of insurance or a certificate of security,

is guilty of an offence.

KEYNOTE

There is no need to show that, in making the false statements above, the person actually gained anything or brought about the desired consequence (see e.g. *Jones* v *Meatyard* [1939] 1 All ER 140).

The offence under s. 174(4)(b) is an offence of specific intent.

3.10.15.4 Issuing False Documents

OFFENCE: **Issue of False Documents—*Road Traffic Act 1988, s. 175***

- Triable summarily • Fine

The Road Traffic Act 1988, s. 175 states:

If a person issues—

(a) any such document as is referred to in section 174(5)(a) or (b) of this Act, or

(b) a test certificate or certificate of conformity (within the meaning of Part II of this Act),

and the document or certificate so issued is to his knowledge false in a material particular, he is guilty of an offence.

KEYNOTE

In proving this offence you must show that the person issuing the documents knew that they were false (see *Ocean Accident etc. Co.* v *Cole* (1932) 96 JP 191).

Test certificates bearing a false stamp or ones which have been backdated are 'false in a material particular' (see *Murphy* v *Griffiths* [1967] 1 All ER 424).

3.10.15.5 Police Powers

The Road Traffic Act 1988, s. 176 states:

(1) If a constable has reasonable cause to believe that a document produced to him—

(a) in pursuance of section 137 of this Act, or

(b) in pursuance of any of the preceding provisions of this Part of this Act,

is a document in relation to which an offence has been committed under section 173, 174 or 175 or this Act or under section 115 of the Road Traffic Regulation Act 1984, he may seize the document.

(1A) Where a licence to drive or a counterpart of any such licence or of any Northern Ireland licence or Community licence may be seized by a constable under subsection (1) above, he may also seize the counterpart, the licence to drive or the Northern Ireland licence or Community licence (as the case may be) produced with it.

(2) When a document is seized under subsection (1) above, the person from whom it was taken shall, unless—

(a) the document has been previously returned to him, or

(b) he has been previously charged with an offence under any of those sections,

be summoned before a magistrates' court . . . to account for his possession of the document.

(3) ...

(4) If a constable, an examiner appointed under section 66A of this Act has reasonable cause to believe that a document or plate carried on a motor vehicle or by the driver of the vehicle is a document or plate to which this subsection applies, he may seize it.

For the purposes of this subsection the power to seize includes power to detach from a vehicle.

(5) Subsection (4) above applies to a document or plate in relation to which an offence has been committed under sections 173, 174 or 175 of this Act in so far as they apply—

(a) to documents evidencing the appointment of examiners under section 66A of this Act, or

(b) to goods vehicle test certificates, plating certificates, certificates of conformity or Minister's approval certificates (within the meaning of Part II of this Act), or

(c) to plates containing plated particulars (within the meaning of that Part) or containing other particulars required to be marked on goods vehicles by sections 54 to 58 of this Act or regulations made under them, or

(d) to records required to be kept by virtue of section 74 of this Act, or

(e) to international road haulage permits.

(6) When a document or plate is seized under subsection (4) above, either the driver or owner of the vehicle shall, if the document or plate is still detained and neither of them has previously been charged with an offence in relation to the document or plate under section 173, 174 or 175 of this Act, be summoned before a magistrates' court . . . to account for his possession of, or the presence on the vehicle of, the document or plate.

KEYNOTE

This extensive power also allows (where appropriate) for the items to be detached from the vehicle (s. 176(4)). The power under subsection (4) is restricted to officers who are authorised vehicle examiners.

The references in s. 137(1) of the Act and s. 115 of the Road Traffic Regulation Act 1984 relate to the registration of driving instructors and the misuse of parking documents respectively.

3.10.16 Other Offences Involving False Records and Forgery

OFFENCE: **Forging or Altering Registration Documents—*Vehicle Excise and Registration Act 1994, ss. 44 and 45***

- Triable either way • Two years' imprisonment and/or a fine on indictment
- Fine summarily

The Vehicle Excise and Registration Act 1994, ss. 44 and 45 state:

44.—(1) A person is guilty of an offence if he forges, fraudulently alters, fraudulently uses, fraudulently lends or fraudulently allows to be used by another person anything to which subsection (2) applies.

(2) This subsection applies to—

(a) a vehicle licence,

(b) a trade licence,

(c) a nil licence,

(d) a registration mark,

(e) a registration document, and

(f) a trade plate (including a replacement trade plate).

45.—(1) A person who in connection with—

(a) an application for a vehicle licence or a trade licence,

(b) a claim for a rebate under section 20, or

(c) an application for an allocation of registration marks,

makes a declaration which to his knowledge is either false or in any material respect misleading is guilty of an offence.

(2) A person who makes a declaration which—
    (a) is required by regulations under this Act to be made in respect of a vehicle which is an exempt vehicle under paragraph 19 of Schedule 2, and
    (b) to his knowledge is either false or in any material respect misleading,
is guilty of an offence.

(2A) A person who makes a declaration or statement which—
    (a) is required to be made in respect of a vehicle by regulations under section 22, and
    (b) to his knowledge is either false or in any material respect misleading,
      is guilty of an offence.

(3) A person who—
    (a) is required by virtue of this Act to furnish particulars relating to, or to the keeper of, a vehicle, and
    (b) furnishes particulars which to his knowledge are either false or in any material respect misleading,
is guilty of an offence.

(3A) A person who, in supplying information or producing documents for the purposes of any regulations made under section 61A or 61B—
    (a) makes a statement which to his knowledge is false or in any material respect misleading or recklessly makes a statement which is false or in any material respect misleading, or
    (b) produces or otherwise makes use of a document which to his knowledge is false or in any material respect misleading,
is guilty of an offence.

(3B) A person who—
    (a) with intent to deceive, forges, alters or uses a certificate issued by virtue of section 61A or 61B;
    (b) knowing or believing that it will be used for deception lends such a certificate to another or allows another to alter or use it; or
    (c) without reasonable excuse makes or has in his possession any document so closely resembling such a certificate as to be calculated to deceive,
is guilty of an offence.

KEYNOTE

'Fraudulently' means dishonestly deceiving someone who has a public duty to examine and enforce items covered by the 1988 Act (including a police officer) and there is no need to prove any intent to cause economic loss (see *R v Terry* [1984] AC 374).

OFFENCE: **Forgery of Documents Relating to Public Service Vehicles—*Public Passenger Vehicles Act 1981, s. 65(2)***

    • Triable either way • Two years' imprisonment on indictment • Fine summarily

The Public Passenger Vehicles Act 1981, s. 65 states:

(1) This section applies to the following documents and other things, namely—
    (a) a licence under Part II of this Act;
    (b) a certificate of initial fitness under section 6 of this Act;
    (c) a certificate under section 10 of this Act that a vehicle conforms to a type vehicle;
    (d) an operator's disc under section 18 of this Act;
    (e) a certificate under section 21 of this Act as to the repute, financial standing or professional competence of any person;
    (ea) a control document issued under Article 6 of Council Regulation (EC) No 12/98 of 11 December 1997.
(2) A person who, with intent to deceive—
    (a) forges or alters, or uses or lends to, or allows to be used by, any other person, a document or other thing to which this section applies, or
    (b) makes or has in his possession any document or other thing so closely resembling a document or other thing to which this section applies as to be calculated to deceive, shall be liable . . .

KEYNOTE

'Forges' means making a false document or other thing in order that it may be used as genuine (s. 65(3)).
The expression 'calculated to deceive' means likely to do so.

OFFENCE: **Forgery or Alteration of Documents Relating to Goods Vehicle Operators—*Goods Vehicles (Licensing of Operators) Act 1995, s. 38***
* Triable either way • Two years' imprisonment and/or a fine on indictment
* Fine summarily

The Goods Vehicles (Licensing of Operators) Act 1995, s. 38 states:

(1) A person is guilty of an offence if, with intent to deceive, he—
   (a) forges, alters or uses a document or other thing to which this section applies;
   (b) lends to, or allows to be used by, any other person a document or other thing to which this sections applies; or
   (c) makes or has in his possession any document or other thing so closely resembling a document or other thing to which this section applies as to be calculated to deceive.
(2) This section applies to the following documents and other things, namely—
   (a) any operator's licence;
   (b) any document, plate, mark or other thing by which, in pursuance of regulations, a vehicle is to be identified as being authorised to be used, or as being used, under an operator's licence;
   (c) any document evidencing the authorisation of any person for the purposes of sections 40 and 41;
   (d) any certificate of qualification under section 49; and
   (e) any certificate or diploma such as is mentioned in paragraph 13(1) of Schedule 3.

KEYNOTE

'Forges' means making a false document or other thing in order that it may be used as genuine (s. 38(4)).
This offence requires proof of an intent to deceive, making it a crime of 'specific intent'.
Section 41 of the 1995 Act gives a power of seizure to police officers.

OFFENCE: **Misuse of Parking Documents and Apparatus—*Road Traffic Regulation Act 1984, s. 115***
* Triable either way • Two years' imprisonment and/or a fine on indictment
* Fine summarily

The Road Traffic Regulation Act 1984, s. 115 states:

(1) A person shall be guilty of an offence who, with intent to deceive—
   (a) uses, or lends to, or allows to be used by, any other person,—
      (i) any parking device or apparatus designed to be used in connection with parking devices;
      (ii) any ticket issued by a parking meter, parking device or apparatus designed to be used in connection with parking devices;
      (iii) any authorisation by way of such a certificate, other means of identification or device as is referred to in any of sections 4(2), 4(3), 7(2) and 7(3) of this Act; or
      (iv) any such permit or token as is referred to in section 46(2)(i) of this Act;
   (b) makes or has in his possession anything so closely resembling any such thing as is mentioned in paragraph (a) above as to be calculated to deceive; . . .
(2) A person who knowingly makes a false statement for the purpose of procuring the grant or issue to himself or any other person of any such authorisation as is mentioned in subsection (1) above shall be guilty of an offence.

3.11 Fixed Penalty System

3.11.1 Introduction

Originally introduced by the Transport Act 1982 the fixed penalty system is intended to speed up the administrative procedure for the prosecution of certain road traffic offences. The process is initiated by serving a person with a fixed penalty notice, attaching such a notice to a stationary vehicle or through the 'conditional offer' system.

The main elements of the first two of these processes are set out briefly below. However reference should be made to the legislation itself for a full explanation of the procedure to be followed in each case. The 'conditional offer' is dealt with at the end of this chapter.

The system described in this chapter has no connection with the system for dealing with other instances of criminal conduct by way of fixed penalties under the Criminal Justice and Police Act 2001.

3.11.2 Extended Fixed Penalty System

The law governing the extended fixed penalty system is to be found under part III of the Road Traffic Offenders Act 1988.

The 'fixed penalty' itself is determined by s. 53 which allows for the setting of the level of any penalty to be imposed under the system. Under s. 53 the Secretary of State may prescribe a different fixed penalty to be applied and amount of points to be endorsed depending on the circumstances. These circumstances in particular include:

(a) the nature of the contravention or failure constituting the offence,
(b) how serious it is,
(c) the area, or sort of place, where it takes place, and
(d) whether the offender appears to have committed any offence or offences of a description specified in the order during a period so specified.

The purpose of the system is to avoid court hearings for the listed offences but, at the same time, to ensure that those committing them receive the appropriate punishment including the endorsement of their licence. The definition of a 'fixed penalty notice', under s. 52, sums up the essence of the system:

(1) 'A 'fixed penalty notice' means a notice offering the opportunity of the discharge of any liability to conviction of the offence to which the notice relates by payment of a fixed penalty. . .

Where a fixed penalty offence (see below) has been committed, the system allows for a procedure other than prosecution to be followed during a specified period. This period, known as the 'suspended enforcement period' (s. 52(3)(a)), is at least 21 days following the date of the fixed penalty notice or such longer period as may be specified in it.

3.11.2.1 Financial Penalty Deposits

The Road Traffic Offenders Act 1988, ss. 90A–F, empowers police officers or vehicle examiners to impose immediate financial penalty deposits on any person who is committing an offence relating to a motor vehicle as may be specified in an order made by the Secretary of State.

Under s. 90A, police officers and vehicle examiners, appointed under s. 66A of the Road Traffic Act 1988, are able to require the payment of a deposit by a person they believe to have committed an offence in relation to a motor vehicle who does not provide a satisfactory address in the United Kingdom at which it is likely they can be found. The police officer or vehicle examiner must also believe that the person, the offence and the circumstances in which the offence is committed are of a description specified in an order made by the Secretary of State (see Road Safety (Financial Penalty Deposit) Order 2009 (SI 2009/491)).

This section enables the deposit scheme to be applied to any driver who cannot satisfy the relevant enforcement officer that he/she could be found in the United Kingdom, when necessary in connection with a fixed penalty or court proceedings. The deposit would be used to pay any uncontested fixed penalty notice. However, drivers will be able to contest the charge in court (including contesting a fixed penalty notice). If the court decided in favour of the driver or if the case did not go to court within a year (or, if shorter, any period after which no prosecution could be commenced in respect of the offence), the deposit would be refunded with the relevant interest. If the court decided against the driver, the deposit would be retained to be offset against all, or part, of the fine imposed.

Section 90D enables police officers or vehicle examiners to prohibit the vehicle from being moved if the deposit is not paid immediately, though the vehicle may be moved to another, specified place by a written direction. The prohibition continues in force until the driver either pays the deposit or (if he/she received a fixed penalty notice or conditional offer) fixed penalty, is charged with the offence or informed he/she will not be prosecuted or payment is made, or the prosecution period comes to an end, whichever occurs first. Failure to comply with the prohibition set by non-payment of a fixed penalty notice is an offence punishable by a fine up to level 5 on the standard scale.

The overall effect of these provisions is to provide a means of enforcement against offenders who avoid payment of fixed penalties and prosecution by not having a satisfactory address in the United Kingdom.

3.11.3 Fixed Penalty Offences

The offences to which the system applies are set out in sch. 3 to the Road Traffic Offenders Act 1988.

Section 51(2) of the 1988 Act, however, provides that an offence specified in the schedule is not a fixed penalty offence if it is committed by *causing* or *permitting* a vehicle to be used by another in contravention of any statutory provision, restriction or prohibition. Effectively this means that defendants reported for causing or permitting offences may not enjoy the administrative provisions made under the fixed penalty system.

Further offences may be added or removed from the system by s. 51(3). There are regular Fixed Penalty Orders to achieve this so the schedule is subject to change.

The Road Traffic (Vehicle Emissions) (Fixed Penalty) (Wales) Regulations 2003 (SI 2003/300) and the Road Traffic (Vehicle Emissions) (Fixed Penalty) (England) Regulations 2002 (SI 2002/1808) in England provide for certain specified local authorities to issue fixed penalty notices to vehicle users who contravene regs 61 and 98 of the Road Vehicles (Construction and Use) Regulations 1986 in relation to the emission of smoke and fumes.

3.11.4 Fixed Penalty Procedure

As mentioned above, the fixed penalty procedure envisages two situations: where the driver is present and where there is a stationary vehicle to which a notice can be fixed. Where the relevant offence is endorsable, the procedure makes provision for the submission by a driver of his/her licence. This is to allow the clerk at the relevant court to record the endorsement on the licence.

Proof of the service of fixed penalty notices by police officers is provided for under s. 79 of the 1988 Act.

3.11.4.1 Procedure where Driver is Present

The Road Traffic Offenders Act 1988, s. 54 states:

(1) This section applies where in England and Wales on any occasion a constable in uniform, or a vehicle examiner who produces his authority, has reason to believe that a person he finds is committing or has on that occasion committed a fixed penalty offence.

(2) Subject to the following provisions of this section, the constable or vehicle examiner may give him a fixed penalty notice in respect of the offence.

(3) Where the offence appears to the constable or vehicle examiner to involve obligatory endorsement, and the person is the holder of a licence, the constable may only give him a fixed penalty notice under subsection (2) above in respect of the offence if—

    (a) he produces his licence and its counterpart for inspection by the constable or vehicle examiner,

    (b) the constable or vehicle examiner is satisfied, on inspecting the licence and its counterpart, that he would not be liable to be disqualified under section 35 of this Act if he were convicted of that offence, and

    (c) he surrenders his licence and its counterpart to the constable or vehicle examiner to be retained and dealt with in accordance with this Part of this Act.

(4) Where—

    (a) the offence appears to the constable or vehicle examiner to involve obligatory endorsement,

    (aa) the person concerned is the holder of a licence, and

    (b) he does not produce his licence and its counterpart for inspection by the constable or vehicle examiner,

the constable or vehicle examiner may give him a notice stating that if, within seven days after the notice is given, he delivers the notice together with his licence and its counterpart in accordance with subsection (4A) below and the requirements of subsection (5)(a) and (b) below are met he will then be given a fixed penalty notice in respect of the offence.

(4A) Delivery must—

    (a) if the notice is given by a constable, be made in person, within seven days after the notice is given, to a constable or authorised person at the police station specified in the notice (being a police station chosen by the person concerned), or

    (b) if the notice is given by a vehicle examiner, be made (either by post or in person), within fourteen days after the notice is given, to the Secretary of State at the place specified in the notice.

(5) If a person to whom a notice has been given under subsection (4) above delivers the notice together with his licence and its counterpart in accordance with subsection (4A) above and the following requirements are met, that is—

(a) the person to whom the notice under subsection (4) above is delivered is satisfied, on inspecting the licence and its counterpart, that he would not be liable to be disqualified under section 35 of this Act if he were convicted of the offence, and

(b) his licence and its counterpart are delivered to be retained and dealt with in accordance with this Part of this Act,

the person to whom the notice under subsection (4) above is delivered must give him a fixed penalty notice in respect of the offence to which the notice under subsection (4) above relates.

(5A) Where the offence appears to the constable or vehicle examiner to involve obligatory endorsement, and the person is not the holder of a licence, the constable or vehicle examiner may only give him a fixed penalty notice under subsection (2) above in respect of the offence if the constable or vehicle examiner is satisfied, on accessing information held on his driving record, that he would not be liable to be disqualified under section 35 of this Act if he were convicted of that offence.

(5B) Subsection (5C) below applies where—

(a) the offence appears to the constable or vehicle examiner to involve obligatory endorsement,

(b) the person concerned is not the holder of a licence, and

(c) the constable or vehicle examiner is unable to satisfy himself, by accessing information held on his driving record, that he would not be liable to be disqualified under section 35 of this Act if he were convicted of that offence.

(5C) Where this subsection applies, the constable or vehicle examiner may give the person a notice stating that if—

(a) he delivers the notice in accordance with subsection (5D) below, and

(b) the person to whom it is delivered is satisfied, on accessing information held on his driving record, that he would not be liable to be disqualified under section 35 of this Act if he were convicted of the offence,

he will then be given a fixed penalty notice in respect of the offence.

(5D) Delivery must—

(a) if the notice is given by a constable, be made in person, within seven days after the notice is given, to a constable or authorised person at the police station specified in the notice (being a police station chosen by the person concerned), or

(b) if the notice is given by a vehicle examiner, be made (either by post or in person), within fourteen days after the notice is given, to the Secretary of State at the place specified in the notice.

(5E) If a person to whom a notice has been given under subsection (5C) above delivers the notice in accordance with subsection (5D) above, and the person to whom it is delivered is satisfied, on accessing information held on his driving record, that he would not be liable to be disqualified under section 35 of this Act if he were convicted of the offence, that person must give him a fixed penalty notice in respect of the offence to which the notice under subsection (5C) relates.

(6) A notice under subsection (4) or (5C) above shall give such particulars of the circumstances alleged to constitute the offence to which it relates as are necessary for giving reasonable information about the alleged offence.

(7) A licence and a counterpart of a licence surrendered or delivered in accordance with this section must be sent to the fixed penalty clerk if the fixed penalty notice was given by a constable or authorised person.

KEYNOTE

The constable must be in uniform in order to give the fixed penalty notice. If the offence is endorsable, the notice can only be given if the person surrenders his/her licence and the penalty incurred will not take him/her up to 12 points or beyond.

If he/she does not produce his/her licence, the person may be issued with a notice to be produced, together with the licence, within seven days at a police station.

If a person surrenders his/her licence and a notice issued under s. 54(4) at the police station within seven days, he/she must be given a fixed penalty notice so long as the total number of points on the licence will not then reach 12 or more (s. 54(5)).

If the person has not paid the fixed penalty, or given notice requesting a court hearing (under s. 55(2)), by the end of the suspended enforcement period, the police can register a sum equal to 1.5 times the amount of the penalty for enforcement against that person (s. 55(3)). Where this happens, the justices' clerk for the area where the person lives will notify the person to that effect (s. 71(6)).

If a person receives such a notification he/she can serve a statutory declaration to the effect that either:

• he/she was not the person who was given the fixed penalty notice, or
• he/she has given notice requesting a court hearing under s. 55(2).

In either case he/she must make and serve this notice within 21 days of receiving the notification from the clerk.

This power is among those that can be conferred on a Police Community Support Officer (PCSO) designated under sch. 4 to the Police Reform Act 2002 and a person accredited under sch. 5 to that Act in relation to offences of cycling on a footway under s. 72 of the Highway Act 1835.

Section 54 of the Road Traffic Offenders Act 1988 has been amended to facilitate the endorsement of a driver's record held at the DVLA for unlicensed and foreign drivers.

It also allows fixed penalty notices to be issued by vehicle examiners.

Previously a fixed penalty notice could only be issued to a person who held a licence issued in Great Britain. The new system enables a fixed penalty notice which carries an endorsement to be issued to anyone provided that they are not liable to be disqualified under s. 35 of the Road Traffic Offenders Act 1988.

To enable officers to determine whether the person may be liable to disqualification the Secretary of State may make arrangements for constables and various other persons to have access to that person's driver record.

3.11.4.2 Where the Driver is not Present

The Road Traffic Offenders Act 1988, s. 62 states:

(1) Where on any occasion a constable or a vehicle examiner has reason to believe in the case of any stationary vehicle that a fixed penalty offence is being or has on that occasion been committed in respect of it, he may fix a fixed penalty notice in respect of the offence to the vehicle unless the offence appears to him to involve obligatory endorsement.

KEYNOTE

Again a person may give notice during the suspended enforcement period, requesting a court hearing (s. 63(3)).

If no such notice has been given and the penalty has not been paid by the end of the suspended enforcement period, the police may serve a 'notice to owner' on the person who appears to be the owner of the vehicle (s. 63(2)).

If there is no response to the 'notice to owner', the police may register a sum equal to 1.5 times the amount of the penalty for enforcement against the person (s. 64(2)).

As in the above case where the person is present, the appropriate justices' clerk must notify the person that this has been done. The recipient can then make a statutory declaration (under sch. 4) to the effect that:

• he/she did not know of the fixed penalty notice until he/she received notification from the clerk, or

- he/she was not the owner of the vehicle at the time, or
- he/she gave notice requesting a court hearing.

If the person served with the 'notice to owner' was not in fact the owner he/she will not be liable if he/she can provide a statutory statement of ownership in relation to the vehicle (s. 64(4)).

Traffic Wardens

Under the Functions of Traffic Wardens (Amendment) Order 1986 (SI 1986/1328), traffic wardens may exercise the functions conferred upon constables by part III of the 1988 Act for certain offences under the fixed penalty system.

3.11.4.3 The Offences

OFFENCE: **Making False Statements in Relation to Notice to Owner—*Road Traffic Offenders Act 1988, s. 67***
- Triable summarily • Fine

The Road Traffic Offenders Act 1988, s. 67 states:

A person who, in response to a notice to owner, provides a statement which is false in a material particular and does so recklessly or knowing it to be false in that particular is guilty of an offence.

KEYNOTE

The statement made must be false in a 'material particular', that is, in relation to some matter which is directly relevant to the information required in the notice to owner.

The Road Traffic Offenders Act 1988, s. 62 states:

(2) A person is guilty of an offence if he removes or interferes with any notice fixed to a vehicle under this section, unless he does so by or under the authority of the driver or person in charge of the vehicle or the person liable for the fixed penalty offence in question.

KEYNOTE

Clearly if the person removing the notice can show that he/she did so on behalf of the person liable for the offence, he/she would not commit this offence.

Given the procedure set out in the 1988 Act, the removal of a notice would not impede the effect of the fixed penalty system; its service can be proved by the officer under s. 79 and the notification of registration by the justices' clerk allows a defendant time to contest the allegation of the particular offence.

3.11.5 Conditional Offers

The introduction of automatic devices for detecting speeding and traffic signal offences (by the Road Traffic Act 1991) created the need for a method of issuing fixed penalty notices where neither of the previous circumstances applied, namely the presence of the defendant or his/her vehicle. The result was the introduction of the 'conditional offer' system.

The Road Traffic Offenders Act 1988, s. 75 states:

(1) Where in England and Wales—
   (a) a constable has reason to believe that a fixed penalty offence has been committed, and
   (b) no fixed penalty notice in respect of the offence has been given under section 54 of this Act or fixed to a vehicle under section 62 of this Act,

   a notice under this section may be sent to the alleged offender by or on behalf of the chief officer of police or, if the constable is a member of the British Transport Police, by or on behalf of the chief constable of the British Transport Police.

   . . .

(6) Where a conditional offer is issued by a person under subsection (1), (2) or (3) above he must notify the designated officer, or in Scotland clerk of court, specified in it of its issue and its terms; and he is referred to in this section and sections 76, 77 and 77A as 'the fixed penalty clerk'.

(7) A conditional offer must—
   (a) give such particulars of the circumstances alleged to constitute the offence to which it relates as are necessary for giving reasonable information about the alleged offence,
   (b) state the amount of the fixed penalty for that offence, and
   (c) state that proceedings against the alleged offender cannot be commenced in respect of that offence until the end of the period of twenty-eight days following the date on which the conditional offer was issued or such longer period as may be specified in the conditional offer.

(8) A conditional offer sent to an alleged offender who is the holder of a licence must indicate that if the following conditions are fulfilled, that is—
   (a) within the period of twenty-eight days following the date on which the offer was issued, or such longer period as may be specified in the offer, the alleged offender—
      (i) makes payment of the fixed penalty to the appropriate person, and
      (ii) where the offence to which the offer relates is an offence involving obligatory endorsement, at the same time delivers his licence and its counterpart to the appropriate person, and
   (b) where his licence and its counterpart are so delivered, the appropriate person is satisfied on inspecting them that, if the alleged offender were convicted of the offence, he would not be liable to be disqualified under section 35 of this Act,

   any liability to conviction of the offence shall be discharged.

KEYNOTE

A conditional offer can be sent through the post but it can only be issued where the defendant has neither been served with a fixed penalty notice in person, nor had such a notice fixed to his/her vehicle.

The offer must state that, if payment is made and—where the offence is endorsable—the defendant's licence surrendered within the specified time, any liability to conviction for the offence(s) shall be discharged.

If the defendant fails to pay the fixed penalty and, where appropriate, surrender his/her licence, the police will be notified (s. 76(5)).

If the defendant is liable to disqualification, the payment and the licence will be returned and the police notified (s. 76(4)).

Where a conditional offer has been issued and the amount of the penalty stated in the offer is not the higher amount applicable by virtue of s. 53 (see para. 3.11.2) but it subsequently appears that that higher amount is in fact applicable, regulations may allow the fixed penalty clerk to issue a further notice (a 'surcharge notice') requiring payment of the difference between the two amounts. At the time of writing no such regulations have been made.

Index